ARENDT ON THE POLITICAL

What is politics? How is politics different from other spheres of human life? What is behind the debasement of political life today? This book argues that the most illuminating answers to these questions have come from Hannah Arendt. Arendt held that Western philosophy has never had a "pure concept of the political," and that political philosophers have been guided and misguided by the assumptions implicit in their metaphysical questions. Her project was "to look at politics ... with eyes unclouded by philosophy," and to retrieve and refine the non-theoretical understanding of politics implicit in ancient Greek literature and history. David Arndt's original and accessible study shows how Arendt reworked some of the basic concepts of political philosophy, which in turn led her to a reinterpretation of the American Revolution and to a profoundly original reading of the US Declaration of Independence.

DAVID ARNDT is Tutor in the Integral Program at Saint Mary's College of California, where he teaches literature, philosophy, and Attic Greek.

ARENDT ON THE POLITICAL

DAVID ARNDT
Saint Mary's College, California

CAMBRIDGE
UNIVERSITY PRESS

University Printing House, Cambridge CB2 8BS, United Kingdom

One Liberty Plaza, 20th Floor, New York, NY 10006, USA

477 Williamstown Road, Port Melbourne, VIC 3207, Australia

314–321, 3rd Floor, Plot 3, Splendor Forum, Jasola District Centre, New Delhi – 110025, India

79 Anson Road, #06–04/06, Singapore 079906

Cambridge University Press is part of the University of Cambridge.

It furthers the University's mission by disseminating knowledge in the pursuit of education, learning, and research at the highest international levels of excellence.

www.cambridge.org
Information on this title: www.cambridge.org/9781108498319
DOI: 10.1017/9781108653282

© David Arndt 2019

This publication is in copyright. Subject to statutory exception and to the provisions of relevant collective licensing agreements, no reproduction of any part may take place without the written permission of Cambridge University Press.

First published 2019

A catalogue record for this publication is available from the British Library.

Library of Congress Cataloging-in-Publication Data
NAMES: Arndt, David, 1965– author.
TITLE: Arendt on the political / David Arndt, Saint Mary's College, California.
DESCRIPTION: New York : Cambridge University Press, 2019. | Includes bibliographical references and index.
IDENTIFIERS: LCCN 2019015912 | ISBN 9781108498319 (hardback : alk. paper) |
ISBN 9781108735704 (pbk. : alk. paper)
SUBJECTS: LCSH: Arendt, Hannah, 1906–1975–Political and social views. | Political science–Philosophy.
CLASSIFICATION: LCC JC251.A74 A83 2019 | DDC 320.5–dc23
LC record available at https://lccn.loc.gov/2019015912

ISBN 978-1-108-49831-9 Hardback

Cambridge University Press has no responsibility for the persistence or accuracy of URLs for external or third-party internet websites referred to in this publication and does not guarantee that any content on such websites is, or will remain, accurate or appropriate.

Contents

Preface	*page* vii
Acknowledgments	ix
List of Abbreviations	x
Introduction	1
1 On Arendt	9
2 A Way of Thought	34
3 A Pure Concept of the Political	47
4 Thinking before Theory	84
5 Classical Political Philosophy	108
6 Rethinking the Classical Legacy	166
7 On Politics and Revolution	190
Conclusion: The Political Today	263
Works Cited	266
Index	273

Preface

Near the end of her life, Hannah Arendt praised Socrates as a philosopher who thought at the highest level and yet spoke in a way that was open to all. He was

> A thinker who was not a professional ... a man who counted himself neither among the many nor among the few ... who had no aspiration to be a ruler of men, no claim even to be particularly well fitted by his superior wisdom to act in an advisory capacity to those in power, but not a man who submitted meekly to being ruled either; in brief, a thinker who always remained a man among men, who did not shun the marketplace, who was a citizen among citizens ...[1]

Socrates taught no doctrine, charged no fee, established no school of thought, she said, because his role as a philosopher in politics was not to teach esoteric truths, but to introduce serious thinking into the public sphere through dialogues open to citizens and strangers alike. "The role of the philosopher, then, is not to rule the city but to be its 'gadfly,' not to tell philosophical truths but to make citizens more truthful."[2]

In her praise of Socrates we glimpse an ideal Arendt set for herself. She aimed to think at the highest level, but she wanted to be more than a professional thinker, a bureaucrat of the intellect, an expert who spoke only to other experts in the esoteric language of a tiny elite. She wanted her thinking to shed light on human existence in a way that was open to all. Her books were written for other political thinkers, of course, but also for the widest possible audience.

In this book I have tried to follow her example. My aim has been to think at her level, and yet to write as simply and clearly as possible. One task of the book is to lay out a reading of Arendt that will offer new

---

[1] *The Life of the Mind*, vol. 1: *Thinking* (New York: Harcourt Brace, 1978), 167.
[2] *The Promise of Politics*, ed. Jerome Kohn (New York: Schocken Books, 2005), 15.

insights to scholars and theorists. But another task is simply to make her work accessible to citizens and strangers alike. Whether I have succeeded is not for me to say. But my hope is the book will speak to several audiences at once: experts on Arendt; political thinkers in general; and anyone who cares about politics and the question of the political.

Acknowledgments

If I had known how hard it would be to write this book, I never would have started. Fortunately, I was inspired from the start by a total lack of realism. In Homeric terms: if Odysseus was most loved by Athena, and Paris was most loved by Aphrodite, the goddesses who love me most are Hope and Delusion. To them I am profoundly grateful.

I owe more than I can say to J. Hillis Miller, Jacques Derrida, Andrzej Warminski, Shoshana Felman, and Juliet Flower MacCannell. Many others also read early versions of this book and freely offered insight and encouragement. I am especially grateful to Rodolphe Gasché, Karsten Harries, Paul Kottman, Sam Zeitlin, Jennifer Forsyth, John Ronan, and Julie Park. Words of gratitude seem inadequate to their generosity.

Arendt has been the subject of a vast secondary literature, without which I could not have written this book. My debts are too numerous to list here; in the footnotes I try to show how much I owe previous writers on Arendt. Heartfelt gratitude to all.

This book was born of research supported by the Strauss Family Foundation, to whom I am deeply grateful.

I would especially like to thank my brother, Michael, who supported and encouraged me without fail for many, many years, and without whom this book might never have seen the light of day.

Above all, I am grateful to Deep Springs College. This book is dedicated to its students and friends.

Abbreviations

BPF	*Between Past and Future* (New York: Penguin Books, 1968)
CR	*Crises of the Republic* (New York: Harcourt Brace, 1972)
EJ	*Eichmann in Jerusalem* (New York: Penguin Books, 1963)
EU	*Essays in Understanding* (New York: Harcourt Brace, 1994)
HA	*Hannah Arendt*, ed. Melvyn Hill (New York: St. Martin's Press, 1979)
JW	*The Jewish Writings* (New York: Schocken Books, 2007)
KPP	*Lectures on Kant's Political Philosophy* (Chicago: University of Chicago Press, 1982)
LMT	*The Life of the Mind*, vol. 1: *Thinking* (New York: Harcourt Brace, 1978)
LMW	*The Life of the Mind*, vol. 2: *Willing* (New York: Harcourt Brace, 1978)
MDT	*Men in Dark Times* (New York: Harcourt Brace, 1968)
OR	*On Revolution* (New York: Penguin Books, 1962)
OT	*The Origins of Totalitarianism* (New York: Harcourt Brace, 1951)
OV	*On Violence* (New York: Harcourt Brace, 1969)
PP	*The Promise of Politics* (New York: Schocken Books, 2005)
RJ	*Responsibility and Judgment* (New York: Schocken Books, 2003)
TWB	*Thinking without a Bannister* (New York: Schocken Books, 2018)
WP	*Was Ist Politik?* (Munich: Piper Verlag, 1993)

Introduction

What has happened to politics in America today?

Our political culture has sunk to the lowest level in living memory. Every time it seems we have hit rock bottom, the bottom falls out and we descend further. Not to put too fine a point on it, politics is now less a matter of debate and action *by* citizens than a struggle for power *over* citizens. There are few spaces where people meet to deliberate on matters of common concern, and our polity has fragmented by class and culture into like-minded communities unwilling or unable to engage the views of others. We tend to see politics less from the perspective of citizens concerned with the common good, and more from the perspective of interest groups, identity movements, single-issue activists, and professional politicians concerned above all with fundraising and reelection. Politics has for the most part become a struggle to seize government power and to advance a partisan agenda by any means: advertising, lobbying, propaganda, disinformation, smear campaigns, dirty tricks, scapegoating, fearmongering, misdirection, deception, and outright lies.

But precisely because our official politics has sunk so low, we are living through a renaissance of active citizenship. Millions of citizens have for the first time spoken out, attended town hall meetings, joined political associations, and marched in the streets. In doing so they are rediscovering what Arendt called the lost treasure of the American Revolution – the public happiness of political action.

The worst realities of American politics today support what Arendt called "prejudices against politics – the idea that domestic policy is a fabric of lies and deceptions woven by shady interests and even shadier ideologies, while foreign policy vacillates between vapid propaganda and the exercise of raw power."[1] The problem with these prejudices is not that they

---

[1] PP, 98.

are inaccurate: "they refer to undeniable realities and faithfully reflect our current situation."[2] The problem is that they make our situation seem necessary and inevitable. In taking them for granted, we fail to see how things could be other than they are. The state of politics seems natural in light of the assumption that politics is ultimately a war for power over others, and this assumption is taken to be a matter of realism rather than a disgraceful betrayal of the deepest principles of the democratic tradition. The heroes of American democracy did not fight and die for a political culture ruled by mendacity, myopia, ruthlessness, incompetence, and stupidity.

These prejudices do not just reflect our political culture, Arendt argued, they also shape it. Politics is not a reality that remains what it is apart from whatever we say and think about it. It is a practice whose character depends on how it is understood by its practitioners. If we come to see politics as a grubby and amoral fight for the perks of government power, that is what our politics will become. And if we lose a genuine understanding of politics – if we abdicate our responsibilities as citizens in exchange for the security and prosperity promised by autocratic demagogues – we may hollow out the sphere of politics to the point where we lose it altogether: "Our prejudices invade our thoughts; they throw out the baby with the bathwater, confuse politics with what would put an end to politics, and present that very catastrophe as if it were inherent in the nature of things and thus inevitable."[3]

But the actual experience of political action does not quite fit these prejudices. People who get organized and take action tend to find that, despite the drudgery of normal politics – making calls, writing letters, raising money, filling out paperwork, knocking on doors, going to gatherings, and sitting through endless committee meetings – political life leads them into a deeper engagement in the world, into the solidarity of strangers working for the same goal, a commitment to a struggle larger than oneself, the responsibility for a future beyond one's life, and the strangely impersonal friendship of citizens who, whatever their different beliefs, share a common love of their community and devotion to its basic principles. And they may also find that, in extraordinary moments, the impossible occurs: political action actually makes something happen. The horizon of what is possible expands. What seemed unalterable fades away. And – beyond anyone's foresight or control – something new comes into the world.

[2] PP, 96.   [3] PP, 96–97.

Introduction

We are situated between cynical prejudices that debase our political culture and political experiences that remain mostly inarticulate because they resist the terms in which we think. This situation itself calls into question common concepts of politics, and calls on us to rethink the meaning of the political.

***

This book is on the question of the political: What is politics? What defines the political sphere? How is politics different from other spheres of human existence – morality, religion, law, economics, and war? What does it mean to say something is political?

At first these questions seem pointless, since we already seem to have the answer: politics is about government and power. But when we try to say exactly what this means we tend to fall silent, and this silence suggests we don't really know what we are talking about.

Recent thinkers have understood the political in different ways. Carl Schmitt defined politics as the sphere of radical antagonism: "The specific political distinction to which political actions and motives can be reduced is that between friend and enemy."[4] Chantal Mouffe has echoed Schmitt: "by 'the political' I mean the dimension of antagonism which I take to be constitutive of human societies."[5] Emmanuel Lévinas saw politics as "the art of foreseeing war and of winning it by every means."[6] Michel Foucault defined the political as "the set of relations of force in a given society."[7] To Michael Oakeshott politics was "the activity of attending to the general arrangements of a set of people whom chance or choice has brought together."[8] And M. I. Finley defined politics as "the art of reaching decisions by public discussion and then of obeying those decisions as a necessary condition of civilized life."[9] Even at the highest levels of theory there is no agreement on the meaning of the word.

---

[4] Carl Schmitt, *The Concept of the Political*, tr. George Schwab (Chicago: University of Chicago Press, 1996), 21.

[5] Chantal Mouffe, *On the Political* (New York: Routledge, 2005), 9.

[6] Emmanuel Lévinas, *Totality and Infinity*, tr. Alphonso Lingis (Pittsburgh: Duquesne University Press, 1969), 21.

[7] Michel Foucault, *Power/Knowledge*, ed. Colin Gordon (New York: Pantheon Books, 1980), 189.

[8] Michael Oakeshott, *Philosophy, Politics, and Society*, ed. P. Laslett (Oxford: Oxford University Press, 1956), 2.

[9] M. I. Finley, *Democracy, Ancient and Modern* (New Brunswick: Rutgers University Press, 1973), 13.

4   Introduction

This disagreement is the symptom of a deep confusion over the meaning of politics, and this confusion underlies four phenomena that mark modern life:

1. *The attempt to expand politics to include everything.* Some thinkers have extended the sphere of politics without limit, following the claim that "everything is political." This claim is based on real insights: that anything can be politicized; that the border between what is political and nonpolitical can always be redrawn; and that justice sometimes demands that matters commonly considered private, personal, natural, or technical should be brought into the political sphere as objects of public debate and concerted action. But we should be wary of the unlimited expansion of politics, in both theory and practice. To claim in theory that everything is political is to risk emptying the word of any precise meaning. To aim in practice to politicize everything is to aim at abolishing the sphere of private life. We should remember, as Jean-Luc Nancy reminds us, that "the claim served as a maxim or slogan as much for the various forms of fascism as for those of communism."[10] A central aim of totalitarian regimes is precisely to revoke the distinction between public and private and to politicize every aspect of life. Arendt noted that at the height of their power the Nazis boasted that "The only person who is still a private individual in Germany is somebody who is asleep."[11] If everything is political then every aspect of life – science, law, religion, art, culture, business, family, etc. – can be subject to political power. The unlimited expansion of the political sphere means the destruction of politics as a limited and distinct realm of existence.

2. *The attempt to reduce politics to something else.* There have been many attempts – in theory and practice – to assimilate politics to another sphere of life. Some thinkers have defined politics as a continuation of war, and practiced politics as a kind of combat. (Foucault argued that political "power is war, a war continued by other means").[12] Others have tried to subordinate politics to morality or religion, and to use political power to enforce moral or religious laws. (Russell Kirk claimed that "Political problems, at bottom, are religious and moral problems").[13] Others have collapsed the difference between the sphere of politics and the sphere of the family. (Hobbes wrote that "cities and kingdoms . . . are

[10] Jean-Luc Nancy, "Is Everything Political?", *The New Centennial Review* 2:3 (Fall 2002): 16.
[11] *The Origins of Totalitarianism* (New York: Harcourt Brace, 1951), 339.
[12] Foucault, *Power/Knowledge*, 90.
[13] Russell Kirk, *The Conservative Mind* (Washington DC: Regnery Publishing, 1985), 8.

Introduction 5

but greater families").[14] In the same way, others have effaced the distinction between politics and economics, and understood political governance on the model of economic management (Arendt argued that this confusion goes back to Plato: "It is a decisive contention of the *Statesman* that no difference existed between the constitution of a large household and that of the *polis* (see 259), so that the same science would cover political and 'economic' or household matters").[15] The reduction of politics to something else means the destruction of politics as a distinct realm of existence.

3. *The attempt to understand politics in nonpolitical terms.* In the absence of a pure concept of the political, political theorists have borrowed concepts, models, and methods from other fields of thought: theology, morality, psychology, social theory, economics, jurisprudence, and natural science. These conceptual "tools" may be useful. But the failure to work out basic concepts of political theory in light of experiences proper to the political realm, and the indiscriminate use in political theory of concepts taken from nonpolitical spheres, has distorted the basic realities of political life and generated confusion even at the highest levels of theory. This confusion increases by several orders of magnitude when political theories filter down to the level of practical political discourse and are debased first into ideologies, then into dogmas, then into slogans, and finally into weapons in the hands of polemicists who, guided blindly by words emptied of meaning, are caught in situations and dominated by events they cannot understand.

4. *The debasement of politics in both theory and practice.* Understanding the political in nonpolitical terms tends to empty politics of any intrinsic worth. Politics appears either as a lamentable necessity or else as a means to achieve nonpolitical ends. From an economic perspective, political institutions appear as instruments created by social groups to protect and advance their interests. From a moral perspective, politics appears as the sphere of power – amoral in itself – that must be used to protect and enforce moral norms. From a Christian perspective, politics has often been seen as an evil made necessary by our fallen condition. And for those who understand politics in terms of war, the political is continuous with all the forms of radical antagonism that mark human life. In each case political life has no dignity of its own.

---

[14] Thomas Hobbes, *Leviathan*, ed. Richard Tuck (Cambridge: Cambridge University Press, 1991), 118.
[15] *The Human Condition* (Chicago: University of Chicago Press, 1958), 223.

6   Introduction

Why does this matter?

The debasement of politics in theory sustains debased forms of political practice. The idea that politics is the sphere of radical *antagonism*, for example, supports a style of politics that is essentially polemical: political action is thought to consist of building alliances, marshaling forces, mobilizing troops, and waging campaigns. Political discourse is understood as polemic and propaganda. Political opponents are seen not as possible partners in a process of negotiation and deliberation, but as enemies whose very existence constitutes a threat and who must be defeated at all costs. American culture is permeated with the rhetoric of politics as warfare, and this rhetoric implicitly justifies the use of any means to achieve political ends.

It is true that politics is about conflict. But conflict may be agonistic without being antagonistic. In the words of Chantal Mouffe, "While antagonism is a we/they relation in which the two sides are enemies who do not share any common ground, agonism is a we/they relation where the conflicting parties ... recognize the legitimacy of their opponents. They are 'adversaries,' not enemies."[16]

The question of the political is not just theoretical, since our understanding of the political largely governs our actual practice of politics. The question is directly linked to the practical question of how we should live together. *What is at stake in the question of the political is our own understanding of the meaning and dignity of political life.*

What then is politics?

The most illuminating response to this question has come from Hannah Arendt. We have to come to terms with her work if we want to clarify, deepen, and refine our understanding of the political. This book tries to rethink the question of politics in dialogue with Arendt.

This is hard for two reasons.

First, while Arendt worked out a distinctive understanding of politics, she never fully articulated this understanding in her published works. The question of politics was at the center of a book she wrote called *Introduction into Politics* (*Einfürung in die Politik*), which she never published and which has not received the attention it deserves (It is not mentioned in Dana Villa's otherwise excellent summary of Arendt's work in *The Cambridge Companion to Hannah Arendt.*).[17] Since her published books

---

[16] Mouffe, *On the Political*, 20.
[17] *The Cambridge Companion to Hannah Arendt*, ed. Dana Villa (New York: Cambridge University Press, 2002), 1–21.

Introduction 7

never explicitly laid out her concept of the political, her understanding of politics has remained in the background of her thought, implicit in her writings but rarely highlighted in itself.

Second, while she worked out a distinctive approach to political theory, she rarely spoke explicitly of her way of thinking. Arendt thought debates over method were a waste of time, according to her friend and biographer Elisabeth Young-Bruehl: "Arendt practiced a kind of phenomenology, though she seldom used the term and usually felt that the less said about method the better."[18] At the same time, she thought the conclusions of her thinking were less important than her way of thought itself. In the preface to a book of essays, she wrote that "their only aim is to gain experience in *how* to think; they do not contain prescriptions on what to think or which truths to hold."[19] To fully understand Arendt we have to grasp both *what* she thought about politics and *the way* she approached political theory.

So this book has several aims. Chapter 1 traces the question of politics throughout Arendt's work. Chapter 2 sketches her way of thought. Chapter 3 shows how she worked out a pure concept of the political by explicating the nontheoretical understanding of politics implicit in classical literature and history. Chapter 4 lays out the differences between theoretical and nontheoretical forms of political thought. Chapter 5 shows how the nontheoretical understanding of politics implicit in classical literature and history was distorted and concealed by the tradition of political philosophy founded by Plato and Aristotle. Chapter 6 shows that Arendt's effort to critically dismantle this tradition allowed her to rethink some basic concepts of political theory. The next chapter shows how this conceptual work made possible an original interpretation of the American Revolution and of the Declaration of Independence. The Conclusion asks how Arendt's thought is still relevant today. The book focuses on *what* Arendt thought about politics, but in doing so it also implicitly follows her *way* of thinking.

In her remarks on thinking Arendt made three points. Thought is always indebted to *tradition* – we tend to follow ways of thinking we have inherited rather than invented. Thought is oriented by *experience* – traditional ways of thinking were born of specific kinds of experience, and yet in our own experience we are sometimes exposed to what resists traditional ways of thought. And thought is provoked by *events*, which

---

[18] Elisabeth Young-Bruehl, *Hannah Arendt: For Love of the World* (New Haven: Yale Press, 1982), 405.
[19] *Between Past and Future* (New York: Penguin Books, 1968), 14.

confront us with what exceeds our understanding. "I do not believe that there is any thought process possible without personal experience. Every thought is an afterthought, that is, a reflection on some matter or event."[20] It is the impact of events that strikes us with wonder; this sense of wonder inspires genuine questions; and it is around a few basic questions that most thinkers construct their concepts and arguments.

To understand Arendt we have to understand not just her concepts and arguments, but the events she lived through, the experiences that oriented her thinking, the traditions she worked within, and the questions that guided her thought. What events made her think? What experiences guided her thought? To what traditions did she belong? What were her basic questions?

[20] Arendt, *Essays in Understanding* (New York: Harcourt Brace, 1994), 20.

CHAPTER I

On Arendt

Events

In the spring of 1933 Arendt was arrested and jailed by the Nazis, who suspected her of actively opposing National Socialism. Their suspicion was in fact correct: she had offered her apartment as a safe house for dissidents fleeing Germany, and she was secretly working to document and publicize Nazi anti-Semitism.[1]

For most of her life Arendt had been profoundly apolitical – by her own account it was hard to convey how deeply she did not care about politics. "I was interested neither in history nor in politics when I was young," she wrote later.[2] "I found the so-called Jewish question boring."[3] Later in life she saw her early political apathy as in part a matter of personal temperament – she freely admitted that she was not a doer but a thinker.[4] But she also saw her early political apathy as part of a social milieu that was largely apolitical. Her family was culturally assimilated but politically passive. The Jewish community to which she belonged could be called political "only with great reservations."[5] The German middle classes were governed by an ethos that valued private life over public life, and that

---

[1] My account of Arendt's life is indebted to Elisabeth Young-Bruehl's biography, *Hannah Arendt: For Love of the World.*

[2] *The Jewish Writings* (New York: Schocken Books, 2007), 466. Her words are from a 1964 letter to Gershom Scholem.

[3] Hannah Arendt, *Hannah Arendt/Karl Jaspers: Correspondence*, ed. Lotte Kohler and Hans Saner, trans. Robert and Rita Kimber (New York: Harcourt Brace, 1992), 197. Her words are from a 1952 letter to Jaspers.

[4] At a conference on her work she said, "Now I will admit one thing. I will admit that I am, of course, primarily interested in understanding. This is absolutely true. And I will admit that there are other people who are primarily interested in doing something. I am not. I can very well live without doing anything. But I cannot live without trying at least to understand whatever happens ... I have acted in my life, a few times, because I couldn't help it. But that is not where my primary impulse is": *Hannah Arendt: The Recovery of the Public World*, ed. Melvyn A. Hill (New York: St. Martin's Press, 1979), 303–304.

[5] EU, 17.

On Arendt

"prevented the growth of a citizenry that felt individually and personally responsible for the rule of the country."[6] In Germany as a whole there was also a widespread cynicism toward politics, which both the left and right regarded as ultimately a struggle for power devoid of any dignity of its own. And this cynicism was supported by political philosophies that "always assumed the identity of politics, economics and society" – philosophies that lacked a pure concept of the political.[7]

Instead of politics she was interested in poetry, theology, and philosophy. At twelve she started learning poems by heart. At fourteen she began to read Jaspers, Kant, and Kierkegaard. At fifteen she led a boycott of a teacher's classes, and was glad to be expelled from school and allowed to prepare for the university entrance exams on her own. Her mother arranged for her to audit courses at the University of Berlin, where she studied Classics and attended lectures by the existentialist theologian Romano Guardini. It was at Berlin that she first heard of a young philosopher who was already famous despite having published almost nothing, and whose reputation alone was enough to draw students from around Germany to the University of Marburg. His name was Martin Heidegger.

Fifty years later Arendt described what drew her to Heidegger's thought. He saw philosophy not as an academic field but as an engagement with basic questions of human existence. His thinking had broken through old debates and reached a new level of understanding. And this breakthrough let him open a real dialogue with the greatest works of the philosophical tradition. Rather than reduce the works to doctrines, he would question them and let them speak.

> There was something strange about this early fame . . . There was nothing tangible on which this fame could be based. There was nothing written, except for notes taken on his lectures, which were passed around among students. These lectures dealt with texts that were generally familiar; they contained no doctrine that could be reproduced or transmitted. There was hardly anything more than a name, but the name travelled through Germany like the rumor of a secret king . . . The rumor said quite simply: Thinking has come alive again; the cultural treasures of the past, believed to be dead, are made to speak, and it turns out that they produce things altogether different than it had been presumed they said. There is a teacher; one can perhaps learn thinking.[8]

[6] OT, 314.   [7] OT, 336.
[8] Hannah Arendt, "For Martin Heidegger's Eightieth Birthday," in *Martin Heidegger and National Socialism*, ed. Gunther Neske and Emil Kettering (New York: Paragon House, 1990), 207–209.

Events 11

In 1924 she enrolled in the University of Marburg and studied closely with Heidegger in the years when he was writing *Being and Time*. What she learned from him, she wrote later, was not doctrines or dogmas but questions and ways of thought.

> He probes the depths, not to discover, let alone bring to light, an ultimate, secure foundation in a dimension of depth that could be said to have been previously undiscovered. Rather, he remains in the depths in order to lay down paths and to set up "pathmarks."[9]

During her time in Marburg she fell in love with Heidegger and they had a secret affair. After the end of their affair, Arendt moved to Freiburg to study with Husserl, and then to Heidelberg to study with Jaspers, under whose aegis she wrote a dissertation on the concept of love in Saint Augustine. Unable to work at a university because of sexism and anti-Semitism, she moved to Berlin in 1929 and married a leftist Jewish philosopher named Günther Stern. She was twenty-three and had devoted her life to the life of the mind.

But in the early 1930s Arendt could not stay above politics. With the collapse of the German economy, the electoral success of the Nazis, and the spreading plague of anti-Semitism, the Jewish question no longer seemed boring. She began work on a biography of an eighteenth-century Jewish intellectual named Rahel Varnhagen, a book that was in part an attempt to understand her own situation. "I wrote it with the idea, 'I want to understand.' I wasn't discussing my personal problems as a Jew. But now, belonging to Judaism had become my own problem, and my own problem was political. Purely political!"[10] Still, even as she turned her attention to politics, she did so as a thinker rather than an activist.

The move from thought to action came in 1933: Hitler came to power in January; her husband fled Berlin for Paris in March, several days after the burning of the Reichstag and the Nazi crackdown on leftists; Heidegger was elected Rector of Freiburg University in April and joined the Nazi Party in May; Jaspers was singled out for his opposition to the Nazis and was later banned from teaching. Arendt stayed in Berlin and did what she could to fight the new regime. She was "delighted" when Kurt Blumenfeld asked her to illegally collect evidence of anti-Semitism in order to publicize the situation of Jews in Nazi Germany, and she worked on Blumenfeld's project until she was arrested by the Nazis and jailed in the police Presidium in Berlin. After eight days of interrogation she was released for

---

[9] Arendt, in Neske and Kettering, *Martin Heidegger and National Socialism*, 210.   [10] EU, 12.

lack of evidence, and a few days later she left Germany illegally, crossing the Czech border at night and settling first in Prague, then in Geneva, and finally in Paris. She was stateless and without citizenship for the next eighteen years.

The year 1933 was for her a time of shattering disillusion. The shock was not that the Nazis took power legally and with widespread support: "We didn't need Hitler's assumption of power to know that the Nazis were our enemies. That had been completely evident for at least four years to everyone who wasn't an idiot."[11] The shock was that her friends failed to see clearly the nature of the Nazi regime or to offer any real resistance. "The problem, the personal problem, was not what our enemies did but what our friends did."[12] In addition to being disillusioned with her intellectual friends – above all with Heidegger – she was also disillusioned with intellectual life itself: it was precisely their disengagement from political realities, their sovereign disdain for the ephemera of public life, she thought, that kept her friends from seeing the emergence of totalitarianism for what it was.

> I lived in an intellectual milieu, but I also knew other people. And among intellectuals accommodation [to the Nazi regime] was the rule, so to speak. But not among the others. And I never forgot that. I left Germany dominated by the idea – of course somewhat exaggerated: Never again! I will never again get involved in any kind of intellectual business.[13]

Arendt turned from theory to practice. "I wanted to go into practical work, exclusively and only Jewish work. With this in mind I then looked for work in France."[14]

In Paris she spent five years working for a Zionist group that helped Jewish teenagers emigrate to Palestine. At first she lived with her husband, but their marriage had ended, and they were divorced in 1936. She became friends with a number of thinkers, including Walter Benjamin, Raymond Aron, Alexander Koyré, and Heinrich Blücher. In January 1940, Arendt and Blücher were married, and four months later they were rounded up with the other refugees in Paris and shipped to concentration camps in the south of France. She spent several weeks in a camp at Gurs near the Pyrenees, while her husband was sent to a separate camp. After the defeat of France, Arendt was able to get liberation papers and leave the camp, and by chance she found Blücher in the town of Montauban. In Marseille they met Walter Benjamin, who entrusted Arendt with a suitcase full of his

---

[11] EU, 10 [translation modified].   [12] EU, 10–11.   [13] EU, 11.   [14] EU, 12.

Experiences

manuscripts. That fall she and her husband were able to get American emergency visas, and in 1941 they took a train to Lisbon and then sailed to America. Later she learned that Benjamin had killed himself to escape capture by the Nazis. She also learned that most of the prisoners who stayed behind at Gurs had been shipped to Auschwitz.

American political culture was unlike any Arendt had known. In a letter to Jaspers she wrote, "There really is such a thing as freedom here and a strong feeling among many people that one cannot live without freedom. The republic is not a vapid illusion ... Then, too, people here feel themselves responsible for public life to an extent I have never seen in any European country."[15] Ten years after her arrival she became an American citizen, and she remained an American for the rest of her life.

In America Arendt returned warily to the life of the mind. At first she found work as a columnist for a German-language newspaper, then as an editor at Schocken Books. In New York she became part of a circle of intellectuals that included W. H. Auden, Randall Jarrell, Mary McCarthy, and Hans Morgenthau. And after the war she reestablished friendships with Jaspers and Heidegger.

Experiences

Arendt rarely spoke of her experience of action, but her few words are revealing. Asked in 1964 if there was a definite event that marked her turn to politics, she said:

> I would say February 27, 1933, the burning of the Reichstag, and the illegal arrests that followed during the same night. The so-called protective custody. As you know, people were taken to Gestapo cellars or to concentration camps. What happened then was monstrous, but it has now been overshadowed by things that happened later. This was an immediate shock for me, and from that moment on I felt responsible. That is, I was no longer of the opinion that one can simply be a bystander. I tried to help in many ways.[16]

In these words we recognize something essential to the experience of political action. There comes a time when, in the face of public events, we can no longer stand by and do nothing. A situation calls for action, and we ourselves feel called upon to act. If we hear this call and make action our vocation, our lives are transformed. Our center of gravity shifts from

---

[15] Arendt, *Hannah Arendt/Karl Jaspers: Correspondence 1926–1969*, 30.   [16] EU, 4–5.

private to public life. We have to renounce solitude in order to work with others, and to exchange the inwardness of thought for an active engagement in the world. In the urgency of the moment we must act without fully knowing what we are doing; intellectual work at such times seems at best an idle luxury, at worst an excuse for doing nothing. One senses something of this experience in Arendt's disillusionment with intellectual life in 1933. When a political situation demands action, the demands of thought seem trivial and weak.

But Arendt later returned to the life of the mind. After the war, her need to act gave way to a need to think, to understand what had happened, and to shed light on dark times. In her first book, she summarized the task of understanding as follows:

> Comprehension does not mean denying the outrageous, deducing the unprecedented from precedents, or explaining phenomena by such analogies and generalities that the impact of reality and the shock of experience are no longer felt. It means, rather, examining and bearing consciously the burden which our century has placed on us – neither denying its existence nor submitting meekly to its weight. Comprehension, in short, means the unpremeditated, attentive facing up to, and resisting of, reality – whatever it may be.[17]

In these words, we recognize something essential to the experience of thought. In practical life we tend to rely on common sense, and for practical purposes common sense is usually enough. But it sometimes happens that events reveal how far reality exceeds our powers of comprehension: either we find ourselves faced with something new and unfamiliar, or else within what is familiar we sense a side of things we can neither see nor grasp. We feel the limits of common sense – not that common forms of thought are useless, but that they fail to get at the essential and to illuminate what really matters. We find ourselves exposed to something real, whose obscurity is veiled by the false clarity of common sense, and whose impact is blunted by the mass of received ideas. It is this experience that provokes us to stop what we are doing, to suspend our trust in familiar concepts, to stray from the commonplaces of shared understanding and the beaten paths of old ways of thought, to pose new questions, to attend to what resists or eludes understanding, and to refine inherited forms of thought in order to grasp and bring to light what had struck us as obscure and unthinkable. The experience of the real itself calls us to the task of thinking.

---

[17] OT, viii.

Experiences 15

Arendt lived both the active life and the life of the mind. There is a hint of autobiography in her remark that the typical thinker of her era had "been forced to turn full circle not once but twice, first when he escaped from thought into action, and then again when action, or rather having acted, forced him back into thought."[18] Part of the allure of her thought is that she recognized the claims of both thought and action. Her commitment to understanding totalitarianism after 1945 was as strong as her earlier commitment to resisting it. One senses that she brought to the task of thinking the same passion that she once brought to political action. And one senses, too, in her work a deep and abiding outrage – an outrage that did not cloud her vision but that fueled a cold and unflinching lucidity.

While she acknowledged the claims of both action and thought, she sensed an essential tension between them.

The active life, in her view, is not conducive to the life of the mind. To devote oneself to action is to renounce two things that make possible serious thought: solitude and free time. Action requires work with others: "Action . . . is never possible in isolation; to be isolated is to be deprived of the capacity to act."[19] And the urgency of the active life precludes the leisure or *schole* required for sustained reflection: "The very urgency, the a-scholia, of human affairs demands provisional judgments, the reliance on custom and habit, that is, on prejudices."[20] Thinking appears pointless in light of the concern to get things done that governs the active life. From the perspective of the active life, to devote oneself to thinking is to devote oneself to doing nothing.

The life of the mind is similarly inimical to the life of action. Thinking requires inaction: "It interrupts any doing, any ordinary activities, no matter what they happen to be. All thinking demands a stop-and-think."[21] To think we have to suspend any concern for usefulness and for results, because thought is useless and without end: "Thinking is out of order because the quest for meaning produces no end result that will survive the activity, that will make sense after the activity has come to its end."[22] Thinking also requires solitude – withdrawal not just from the company of others but from the common sense that we share with them: "For while, for whatever reason, a man indulges in sheer thinking, and no matter on what subject, he lives completely in the singular, that is, in complete

---

[18] BPF, 9.   [19] HC, 188.   [20] LMT, 71.   [21] LMT, 78.   [22] LMT, 123.

solitude, as though not men but Man inhabited the earth."[23] Thinking requires us to turn away from particular realities toward what was traditionally called their nature or essence: "For thinking ... withdrawal from the world of appearances is the only essential precondition."[24] For those who devote themselves to the search for truth, action seems to have value only insofar as it makes the life of the mind possible. In light of the concern for truth that governs the life of the mind, the active life seems like mindless busyness.

Arendt did not think action and thought were antithetical. While thinking does not effect anything, she thought, the illuminating power of thought makes effective action possible. And while practical experience does not necessarily lead to insight, insight is only possible when thought adheres to reality as revealed in experience: "All thought arises out of experience, but no experience yields any meaning or even coherence without undergoing the operations of imagination and thinking."[25]

But she saw a tension between the claims of thought and action. Thinking and acting require different stances toward the world, different kinds of attention, a different sense of what matters, and ultimately different ways of seeing. Things appear differently to us depending on whether we approach them from the perspective of thinking or doing. This difference of perspective helps to explain the limitations of both thinkers and doers – both the theoretical naïveté of "men of action" and the notorious myopia of philosophers in the realm of human affairs. It makes sense of the disdain with which philosophers have traditionally regarded the worldly life and with which "men of action" have regarded philosophy: "Seen from the perspective of thinking, life in its sheer thereness is meaningless; seen from the perspective of the immediacy of life and the world given to the senses, thinking is ... a living death."[26]

One of Arendt's strengths as a thinker was her ability to "invert perspectives" – to see philosophy from the viewpoint of the active life, and to see politics with the eyes of a thinker. What was decisive for her was not the experience of thought itself, nor the experience of action, but the experience of moving from one to the other and back again. These experiences – of thought, action, and the movement between them – underlie all her work.

---

[23] LMT, 47.   [24] LMT, 78.   [25] LMT, 87.   [26] LMT, 87.

Traditions

When Arendt spoke of "tradition," the word had several senses. In the most common sense, it simply meant inherited ways of doing and thinking. Tradition in this sense is a basic trait of human existence. She also used the word as a proper name for "the" tradition ("the Western Tradition") – the forms of thought and practice that Europe inherited from antiquity. In this sense "tradition" named the canon of Greek, Roman, Jewish, and Christian texts in which she had been educated and in whose terms she had learned to think.[27] But Arendt often used the word in the Roman sense of *traditio* – a relation to history that interprets the present in terms of concepts and examples handed down from the past. For the Romans, she thought, the words and the deeds of the ancestors had unquestionable authority, and it was only natural and right to see the past and the present in light of this inheritance: "To act without authority and tradition, without accepted, time-honored standards and models, without the help of the wisdom of the founding fathers, was inconceivable."[28] Tradition in this sense named a stance toward the past – not just inherited forms of thinking and doing, but the conservation of this inheritance as an authoritative guide to thought and action.

Despite her traditional education, Arendt emphasized the limitations of traditional political theory. In her view, many inherited concepts failed to fully grasp the nature of political phenomena. Theories of civil disobedience failed "to come to terms with and to understand the true character of the phenomenon."[29] The realities of revolution were obscured rather than illuminated by the inherited concepts of political theory, and "the gap between theory and reality is perhaps best illustrated by the phenomenon of revolution" itself.[30] And totalitarianism eluded the terms of traditional political theory: "Not only are all our political concepts and definitions insufficient for an understanding of totalitarian phenomena, but also all our categories of thought and standards for judgment seem to explode in our hands the instant we try to apply them here."[31]

Arendt explained these limitations in two ways.

First, she argued that traditional concepts were based on premodern political institutions and experiences, and so were simply not suited to the

---

[27] Arendt stressed that this tradition is riven with internal differences. In her book *On Violence* she suggests that "the Western Tradition" is a unity in name only, and that in fact this name covers a plurality of heterogeneous traditions. Arendt, *On Violence* (New York: Harcourt Brace: 1969), 40.

[28] BPF, 124.   [29] *Crises of the Republic* (New York: Harcourt Brace, 1972), 55.   [30] OV, 47.

[31] EU, 302.

On Arendt

new political phenomena that emerged in the modern age. The realities of modern politics exceed the concepts and models handed down from other times. We are living through a crisis in the Western tradition, she thought, not because modern thinkers have questioned the tradition, but because events have shown it is no longer possible to rely uncritically on inherited forms of thought. The decisive event in this respect is the emergence of totalitarianism:

> Totalitarian domination as an established fact, which in its unprecedentedness cannot be comprehended through the usual categories of political thought, and whose "crimes" cannot be judged by traditional moral standards or punished within the legal framework of our civilization, has broken the continuity of Occidental history. The break in our tradition is now an accomplished fact. It is neither the result of anyone's deliberate choice nor subject to further decision.[32]

Modern thinkers did not create this crisis, she argued, but only responded to it. They called into question the authority of traditional theories not because they were nihilists or relativists, but because "they perceived their world as one invaded by new problems and perplexities which our tradition of thought was unable to cope with."[33] Their questions were a response to the failures of traditional ways of thought: "Elementary and direct questions [such] as What is authority? What is freedom? can arise only if no answers, handed down by tradition, are available and valid any longer."[34]

Second, Arendt argued that traditional political philosophy has always had certain limitations, and that these limitations have to be understood in light of the inherent tension between politics and philosophy. Political philosophy has approached politics from the perspective of philosophers, and philosophers have rightly found the demands of political life inimical to the conditions of philosophical contemplation. So the stance of philosophers towards politics has generally ranged from active indifference to outright hostility. The traditional task of political philosophy has been to discover truths that transcend the political sphere, and to use those truths as ideal standards by which actual communities can be measured and according to which they can be remade. "Political philosophy necessarily implies the attitude of the philosopher towards politics; its tradition began with the philosopher's turning away from politics and then returning in order to impose his standards on human affairs."[35]

---

[32] BPF, 26.   [33] BPF, 27.   [34] BPF, 15.   [35] BPF, 17–18.

Traditions 19

The decisive point for Arendt is that philosophers typically have not understood politics from the inside as active participants, but have contemplated politics from the outside as spectators and judges. They have not worked out their political theories on the basis of experiences proper to the sphere of politics, but have viewed politics in light of nonpolitical concerns, and have interpreted political phenomena in terms taken from nonpolitical spheres of life. Philosophers have conceived of politics in terms abstracted from the sphere of the family, the sphere of the household, the sphere of the workshop, and in architectural terms, in military terms, in nautical terms, and in terms of psychology, biology, economics, morality, and religion. This process of abstraction – in which words are borrowed from nonpolitical spheres and applied to political matters – has prevented philosophers from rigorously and precisely distinguishing the political realm from other spheres of life. The attempt to conceive of political phenomena in nonpolitical terms has led philosophers to misconceive the basic realities of political life.

If traditional forms of thought limit our thinking, Arendt argued, we cannot get free of them simply by ignoring the tradition. It is not possible to suspend all preconceptions and invent new concepts from scratch. Thinking is always guided in advance by inherited preconceptions, even when we are unaware of them: "The strength of this tradition, its hold on Western man's thought, has never depended on his consciousness of it."[36] We may transcend the limits of traditional thought only by first seeing how deeply we are indebted to tradition.

The crisis in the Western tradition is not simply negative for Arendt. There is the danger of disinheritance – as inherited forms of thought lose their authority, thinkers may lose sight of the traditions whose deepest assumptions continue to guide or misguide their thinking. But the crisis also has a positive side.

> With the loss of tradition we have lost the thread which safely guided us through the vast realms of the past, but this thread was also the chain fettering each successive generation to a predetermined aspect of the past. It could be that only now will the past open up to us with unexpected freshness and tell us things that no one as yet has had ears to hear.[37]

The break in tradition offers "the great chance to look upon the past with eyes undistracted by any tradition, with a directness which has disappeared

---

[36] BPF, 25.   [37] BPF, 94.

20 On Arendt

from Occidental reading and hearing ever since Roman civilization submitted to the authority of Greek thought."[38]

This concept of tradition framed her view of her own situation. Arendt was indebted to tradition for the concepts in which she thought, but these concepts seemed inadequate to the events through which she had lived. This situation oriented the aims of her thought. Thought must be aware that it works with concepts that it has inherited rather than produced, that both guide and limit its powers of comprehension, and which it cannot simply renounce or discard without losing its powers: "the human mind stands in need of concepts if it is to function at all."[39] Thinking must constantly turn towards what exceeds the grasp of inherited concepts and, through a reflection on experience and the study of actual events, must refine these concepts in order to bring to light what has been obscure or invisible within the tradition. Hence the specific virtues of Arendt's thought: her vast knowledge of political theory; her distrust of theorizing; her attentiveness towards actual events; the tentative character of her thought; and above all the extreme care with which she handles basic concepts. So too the task she set herself as a political thinker: to free political theory from the distortions inherited from the philosophical tradition: "I want to look at politics, so to speak, with eyes unclouded by philosophy."[40]

Works

Arendt devoted her first published book to "the questions with which my generation had been forced to live for the better part of its adult life: What happened? Why did it happen? How could it have happened?"[41] As she studied Nazism and Bolshevism, she came to think they were without precedent in human history: "Totalitarianism differs essentially from other forms of political oppression known to us such as despotism, tyranny, and dictatorship."[42] To grasp what had happened, it was necessary to bring together historical research and theoretical refinement – to trace the origins of totalitarianism out of familiar phenomena (racism, imperialism, etc.), and to distinguish in totalitarian regimes what was essentially new. The aim of her book was not to trace the history of totalitarianism, but to grasp what it is in essence.

But what is essential to totalitarian movements?

---

[38] BPF, 27–28. [39] *On Revolution* (New York: Penguin, 1962), 220. [40] EU, 2.
[41] OT, xxiv. [42] OT, 465.

The Origins of Totalitarianism approached this question in three ways. One approach focused on political ideology – the origins of Nazi racism and anti-Semitism. But the limits of this focus became evident as her study expanded to include Bolshevism, whose political ideology centered not on race but on class. A second approach focused on the objective traits shared by both Nazi and Bolshevik regimes: an ideology that precludes open debate; a single party in control of an all-powerful bureaucracy; techniques of terror that eliminate plurality and opposition; and the "politicization" of all spheres of life. But the limits of this focus were also evident: the objective traits of totalitarian regimes are unintelligible if they are abstracted from the political culture in which they seem to make sense. A third approach looked past the objective traits of totalitarian regimes and focused on their under-lying political culture. A political culture is not just a matter of explicit theories or doctrines. Nor is it the practical know-how that guides collective behavior. It is the mostly unthought and inarticulate background under-standing that makes political life meaningful. It includes an understanding of the political; a sense of what unites members of a community; a view of what distinguishes them from others; a stance toward political conflict; a story of what has made the community what it is; an ideal the community seeks to realize; the ethos necessary to realize that ideal; and a basic concept of the realities of political life. What is essential to totalitarianism, on this level, is a culture that sees politics as ultimately a struggle for dominance; that divides humanity into a movement destined to lead the world and a surrounding mass of implacable enemies, and that blames these enemies for current failures and humiliations; that explains all of history in terms of this conflict; that locates political differences in deep natural or social sources beyond individual control and impervious to reasoned resolution; that aspires to a uniform community under the rule of one leader; that under-stands government, power, and law in terms of command and obedience; and that therefore demands uncritical loyalty, submission, and self-sacrifice. This culture is distinct from the political doctrines proper to various totalitarian movements, whether of the left (Bolshevism) or the right (Nazism). But it is integral to the practices and institutions essential to totalitarianism: the forms of organization, structures of power, techniques of terror, and styles of thought and discourse.

For Arendt, "totalitarian politics" is actually an oxymoron. Since totali-tarians claim an ideology whose truth is beyond question, they eliminate or monopolize all institutions of public life. And since they aim to remake human society, they subject all aspects of private life to the control of the regime. Their ultimate aim is total domination of both public and private spheres. Hence the strange status of "politics" under totalitarian rule: on the one hand everything is "politicized" in the sense that everything is subject to state power; on the other hand, there is no place for politics in the original sense, since public debate and common deliberation are replaced by ideological dogma and bureaucratic administration. Totalitarianism is less a kind of politics than the death of politics.

Once her first book was published in English, Arendt was invited to teach at Princeton, Berkeley, Chicago, and the New School for Social Research. But she "never really wanted to be a professor," and always managed to reserve half of each year to travel to Europe and to work full time on her books.[43]

The Origins left open a question. Arendt thought Nazi ideology was crude and racist pseudoscience. But Bolshevism was inspired by the work of one of the greatest political philosophers of the Western tradition, Karl Marx. Marx was guided by Enlightenment ideals of liberation, brotherhood, equality, and reason. How could his work become a source of a totalitarian ideology? Was Bolshevism merely a perversion of Marx? Or was there something in Marxism that lent itself to totalitarian thought?

In 1951 Arendt began work on "The Totalitarian Elements in Marxism," a project she never finished. She carefully distinguished Marx's thought from Marxist doctrine and Bolshevik ideology: "Marx cannot stand accused of having brought forth the specifically totalitarian aspects of Bolshevik domination."[44] But she argued that elements of Marxism could be used to support a totalitarian ideology. In particular she criticized two basic concepts. On the one hand, she was critical of the Marxist concept of theory, which Marx conceived on the model of natural science. This scientistic conception of theory supported the notion that Marx had discovered the laws of history, and that Marxist doctrine was not a matter of opinion but of knowledge. This concept of theory could be used to support totalitarian ideologies that claimed to transcend mere opinion, and so dispensed with the public deliberation essential to politics. On the other hand, Arendt was critical of the Marxist concept of political action, which Marx conceived on the model of production, as a means to an end discovered in advance by political theory. This instrumental concept of action could be used by totalitarian regimes to justify any means to achieve the right ends. In a

---

[43] Young-Bruehl, *Hannah Arendt*, 296.
[44] Hannah Arendt, "Karl Marx and the Tradition of Western Political Thought," in *Thinking without a Banister: Essays in Understanding 1953–75*, ed. Jerome Kohn (New York: Schocken Books, 2018), 5.

Works

1953 essay she argued that "Marxism could be developed into a totalitarian ideology because of its perversion, or misunderstanding, of political action as the making of history."[45] The totalitarian elements in Marxism lay not on the surface level of theses, but in its underlying stratum of basic concepts or misconceptions. These misconceptions left Marxism open to be appropriated by regimes that did away with politics and replaced open debate and rule of law with ideology and terror.

This conclusion raised more questions. Marx did not invent his language; he articulated his concepts in traditional terms. To ask about the totalitarian elements of Marxism raised questions about that tradition: Was there an anti-political bias in some of the basic terms of traditional political theory, a bias that informed elements of Marx's thinking and that allowed Marxism to support a totalitarian ideology? To what extent were the anti-political elements of Marx's thought part of the tradition?

In a series of lectures on "Karl Marx and the Great Tradition" (1953), Arendt argued that elements of Marx's work could already be found at the very start of the tradition, in the writings of Plato and Aristotle. Both Plato and Aristotle considered political action merely a means to a higher end: "In Aristotelian terms, politics is a means to an end; it has no end in and by itself."[46] Both conceived of action on the model of production; Aristotle explicitly likened statesmen to craftsmen, and compared the population and territory of the polis to the raw material from which they make their products.[47] Plato and Aristotle both conceived of political theory as a science whose truth transcended the play of opinions in the political sphere. Plato claimed to have discovered the idea of the polis, an ideal form against which actual polities could be measured and according to which they could be remade. Aristotle claimed to have discovered the origin and end of political life: politics originates in the activities necessary for survival and prosperity, and has its end in making possible the highest human happiness, the life of contemplation:

> Politics, in other words, is derivative in a twofold sense: it has its origin in the pre-political data of biological life, and it has its end in the post-political, highest possibility of human destiny ... Politics is supposed to watch and manage the livelihood and the base necessities of labor on the one hand, and to take its orders from the apolitical *theoria* of philosophy on the other.[48]

---

[45] EU, 396.   [46] PP, 82.

[47] Aristotle, *Politics*, trans. H. Rackham (Cambridge, MA: Harvard University Press, 1932), 553 (1326a1–5).

[48] PP, 83–84.

24 On Arendt

Arendt began to think both Plato and Aristotle had failed to grasp the meaning of politics. Their theories had distorted the nature of political life, and their legacy had dominated political philosophy up to Marx. Perhaps philosophers had never fully understood the essence of politics. To Karl Jaspers she wrote, "Western philosophy has never had a pure concept of the political [*einen reinen Begriff des Politischen*]."[49]

The question of totalitarianism led her to the question of the political. In 1955, she began *Introduction into Politics* (*Einfürung in die Politik*), another book she never finished.[50] Arendt argued that politics was first seen as such in the classical Greek polis, but that the original Greek understanding of politics had been distorted by ancient philosophers and buried by modern prejudices about the political. Her book tried to clarify the meaning of politics and to work out a pure concept of the political by retrieving the understanding of politics implicit in the non-philosophical writings of the Greeks. The book was never completed, but the question of the political remained a central focus of her work.

At the same time, her reading of the classics led her to question the relations between politics and philosophy. Arendt noted that politics and philosophy have traditionally been seen as ways of life – the *vita activa* and the *vita contemplativa* – and that philosophers have seen these ways of life as opposed. This opposition was articulated by Plato in the *Gorgias*:

> The subject we are discussing is one about which even a man of small intelligence should be seriously concerned; it is nothing less than how a person should live. Is he to adopt the life to which you invite me, doing what you call manly activities, speaking in the Assembly and practicing oratory and engaging in politics on the principles at present in fashion among you politicians? Or should he lead this life – that of a philosopher? And how does the latter life differ from the former?[51]

In a later work, she cited a passage from Hugh of St. Victor that lays out the terms of the opposition:

> There are two lives, the active and the contemplative. The active is laborious, the contemplative is sheer quietness. The active life goes on in public,

---

[49] Arendt, *Hannah Arendt/Karl Jaspers: Correspondence 1926–1969*, 166. The original German is quoted by Ernst Vollrath in "Hannah Arendt: A German-American Jewess Views the United States–and Looks Back to Germany," *in Hannah Arendt and Leo Strauss: German Emigres and American Political Thought after World War II*, ed. Peter Graf Kielmansegg, Horst Mewes, and Elizabeth Glaser-Schmidt (New York: Cambridge University Press, 1997), 47.

[50] The German version of this text was published in 1993 under the title *Was ist Politik?* Arendt, *Was ist Politik?* , ed. Ursula Ludz (Munich: Piper Verlag, 1993).

[51] Plato, *Gorgias*, trans. Walter Hamilton and Chris Emlyn-Jones (New York: Penguin, 1960), 95 (500c).

Works 25

the contemplative life in the desert. The active one is devoted to the necessity of one's neighbor, the contemplative one to the vision of God.[52]

Politics belongs to the active life, and so it has been a philosophical cliché that the philosopher has to renounce politics in order to devote himself to the life of the mind. The political realm has been commonly viewed by philosophers as a kind of cave or a madhouse from which thinkers must withdraw in order to reach the realm of truth.

A hostility towards politics runs through the philosophical tradition like a red thread, according to Arendt. Plato dismissed "the littlenesses and nothingnesses of human things."[53] Epicurus said that "We must free ourselves from the prison of everyday affairs and politics."[54] Pascal argued that "if [Plato and Aristotle] wrote on politics, it was as if laying down rules for a lunatic asylum."[55] Nietzsche wrote that to live as a philosopher "one must be skilled in living on mountains – seeing the wretched ephemeral babble of politics and national self-seeking beneath oneself."[56] Arendt thought that Nietzsche had revealed what "most philosophers before him had carefully hidden from the multitude" – the sense that (in Nietzsche's own words) "politics should be arranged in such a way that mediocre minds are sufficient for it and not everyone needs to be aware of it every day."[57] When philosophers have turned their attention to politics, she thought, it has typically been not to reflect on the nature of political phenomena in light of their own experience of politics, but rather to contemplate the political realm from the outside and to lay down the standards that ought to govern human affairs. Drawing on her own experience of thought and action, Arendt came to think this tension between philosophy and politics was not just a matter of temperament. It is based in an intrinsic tension between action and thought:

> There is a vital tension between philosophy and politics. That is, between man as a thinking being and man as an acting being, there is a tension that does not exist in natural philosophy, for example ... There is a kind of enmity against all politics in most philosophers, with very few exceptions.

---

[52] LMT, 6.

[53] Plato, *Theaetetus,* trans. Harold North Fowler (Cambridge, MA: Harvard University Press, 1987), 121 [173e].

[54] Epicurus, *The Essential Epicurus,* trans. Eugene O'Connor (Buffalo, NY: Prometheus Books, 1993), 83.

[55] EU, 429.

[56] Nietzsche, *Twilight of the Idols/The AntiChrist,* trans. R. J. Hollingdale (New York: Penguin, 1990), 124.

[57] EU, 429.

26 On Arendt

> Kant is an exception. This enmity is extremely important for the whole problem, because it is not a personal question. It lies in the nature of the subject itself.[58]

Action requires engagement in human affairs, while thought requires withdrawal from the world. Those who devote their lives to politics typically have neither the time nor the inclination to philosophize about the political. And those who devote themselves to philosophy typically have no firsthand experience of political life. Thinking "is always paid for by a withdrawal from the world of human affairs; this is even true, and is, indeed, especially true, when thinking, in its own isolated stillness, reflects on just these affairs."[59]

Introduction into Politics approached politics through the phenomenology Arendt had learned from Heidegger, but it diverged sharply from Heidegger's view of politics. If anyone had "paid for" his thinking "by a withdrawal from the world of human affairs," it was Heidegger. Arendt both extended Heidegger's thinking and turned it against him. She used his way of thought to reach a non-Heideggerian concept of the political.

This tension between politics and philosophy raised questions about political philosophy itself. If philosophers since Plato have renounced politics and stood outside the political realm, how has this outside perspective framed their views of political life? What experiences underlie their political theories? How has their lack of political experience guided or misguided their understanding of politics? In what ways has a philosophical perspective limited or distorted their understanding of action? How has the general notion of the *vita activa* blurred the specific differences between various kinds of activity, such as labor, work, and political action?

Arendt dealt with these questions in her second book, *The Human Condition*, whose original title was *Vita Activa*. Later she summarized her concerns:

> I had been concerned with the problem of Action, the oldest concern of political theory, and what had always troubled me about it was that the very term I adopted for my reflections on the matter, namely, *vita activa*, was coined by men who were devoted to the contemplative way of life and who looked upon all kinds of being alive from that perspective.[60]

The book argued that philosophers have failed to fully distinguish action from labor and work, and that this failure has obscured the specificity of the political sphere. Its aim was to refine these distinctions in order to

---

[58] EU, 2.   [59] Arendt, "For Martin Heidegger's Eightieth Birthday," 215.   [60] LMT, 6.

Works 27

clarify the meaning of politics. Arendt both followed and deviated from the way of thought she had learned from Heidegger. In a letter sent to him when *The Human Condition* was published in Germany, she wrote that the book "came directly out of the first Freiburg days and hence owes practically everything to you in every respect."[61] But in public she was discreet about what she owed to his work.

Arendt came to think that the failure to grasp the specificity of politics had led philosophers to misconceive the realities of political life. Over the next fourteen years she wrote a series of essays devoted to essential questions of political theory: What is freedom? What is authority? What is action? What is history? What is power? What is government? What is law? What is civil disobedience? What is the role of truth in politics? These essays were collected in her third and seventh books, *Between Past and Future* (1961) and *Crises of the Republic* (1972).

Along with these essays, Arendt also published *On Revolution* (1963), an interpretation of the American and French Revolutions. The book was inspired by her experience of American politics and her readings of the American revolutionaries, but also by two recent events. The first was the Hungarian Revolution of 1956, when mass protests unexpectedly led to a collapse of the communist regime, and when the rule of the Communist party was briefly replaced by citizen councils that were quickly crushed by Russian troops. The events of 1956 exposed in the starkest way a contest between different concepts of revolution, since the revolution in Hungary was destroyed by a regime that claimed to be the true heir of the revolutionary tradition. The second event was the Cuban revolution, in which leftist guerrillas seized control of the Cuban state through a violent coup. The overarching question of the book was the question of revolution: What is a revolution? But the book also dealt with a number of subordinate questions: What is the genealogy of concepts of revolution? How did the meaning of revolution change from 1688 through 1776, 1789, 1848, 1917, 1949, 1956, and 1959? Why was the American Revolution the only one to establish a stable republic? What is the distinctive character of American politics, and what does it owe to the American revolutionaries?

At the same time, events led Arendt beyond political questions. In 1960, when she learned that Israel had kidnapped Adolf Eichmann to put him on trial in Jerusalem, she persuaded New Yorker editor William Shawn to send her to the trial as a reporter. In the background of her work on

---

[61] Hannah Arendt and Martin Heidegger, *Letters 1925–1975*, ed. Ursula Ludz, trans. Andrew Shields (New York: Harcourt Inc., 2004), 124.

28   On Arendt

Eichmann were the questions that had inspired her book on totalitarianism: What happened? Why did it happen? How could it have happened? But in the foreground was another question: Who was Adolf Eichmann? What kind of person had organized the murder of millions of innocent people? Arendt went to the courthouse expecting Eichmann to be a terrible but extraordinary man – a malevolent genius, a sadist, a monster. Instead she found him shockingly ordinary. After attending the trial and reading the transcripts of his police interrogations, she concluded that his most notable traits were not wickedness and malevolence, but shallowness and thoughtlessness. Eichmann's thoughtlessness was not just the mindless obedience of a bureaucrat who was "just following orders." Arendt stressed that he "sabotaged" orders from Himmler, and "had not obeyed" orders from Nikolaus von Horthy to stop the deportations of Jews from Hungary.[62] Instead, his thoughtlessness was the blind commitment of a true believer. His view of the world derived from Nazi slogans rather than from any authentic reflection on his own experience, or any real engagement with other perspectives. He did not lack a conscience in the common sense of the term, but his conscience only told him to do what Hitler ordered and what the Nazi movement demanded: "He would have had a bad conscience only if he had not done what he had been ordered [by Hitler] to do."[63] Eichmann thought he was acting in the service of a higher good. He had done his job in good conscience because he was "perfectly incapable of telling right from wrong."[64] In her view, the trial made visible the limitations of inherited moral and legal thinking, and it did so by revealing a form of evil that was neither malevolent, nor wicked, nor monstrous, nor demonic: an evil that was appallingly banal.

Eichmann in Jerusalem was widely misunderstood. Arendt was criticized for portraying Eichmann as a bureaucrat who was just doing his job, as if he were the same as the Nazi soldiers at Nuremberg who invoked the defense of superior orders. But Arendt said explicitly Eichmann was different: "The case of the conscience of Adolf Eichmann ... is scarcely comparable to the case of the German generals ... at Nuremberg."[65] In her view, Eichmann was not just a cog in a bureaucratic machine, but a zealot who acted on his own initiative and actually *disobeyed* orders that would have interfered with the Final Solution. He was thoughtless not because he was just following orders, but because he was fanatically

---

[62] *Eichmann in Jerusalem* (New York: Penguin, 1963), 145, 201.   [63] EJ, 25.   [64] EJ, 26.
[65] EJ, 149.

Works   29

committed to Nazism, and had no capacity to see the world on his own rather than in terms of Nazi clichés.[66]

Eichmann led Arendt to focus on questions of thinking, conscience, and judgment. In a 1971 essay, "Thinking and Moral Considerations," she explained her idea of the banality of evil, and laid out the questions raised by Eichmann's trial:

> Some years ago, reporting on the trial of Eichmann in Jerusalem, I spoke of "the banality of evil" and meant with this no theory or doctrine but something quite factual: the phenomenon of evil deeds, committed on a gigantic scale, which could not be traced to any particularity of wickedness, pathology, or ideological conviction in the doer, whose only personal distinction was a perhaps extraordinary shallowness. However monstrous the deeds were, the doer was neither monstrous nor demonic, and the only specific characteristic one could detect in his past as well as in his behavior during the trial and the preceding police examination was something entirely negative: it was not stupidity but a curious, quite authentic inability to think ... This total absence of thinking attracted my interest. Is evildoing, not just the sins of omission but the sins of commission, possible in the absence of not merely "base motives" (as the law calls it) but of any motives at all, any particular prompting of interest or volition? Is wickedness ... not a condition for evildoing? Is our ability to judge, to tell right from wrong, beautiful from ugly, dependent upon our faculty of thought? Do the inability to think and a disastrous failure of what we commonly call conscience coincide? The question that imposed itself was, could the activity of thinking, the habit of examining and reflecting upon whatever happens to come to pass, regardless of specific content and quite independent of results, could this activity be of such a nature that it "conditions" men against evildoing?[67]

Arendt came to think the case of Eichmann showed the general collapse of morality in Nazi Germany had three sides. First, the true believers among the Nazis had rejected traditional moral standards and proclaimed a murderous new set of values. Second, and more importantly, those who faithfully adhered to traditional moral concepts and standards were ill-prepared to understand and respond effectively to the new situation: "All those who were fully qualified in matters of morality and held them in the highest esteem ... demonstrated through their application of traditional concepts and yardsticks during and after the fact, how inadequate these had become, how little, as we shall see, they had been framed or

---

[66] I am indebted here to Roger Berkowitz, "Misreading 'Eichmann in Jerusalem,'" *New York Times*, July 7, 2013.

[67] *Responsibility and Judgment*, ed. Jerome Kohn (New York: Schocken, 2003), 159–160.

30 On Arendt

intended to be applied to conditions as they actually arose."[68] And third, the most important side of this collapse, for Arendt, was that so many ordinary citizens were able to adjust to the new values by supporting Nazi laws and obeying Nazi orders. The problem had not been amorality, but the appalling ease with which people exchanged one set of mores for another:

> The total moral collapse of respectable society during the Hitler regime may teach us that under such circumstances those who cherish values and hold fast to moral norms and standards are not reliable; we now know that moral norms and standards can be changed overnight, and that all that will be left is the mere habit of holding fast to something.[69]

The moral collapse raised questions about the limits of traditional moral concepts and standards. But it also raised questions about the traditional view of morality as a set of concepts and standards. Arendt called into question the assumption that moral life is a matter of applying concepts and obeying laws. But what could moral thinking be except a search for general concepts and standards? "How can you think, and even more important in our context, how can you judge without holding on to preconceived standards, norms, and general rules under which the particular cases and instances can be subsumed?"[70] The questions raised by the Eichmann trial led Arendt to mistrust inherited forms of moral thought, and her reflections on morality led her to questions about the nature of thought itself. What does it mean to think? What does it mean to judge? What is the relation between theoretical and practical thought? What is the relation between judgment, thought, and action?

Arendt turned to these questions in her final book, *The Life of the Mind* (1978). She argued that philosophers had failed to clearly distinguish the different powers of the mind, and had failed to adequately conceive of these powers on the basis of their own inner experiences. There had been a systematic confusion of the faculties of thought: understanding had been confused with knowing; thinking had been confused with willing; and judgment had been confused with cognition. The aim of the book was to distinguish and clarify the powers of the mind through a meditation on inner experience. From 1973 to 1975 she wrote two series of lectures that became the first two volumes of the book, "Thinking" and "Willing." She planned to turn lectures on Kant's Third Critique into a volume on

---

[68] RJ, 25.   [69] RJ, 45.   [70] RJ, 26.

Basic Questions 31

"Judging," but fate called her before she could begin to write. Arendt died of heart failure in December 1975.

Basic Questions

Underlying Arendt's work are two basic questions – implicit in her concerns but not explicit on the page – that exerted a constant pull on her attention. These questions were the points around which her thought turned and returned – the hidden foci of her work.

1. The question of *thinking*. Arendt wanted to avoid the kind of intellectual life and the ways of thought that had led her friends to misjudge the Nazi regime. Her approach to political theory was guided by three rejections: (a) She rejected the disengagement of theory from action – the separation of intellectual life from political life, and the claim of theory to stand outside and above the realm of politics. (b) She rejected the priority of theory over action – the claim that effective action needs the guidance of theory, and that theory can and should tell us what to do. In her view, political action does not need theory as much as it needs experience and knowledge: "Many people say that one cannot fight totalitarianism without understanding it. Fortunately this is not true; if it were, our case would be hopeless."[71] (c) She rejected the assimilation of theory to action – the claim that thinking itself can be a kind of political action, and that the role of theory is to fight wars of ideas. Arendt knew that ideas can be used as weapons, but she saw this as a matter not of thinking but of indoctrination, and indoctrination could not further understanding in the fight against totalitarianism, but "can only further the totalitarian fight against understanding."[72] In her later work she returned to theory and reaffirmed the dignity of pure thought. But in her work there is a constant engagement with questions of theory: What is theory? What is the relation of theory to politics? How is thought related to action? How to think?

2. The question of the *political*. Her experience in Germany and America raised other questions: Why was political life in America different from politics in Germany? What exactly was different? The difference was not just a matter of institutions, since Germany had been a republic after World War I, and the Nazis had taken power by democratic means. Nor was it a matter of political theories, since the question was precisely why specific theories thrived or failed to thrive in different places. The difference was rooted in

---

[71] EU, 307.   [72] EU, 309.

32 On Arendt

what we could call "political culture" – the mostly inarticulate and unthought background understanding on whose basis inherited forms of political thought and practice make sense. This background understanding includes practical know-how (how to vote, how to protest, how to deliberate), concepts of basic political realities (power, law, government, freedom), a self-understanding (who we are as a polity, where we have come from, what unifies us as a people), and a shared ethos (a sense of the way things should be, the goods for which we live together, the ideals we share, and the virtues needed to make them real). Political life is guided by this level of understanding, not in the sense that it determines what people think and do, but in the sense that it makes some forms of thought and action seem sensible and natural, and makes others seem impossible or absurd. At the heart of any politics is an understanding of the political.

This starting point entailed a distinctive approach to political theory. To work out an adequate account of totalitarianism, Arendt first had to understand it from within – to explicate and clarify the understanding of politics within which totalitarian doctrines and practices seem to make sense. But it was not enough to understand what she was fighting against; she had to understand what she was fighting for. To work out an adequate account of democratic politics she had to understand democratic politics from within – to explicate and clarify the understanding of politics within which democratic doctrines and practices make sense. The fight against totalitarianism required both factual knowledge and pure theory. Theory was necessary not to direct but to illuminate the struggle:

> Understanding, while it cannot be expected to provide results which are specifically helpful or inspiring in the fight against totalitarianism, must accompany this fight if it is to be more than a fight for survival. Insofar as totalitarian movements have sprung up in the non-totalitarian world . . . the process of understanding is clearly, and perhaps primarily, also a process of self-understanding. For, although we merely know, but do not yet understand, what we are fighting against, we know and understand even less what we are fighting for . . . In this sense the activity of understanding is necessary; while it can never directly inspire the fight or provide otherwise missing objectives, it alone can make it meaningful and prepare a new resourcefulness of the human mind and heart . . .[73]

Her work was an effort to understand the deepest differences between democratic politics and the anti-politics of totalitarianism.

[73] EU, 310.

Basic Questions 33

This effort did not lead Arendt to a liberal understanding of politics.[74] Liberal concepts of politics seemed inadequate to her in several ways. They failed to distinguish rigorously between politics and other spheres of existence. They interpreted political history in ahistorical terms. They simplified the actual history of politics from the Greeks to the present. They supported superficial concepts of basic political realities. They failed to adequately grasp the actual practice of democratic politics. Another concept of the political was necessary, not only to fight totalitarianism but also to clarify and renew the practice of democratic politics.

But how to answer this question? What way of thought could lead her to another concept of the political?

[74] The core of her critique was that liberalism lacked a pure concept of the political since "it always assumed an identity of politics, economics, and society" (OT, 336).

CHAPTER 2

A Way of Thought

Critical Dismantling

Arendt approached politics through a kind of phenomenology: "I am a sort of phenomenologist, but, ach, not in Hegel's way – or Husserl's."[1] She learned phenomenology from Heidegger, whose way of thought was grounded in his view of human existence. This "existential" phenomenology aimed at a "critical dismantling" ("*Kritische Abbau*") of concepts inherited from the philosophical tradition. Heidegger wrote that critical dismantling consisted of three tasks: *Destruktion*, *Reduktion*, and *Konstruktion*: "These three basic components of phenomenological method – reduction, construction, destruction – belong together in their content and must receive grounding in their mutual pertinence."[2] If we follow *the way* Arendt thought, and if we unpack her few comments on *how* to think, it is clear that she worked through these three tasks in her attempt to construct a pure concept of the political.

Destruktion names the attempt to lay out the inherited terms in which we think of something, and to trace the genealogy of those terms back to the native sphere and the original experiences from which they were born. Heidegger described *Destruktion* as "a critical process in which traditional concepts, which at first must necessarily be employed, are de-constructed down to the sources from which they were drawn."[3] His *Destruktion* of the concepts of form and matter, for example, aimed to uncover their original sense by tracing the words back to their source in the experience of production and the sphere of equipment. In his essay on *The Origin of the Work of Art*, he argued that the concepts of "matter and form are

---

[1] Arendt, quoted in Young-Bruehl, *Hannah Arendt: For Love of the World*, 405.
[2] Heidegger, *Basic Problems of Phenomenology*, 23. I am indebted to Rodolphe Gasché's lucid discussion of Heidegger's early method of phenomenology in "Abbau, *Destruktion*, Deconstruction," in *The Tain of the Mirror* (Cambridge, MA: Harvard University Press, 1986).
[3] Heidegger, *Basic Problems of Phenomenology*, 23.

determinations of beings which find their true home in the essential nature of equipment," and that these concepts are bound to mislead our thinking if we abstract them from their native sphere and force them onto works of art.[4] To critically dismantle traditional concepts does not mean to trash them. It means to recover their original sense, to locate their native sphere, and to demarcate the limits within which they make sense and beyond which they tend to misguide our thought. *Destruktion* does not destroy tradition, but renews it by retrieving the original sense of inherited concepts. "And this is not a negation of the tradition or a condemnation of it as worthless; quite the reverse, it signifies precisely a positive appropriation of the tradition."[5] *Destruktion* shows the lineage of traditional concepts in order to clarify their sense and to deprive them of their seeming self-evidence.

Arendt made this task of thought her own. She argued that philosophical concepts are always formulated in words abstracted from a particular sphere of experience, and their abstract meanings always retain traces of their original sense. "All philosophical terms are metaphors, frozen analogies, as it were, whose true meaning discloses itself when we dissolve the term into the original context, which must have been vividly in the mind of the first philosopher to use it."[6] She described her work as a form of "conceptual analysis" whose first aim was to find out "where concepts come from."[7] Her first step is typically to lay out the common concepts we take for granted, to trace their lineage back to the native sphere from which they came, to uncover the experiences on which they were based, and so to illuminate their original sense. Her task as a thinker was:

> to discover the real origins of traditional concepts in order to distill from them anew their original spirit which has so sadly evaporated from the very key words of political language – such as freedom and justice, authority and reason, responsibility and virtue, power and glory – leaving behind empty shells with which to settle almost all accounts, regardless of their underlying phenomenal reality.[8]

This genealogy of concepts can have two outcomes. It can reveal that some of the words in which we think about politics first originated in nonpolitical experiences and were later abstracted from their native sphere and transposed into political thought; the effect is to deprive these words of

---

[4] Martin Heidegger, *Off the Beaten Track,* ed. and trans. Julian Young and Kenneth Haynes (New York: Cambridge University Press, 2002), 10.
[5] Heidegger, *Basic Problems of Phenomenology,* 23.   [6] LMT, 104.
[7] Arendt, quoted in Young-Bruehl, *Hannah Arendt: For Love of the World,* 318.   [8] BPF, 15.

36 A Way of Thought

their self-evidence and to raise questions about whether they limit or mislead our thinking. But a *Destruktion* of traditional concepts can also reveal the specific political experiences that originally gave inherited words their meaning; the effect is to illuminate more clearly the original sense of words.

Reduktion is the attempt to understand a single, prime example of a phenomenon by describing how it appears in experience, and then to move from that particular experience toward a general understanding of the phenomenon's essential traits. Heidegger described it as the move from descriptions of specific beings toward an understanding of their Being: "For us phenomenological reduction means leading phenomenological vision back from the apprehension of a being, whatever may be the character of that apprehension, to the understanding of the Being of this being."[9] In this sense, to "reduce" a work of art is to move from a description of a particular work of art as it actually appears in experience towards a reflection on the nature of artworks in general. This is why Heidegger began his reflections on art with a description of an actual work – van Gogh's painting of peasant shoes – on whose basis he constructed a general concept of art. *Reduktion* follows from the basic imperative of phenomenology: thought has to start with concrete examples and orient itself by the way they appear in experience. The effort to grasp what beings are in essence must begin from an ever-renewed "return to the things themselves."

Arendt followed this movement in her work. While she rarely highlighted the experiences that informed her thought, she believed that to understand what beings are in essence we must always start from and be guided by the way concrete examples appear in actual experience. In *Between Past and Future* she wrote:

> These are exercises in political thought as it arises out of the actuality of political incidents (though such incidents are mentioned only occasionally), and my assumption is that thought itself arises out of incidents of living experience and must remain bound to them as the only guideposts by which to take its bearings.[10]

This movement of thought can have two starting points. On the one hand, it can start from the direct, personal experience of the thinker. This was often Arendt's point of departure: her work on totalitarianism started from her experience of Nazism; her thoughts on the banality of evil came from

---

[9] Heidegger, *Basic Problems of Phenomenology*, 21.   [10] BPF, 60.1014.

Critical Dismantling

37

her being at the trial of Adolf Eichmann; her reflections on thinking, willing, and judging were guided by her own experience of the life of the mind. But when personal experience is limited or impossible, on the other hand, thinking can start from the testimony of those who have experienced a phenomenon first hand. Arendt worked this way as well: her thoughts on revolution were guided by the testimonies of the American revolutionaries; her concepts of power and violence were informed by the news of the Hungarian Revolution; her reflections on the political started with the experience of politics expressed in the nontheoretical writings of classical Athens.

Konstruktion is the attempt to interpret or construe what something is in essence, by sensing the limits of traditional concepts, discerning what resists or eludes them, and rethinking these concepts in order to more fully grasp and bring to light what they have distorted or concealed. Heidegger described *Konstruktion* in typically cryptic terms: "Being does not become accessible like a being. We do not simply find it in front of us. As is to be shown, it must always be brought to view in a free projection. This projecting of the antecedently given being upon its Being and the structures of its Being we call phenomenological construction."[11] It is easier to see what *Konstruktion* is if we look at what Heidegger actually did in his own thinking. In his essay on art, for example, he first points out two traits of artworks that elude the concepts of form and matter – the power of artworks to illuminate the world, and their irreducible resistance to final understanding. He then tries to bring to light and grasp these two traits by refining and redefining the words "world" and "earth." The task of *Konstruktion* has to start from the meanings of words in everyday speech, since everyday language may hold prejudices that misguide our thinking, but it may also contain insights that are deeper and more illuminating than traditional concepts: "All ontological inquiries into phenomena ... must start from what everyday *Dasein* 'says' about them."[12]

Arendt's thinking was also *konstruktiv* in this sense. She aimed to locate the limits that inherited concepts impose on our thinking, to show what those concepts have been unable to grasp, and to refine or redefine the terms in which we think in order to more fully comprehend what has been beyond the reach of conceptual thought. In her view, political theory has

[11] Heidegger, *Basic Problems in Phenomenology*, 21–22.
[12] Martin Heidegger, *Being and Time*, trans, Joan Stambaugh (Albany, NY: State University of New York Press, 1996), 259.

38 A Way of Thought

been led astray by basic concepts of political philosophy; but it has also been led astray by the metaphysical assumptions that have guided the way essential questions have been traditionally framed and understood. The problem is "not that the old questions which are coeval with the appearance of men on earth have become 'meaningless,' but that the way they were framed and answered has lost plausibility."[13] Her aim was not just to critique political philosophy, but to critically dismantle the metaphysical concepts that political philosophers have used to frame their questions:

> I have clearly joined the ranks of those who for some time now have been attempting to dismantle metaphysics, and philosophy with all its categories, as we have known them from their beginning in Greece until today.[14]

She insisted that critical dismantling is not simply negative: "the dismantling process itself is not destructive."[15] Her thinking was *konstruktiv* – it aimed to reinterpret political phenomena by reconstructing inherited concepts.

Theory and Nontheory

Arendt's way of thought exceeds common concepts of theory. The word "theorist" comes from the Greek word for "spectator," she noted, and "theory" has traditionally implied the stance of an outside observer: "From the Greek word for spectators, *theatai*, the later philosophical term 'theory' was derived, and the word 'theoretical' until a few hundred years ago meant 'contemplating,' looking upon something from the outside, from a position implying a view that is hidden from those who take part in the spectacle and actualize it."[16] To theorize is to disengage from active involvement with beings in order to see them from a detached and outside perspective. As theory in this sense is a privileged form of knowledge, theoretical language is a privileged form of discourse. Just as the task of the theorist is to withdraw from active engagement with phenomena in order to see them as they appear in the experience of disinterested contemplation, so the task of theoretical discourse is to abstract words from the prejudices and confusions of traditional language, and to invent a terminology in which each term has a precise and definite sense.

Heidegger challenged this view of theory in *Being and Time*. Things do not always appear most clearly when we suspend our active involvement with them, he said. Think of a piece of chalk at a blackboard. When I use

[13] RJ, 162.   [14] LMT, 212.   [15] LMT, 212.   [16] LMT, 93.

Theory and Nontheory

it, I see clearly how it relates to the context of the classroom, and these contextual relations are precisely what make it a tool. If I stop using it and adopt a theoretical stance to the chalk, seeing it from outside the activity of writing, I can learn to see and describe it as a chemical substance with objective properties. But this theoretical perspective and discourse necessarily overlook the relational context that is essential to the piece of chalk as a tool of writing. Heidegger asked: "Why does what we are talking about ... show itself differently when our way of talking is modified? Not because we are keeping our distance from handling, nor because we are only looking *away* from the useful character of this being, but because we are looking *at* the thing at hand encountered in a 'new' way, as something objectively present."[17] This kind of theoretical stance does *not* give us a privileged view of the chalk. Instead, it changes the way the chalk appears, so that we see it not as a tool that is ready-to-hand but as a substance that is objectively present. This kind of theory lets us see the chalk *as a natural substance* (calcium carbonate), but it blinds us to the relational context essential the piece of chalk *as a tool.*

Theory does not have to distort our view of the Being of beings, for Heidegger: "A modification of our understanding of Being seems not to be necessarily constitutive for the genesis of the theoretical mode of behavior 'towards things.'"[18] We can avoid such distortion by adopting a different kind of theory. Instead of abstaining from active involvement with things in order to see how they appear in the experience of detached and disinterested contemplation, we can suspend our active involvement with things in order to reflect through memory on how they appeared *in the experience of active involvement.* This kind of theory is exemplified by *Being and Time* itself. Heidegger theorized the nature of tools not by abstracting them from the experience of work and focusing on their objective properties, but by reflecting on the contextual relations that make tools what they are, and that are most apparent in the experience of engaged and interested practical activity. He started from nontheoretical insights, and translated those insights into theoretical terms.

This kind of theory is central to existential phenomenology. A basic trait of human existence is self-understanding. Our self-understanding guides the way we live. Ways of life center on distinctive forms of practice, in light of which the world is relevant and meaningful to us in distinctive ways. To comprehend a way of life we cannot adopt the stance of an observer who sees that way of life from the outside, as if it were a natural reality existing

---

[17] Heidegger, *Being and Time*, 344.   [18] Heidegger, *Being and Time*, 344.

40   A Way of Thought

in and of itself. Instead, we have to start by understanding ways of life from within, by entering the self-understanding of its practitioners, and by explicating, clarifying, and refining their understanding of the world.

This approach to theory alters the relation of theoretical and nontheoretical discourse. Nontheoretical discourse is not just a crude or primitive form of language, rife with prejudice and confusion, from which one must cobble together a precise and definite theoretical terminology. Instead, nontheoretical discourse may articulate genuine insights reached through nontheoretical forms of thought. In *Being and Time*, Heidegger drew on the insights of philosophers, of course, but also on the insights of nontheoretical thinkers such as Thucydides, Augustine, Luther, and Tolstoy. A Latin myth about Care, for example, was cited as a nontheoretical interpretation of human existence: "in this document human existence expresses itself about itself 'primordially,' unaffected by any theoretical interpretation and without aiming to propose any."[19] One task of theory is to find genuine insights in nontheoretical discourse, and to translate those insights into the conceptually articulate language of theory.

Arendt took from Heidegger this existential approach to theory. But she saw in it something Heidegger did not see: its implications for political philosophy. In *The Human Condition*, she argued that political philosophers have generally not understood politics from within, on the basis of an active engagement in political life, but have seen the active life from the outside perspective of the contemplative life.

> I had been concerned with the problem of Action, the oldest concern of political theory, and what had always troubled me about it was that the very term I adopted for my reflections on the matter, namely, *vita activa*, was coined by men who were devoted to the contemplative way of life and who looked upon all kinds of being alive from that perspective.[20]

Existential phenomenology opened up a new approach to political theory: rather than withdrawing from political life and adopting the outside perspective of a spectator in order to see politics as a reality existing in and of itself, the political theorist should suspend active engagement with politics, or study the first-hand testimonies of political actors, in order to reflect on the meaning of political phenomena as they appeared in the experience of active engagement. Instead of viewing politics as an objective reality independent of human understanding, theorists should see politics as a possibility of human existence that depends on a certain

---

[19] Heidegger, *Being and Time*, 190.   [20] LMT, 6.

Theory and Nontheory

self-understanding, a self-understanding implicit in the nontheoretical language and literature of political communities.

For Arendt, politics cannot be understood as if it were a natural phenomenon. Theorists have to start not by looking for timeless, universal, and objective traits of politics, but by explicating, clarifying, and refining the self-understanding of people living political lives: "The sources talk, and what they reveal is the self-understanding as well as the self-interpretation of people who act and who believe they know what they are doing."[21] In her view, this "self-understanding and self-interpretation are the very foundation of all analysis and understanding."[22] Just as Heidegger argued that "All ontological inquiries into phenomena ... must start from what everyday *Dasein* 'says' about them,"[23] so Arendt argued that thinking must start from the sense of words in everyday speech:

> Popular language, as it expresses preliminary understanding, thus starts the process of true understanding. Its discovery must always remain the content of true understanding, if it is not to lose itself in the clouds of mere speculation–a danger always present.[24]

Arendt knew that everyday speech usually expresses an average understanding of things, and one task of thought is to discern and to point out what resists or eludes popular language. But everyday speech can also articulate nontheoretical insights that are more illuminating than inherited theoretical concepts. In this case, the task of thought is to explicate the insights implicit in nontheoretical language, and to refine or redefine inherited words in order to distill those insights into adequate concepts.

Arendt's approach to theory is clearest in her book *On Revolution*. Her thoughts on revolution started from the words of actual revolutionaries. Instead of focusing on their theories, she focused on their nontheoretical discourse. Her task as a theorist was not to recover or critique the theories of the revolutionaries, but to locate the authentic insights implicit in their nontheoretical discourse, and to "translate" these insights "into the less direct but more articulate language of political thought."[25]

Arendt took the same approach to the question of the political. She was concerned with the political theories of philosophers, of course, but she also aimed to find the authentic insights implicit in the nontheoretical writings of Greek poets, orators, and historians. In an essay on freedom,

---

[21] EU, 338.   [22] EU, 339.   [23] Heidegger, *Being and Time*, 259.   [24] EU, 312.
[25] OR, 174.

A Way of Thought

for example, she tried to retrieve an authentic understanding of freedom articulated in the texts of classical antiquity – not in the theories of philosophers ("this articulation is nowhere more difficult to grasp than in the writings of the philosophers"), but in the nontheoretical discourse of "political and pre-philosophical traditions."[26] One task of political theory, in her view, is,

> To try to distill, as it were, adequate concepts from the body of non-philosophical literature, from poetic, dramatic, historical, and political writings, whose articulation lifts experiences into a realm of splendor which is not the realm of conceptual thought.[27]

Arendt also stressed that true insight may be implicit in language itself. Another task of theory is to retrieve and refine the nontheoretical understanding of political phenomena implicit in the language of politics.

Tasks of Thought

So Arendt's approach to political theory consisted of six tasks:

Destruktion
(1)   To lay out the terms in which political matters are understood.
(2)   To trace them back to the experiences from which they emerged.

Reduktion
(3)   To describe an example given in experience or first-hand testimony.
(4)   To move from this description to a reflection on what it is in essence.

Konstruktion
(5)   To find the limits of concepts by showing what they obscure.
(6)   To rethink these concepts in order to better grasp what things are.

These are tasks in a way of thought, not steps in a rigid procedure. Arendt never slogged through them step by step. But when she thought through questions of political theory, explicitly or implicitly she worked through each of these tasks. Her way of thought is especially clear in her effort to critically dismantle traditional concepts of "rule."[28]

---

[26] BPF, 165.   [27] BPF, 165.
[28] See especially "Ruling and Being Ruled," in *Thinking without a Bannister*, ed. Jerome Kohn (New York: Schocken Books, 2018), 56–68.

Tasks of Thought

(1) The first task of *Destruktion* is to lay out the basic terms in which we think. Arendt argued that we tend to think of politics in terms of "rule" (*archein* or *kratein*), and to conceive of forms of government as forms of rule (monarchy, democracy). The language of political philosophy has been shaped by "the commonplace notion already to be found in Plato and Aristotle that every political community consists of those who rule and those who are ruled (on which assumption in turn are based the current definitions of forms of government – rule by one or monarchy, rule by few or oligarchy, rule by many or democracy)."[29] These terms have led theorists to think of politics as a matter of sovereignty, command, and domination – vertical power relations of control and obedience.

(2) The second task of *Destruktion* is to trace terms back to their native sphere. In the case of "rule," Arendt argued, etymology suggests that words for rule did not originate in the political sphere but in the sphere of the household. "All Greek and Latin words which express some rulership over others, such as *rex, pater, anax, basileus,* refer originally to household relationships and were names the slaves gave to their masters."[30] We have come to think of politics in terms of rule in part because the words that express power over others have been abstracted from their native sphere, transposed into the political sphere, and applied indifferently to the realities of politics.

(3) The first task of *Reduktion* is to describe a prime example of a phenomenon. Arendt argued the classical polis was the prime example of a political community, and that if we want to understand the essence of politics it helps to understand the experiences and language of the polis: "The very word [politics] ... echoes the experiences of the community which first discovered the essence and the realm of the political. It is indeed difficult and even misleading to talk about politics and its innermost principles without drawing to some extent upon the experiences of Greek and Roman antiquity, and this for no other reason than that men have never, either before or after, thought so highly of political activity and bestowed so much dignity on its realm."[31] For this reason, much of her work focused on understanding the history, institutions, and language of the classical polis.

(4) The second task of *Reduktion,* in this case, is to move from the example of the polis to the essence of politics. Arendt's thinking started

---

[29] HC, 222.   [30] HC, 32.   [31] BPF, 154.

44 A Way of Thought

from politics as it was understood in classical Athens and moved toward understanding the political as a universal possibility of human existence. One of the things that distinguished the Greek polis from other forms of community, she argued, was that it excluded relations of rule between male citizens:

> Since Herodotus, [freedom] was understood as a form of political organization in which the citizens lived together under conditions of no-rule, *without a division between rulers and ruled.* This notion of no-rule was expressed by the word *isonomy,* whose outstanding characteristic among the forms of government, as the ancients had enumerated them, was that *the notion of rule* (the 'archy' from ἄρχειν in monarchy and oligarchy, or the 'cracy' from κρατεῖν in democracy) *was entirely absent from it.* The *polis* was supposed to be an isonomy, not a democracy.[32]

From this attempt to grasp what distinguishes the polis from other kinds of community, Arendt tried to grasp the traits that distinguish politics from other ways of being together. One trait essential to politics, in her view, is that it excludes relations of rule among equals:

> The meaning of politics ... is that men in their freedom can interact with one another without compulsion, force, and *rule* over one another, as equals among equals, commanding and obeying one another only in emergencies – that is, in times of war–but otherwise managing all their affairs by speaking with and persuading one another.[33]

This is the *reduktiv* movement of existential phenomenology: Arendt started with a prime example of a polity – the Athenian polis – and moved towards a concept of politics as such. This kind of theory is grounded in history, but looks to the essential. *Reduktion* starts from the singular but aims at the universal.

(5) The first task of *Konstruktion* is to locate the limits of traditional concepts by showing what they distort or conceal. Arendt argued that the notion of rule has obscured the nature of political power, and has led theorists to confuse power, strength, force, authority, and violence. Underlying this confusion was

> the conviction that the most crucial political issue is, and always has been, the question of Who rules Whom? Power, strength, force, authority, violence – these are [thought to be] but words to indicate the means

---

[32] OR, 30 (italics added).   [33] PP, 117 (italics added).

Tasks of Thought 45

by which man rules over man; they are held to be synonyms because they have the same function. It is only after one ceases to reduce public affairs to the business of dominion that the original data in the realm of human affairs will appear, or, rather, reappear, in their authentic diversity.[34]

The notion of rule has led theorists to conceive of power in terms of vertical relations of command and obedience. But this concept of power has its limits, Arendt argued. If we conceive of power in terms of rule, we cannot grasp what happens in revolutionary situations when a ruler loses popular support and the command/obedience relation collapses. Revolutionary situations elude traditional concepts of power. The task of *Konstruktion* is thus to point to what exceeds the scope of inherited concepts. In this way, she marked the limits of traditional concepts of power by pointing out their failure to grasp and illuminate the phenomenon of revolution.

(6) The second task of *Konstruktion* is to refine inherited concepts in order to better grasp what things are. In her thoughts on violence, Arendt tried to unearth a level of power that precedes and makes possible the power to rule. The power to rule (the vertical structure of command and obedience) depends on the ability of a group to act in concert through their common support of a ruler. This ability is the condition of possibility of the power of the ruler. So the power of a ruler ultimately depends on the power of a group to act in concert. "Power is never the property of an individual; it belongs to a group and remains in existence only so long as the group stays together."[35] When a group can no longer act in concert, or when it stops supporting the ruler, the power of the ruler to command obedience is bound to collapse. Traditional concepts of power focus on rule but obscure its conditions of possibility.

Traditional concepts obscure another kind of power as well. If power at the most basic level is the ability of a group to act in concert, then power can be generated not only by vertical promises of allegiance between rulers and supporters; it can also be generated by horizontal promises of mutual commitment among equals. So traditional concepts of power also obscure the possibility of non-hierarchical power structures.

[34] OV, 44.   [35] OR, 44.

In short, Arendt aimed to free political thought from the limitations imposed on it by traditional concepts of rule. She used a threefold method of *Destruktion*, *Reduktion*, and *Konstruktion* to uncover the condition of possibility of power in the sense of rule, and also to bring to light the possibility of a kind of power that exceeds altogether the vertical structure of command and obedience. The aim of her thought was to clarify, sharpen, and refine the sense of words in order to better grasp what political phenomena are in essence.

How then did Arendt use this way of thinking to work through the question of the political? Let us follow her path of thought one task at a time.

CHAPTER 3

A Pure Concept of the Political

> Politics is based on the fact of human plurality ... Because philosophy and theology are always concerned with *man* ... they have found no valid philosophical answer to the question: What is politics?[1]

> This occidental philosophy has never had a pure concept of the political [*einen reinen Begriff des Politischen*] and could never have one since, by necessity, philosophy has spoken of Man in the singular, and has simply neglected the fact of plurality.[2]

If Western philosophy has never had a pure concept of the political, we cannot grasp the meaning of politics simply by returning to the philosophical tradition and recovering a ready-made concept. Arendt aimed instead to retrieve the authentic insights implicit in the nontheoretical discourse of people who experienced political life first hand, and to articulate those insights in the conceptual language of theory: "to try to distill, as it were, adequate concepts from the body of non-philosophical literature, from poetic, dramatic, historical, and political writings, whose articulation lifts experiences into a realm of splendor which is not the realm of conceptual thought."[3]

Arendt never defined the political. Definitions went against the grain of her thought, which aimed not to foreclose questions but to keep them open. But questions stay open as long as we try to answer them; they are foreclosed not just by claims to definitive answers, but also by the refusal to venture any answer at all. So – against the grain of her thought – let me try to lay out the understanding of politics implicit in Arendt's writings.

---

[1] PP, 93. The original German is in WP, 9.
[2] Arendt in a letter to Karl Jaspers, March 4, 1951. The English edition translates her words as "a clear concept" of the political (166). In the German, she actually speaks of a "pure" concept: "einen reinen Begriff." *Hannah Arendt and Karl Jaspers, Briefwechsel* 1926–1969, ed. Lotte Köhler and Hans Saner (Munich: Piper Verlag, 1985), 203.
[3] BPF, 165.

47

A Pure Concept of the Political

What then is politics? How does it differ from ethics, law, economics, religion? What defines the realm of the political and marks its limits? What makes it possible?[4]

Prejudices

The first task of thinking, for Arendt, is to make explicit what we take for granted:

> If we want to talk about politics today we have to start with the prejudices that we all have against politics ... We cannot ignore them because they are mixed up in our own words, and we cannot fight them with arguments because they draw on undeniable realities and reflect faithfully the political aspects of our real, current situation.[5]

These prejudices are not groundless assumptions – they are grounded in the realities of our time. But the reality of our time is that politics has been utterly debased. The danger of these prejudices is not that they distort our situation but that they make it seem natural and inevitable, and that by concealing the meaning of politics they may contribute to its utter disappearance.

> The danger is that the political may disappear completely from the world. But these prejudices anticipate this disappearance, they throw out the baby with the bath water, they substitute for politics what would end politics, and they represent what would be a catastrophe as if it were inscribed in the nature of things and therefore inescapable.[6]

By explicitly laying out these prejudices we can begin to gain a certain critical distance from them and start to see the realities of our time in a new light.

These prejudices are as follows:

Politics is a universal and necessary part of human life. There are now many answers to the question of the political, but "What all these answers have in common is that they take for granted that politics exists and has existed always and everywhere that men live together in a historico-cultural sense."[7] This is "the modern prejudice according to which politics would be an absolute necessity that has existed always and everywhere."[8]

---

[4] The necessity of essential questions was laid out by Jacques Derrida: "The political is to be understood as the essence of what is political ... A certain unity of meaning is indeed necessary: do we actually know what 'politics' means, plain and simple." Jacques Derrida, paraphrased in Philippe Lacoue-Labarthe and Jean-Luc Nancy, *Retreating the Political*, ed. Simon Sparks (New York: Routledge, 1997), 142.

[5] PP, 96. WP, 13.   [6] PP, 96–97. WP, 13–14.   [7] PP, 115. WP, 37.   [8] PP, 119. WP, 41.

Politics is a means to an end. "All the determinations or definitions of politics that we find in our tradition constitute, in their authentic content, justifications of politics. To speak very generally, all these justifications and definitions end up defining politics as a means to a higher end, even if this end has naturally been interpreted very differently over the course of the centuries."[9] The means/end schema has dominated political thought.

In the modern age there are two main interpretations of this end.

The end of politics is life itself. Politics is supposed to secure survival and prosperity. "Politics, we hear, is an absolute necessity for human life, whether it is a matter of individual existence or the existence of society. Since man is not self-sufficient [*autark*], but depends on others for his own existence, he has to care about this social existence which concerns everyone, and without which communal life would not be possible. The task and the end of politics is to secure life in the broadest sense."[10] Arendt stressed that "life" here does not mean a specific way of living, but merely the bare life of animal existence.

The end of politics is liberty. "Politics permits the individual to pursue his objectives in peace and quiet, that is to say, without being bothered with politics."[11] While liberty is conceived in many ways, she argued, it is commonly seen as external to politics. Politics secures liberty, and liberty exists outside the political realm.

Politics is a matter of rule. Strictly speaking, to rule is to be sovereign, to be master of a domain, not to be subject to a higher power, to command obedience. More generally, to rule means to have power over others, to be able to control their actions, to be able to make them do as one wills. Arendt argued the hallmark of most political philosophy since Plato is "the concept of rule, that is, the notion that men can lawfully and politically live together only when some are entitled to command and others are forced to obey."[12] The prejudice that politics is a matter of rule underlies the belief that different forms of government are simply different kinds of rule, and this belief is to some extent implicit in the very words with which we conceive and classify forms of government: "monarchy" means rule of one and "oligarchy" means rule by a few. "Democracy" is commonly interpreted as "rule of the people"; "plutocracy" as rule of the rich; "theocracy" as rule of God; "aristocracy" as rule of the best. This prejudice underlies the assumption that the most basic question of political philosophy is "Who should rule whom?"

---

[9] PP, 115. WP, 36.   [10] PP, 115. WP, 36.   [11] PP, 115. WP, 36.   [12] HC, 222.

50 A Pure Concept of the Political

Politics is ultimately a struggle for the power to rule. While politics in the broadest sense is supposed to concern the organization of power in communities, in a narrow sense politics is thought to be the pursuit of power itself. This is the sense in which "politics" is most commonly used today – we speak of party politics as a contest for control of the government, international politics as a fight for global hegemony, politics in general as merely an arena for class struggle, or as the struggle in which the powerful try to sustain their dominance and the powerless seek to resist and subvert it. This notion of politics supports what she called "the prejudices against politics – the idea that politics at bottom is a tissue of lies and deceptions at the service of shabby interests and even shabbier ideologies, while international politics oscillates between empty propaganda and naked violence."[13]

These assumptions are not just errors, according to Arendt. They are based on experience and reflect the realities of our time. The question is not whether they are inaccurate, but whether they are superficial. What is at stake is not whether they correctly describe the obvious features of politics today, but whether they fail to grasp the distinctive character of the political realm – not whether they blind us to the facts, but whether they prevent us from understanding our situation.

Arendt thought these prejudices obscure the meaning of politics. Their prevalence shows that we have for the most part lost a genuine understanding of political life. Our task as thinkers is to suspend belief in our prejudices and to gain a critical distance from common conceptions of politics. But how is this possible?

A Return to Antiquity

In her reflections on politics, Arendt both followed and strayed from Heidegger's way of thought. Heidegger had no definite answer to the question of the political. In a 1942 lecture he wrote: "The 'political' is what belongs to the polis and can therefore be determined only in terms of the polis ... Yet what is the polis of the Greeks? No 'definition' can ever answer such questions; or rather the 'definition,' even if it points in the right direction, provides no guarantee of an adequate relation to what is essential."[14] Heidegger was less concerned with answering the question of

---

[13] PP, 98. WP, 15.
[14] Martin Heidegger, *Hölderlin's Hymn "The Ister,"* trans. William McNeill and Julia Davis (Bloomington: Indiana University Press, 1996), 80.

A Return to Antiquity

the political than with keeping the question open. To keep it open, in his view, we have to avoid two ways in which the question is commonly foreclosed.

On the one hand, we cannot take for granted a modern concept of the political, and project it back onto the ancient Greek polis. "If the 'political' is what belongs to the polis . . . then it is of little help to us to arm ourselves with any ideas whatsoever of the 'political' so as to delimit the essence of the polis using such weapons."[15] To do so is simply to impose our preconceptions on the polis, and to foreclose the possibility that a study of the polis might actually lead us to rethink our current prejudices. Heidegger's target here was the Nazi view of the polis in light of Carl Schmitt's concept of the political, a view in which the Greeks started to look suspiciously like Nazis. "Today . . . one can scarcely read a treatise or book on the Greeks without everywhere being assured that here, with the Greeks, 'everything' is determined 'politically'. In most 'research results,' the Greeks appear as the pure National Socialists."[16]

On the other hand, we cannot just recover a Greek theory of politics and assume that it adequately captures the essence of the polis. To think through the question of the political we have to start with the Greek understanding of the polis, but we cannot assume that Greek philosophy fully grasped the nature of politics. Heidegger makes this point in a passage worth quoting at length:

> Who says the Greeks, because they 'lived' in the polis, were also in the clear as to the essence of the polis? . . . If we therefore ask: What is the polis of the Greeks? then we must not presuppose that the Greeks must have known this, as though all we had to do was to inquire among them. Yet are not extensive reflections on the polis handed down to us in Greek thought– Plato's comprehensive dialogue on the *politeia*, that is, on everything that concerns the polis; the far-reaching lecture course by Aristotle, *episteme politike*, "The Politics"? Certainly. Yet the question remains: From where do these thinkers think the essence of the polis? The question remains whether the foundations and fundamental perspectives of this Greek thought at the end of the great Greek era were then adequate even to the question of the polis at all . . . Perhaps there lies precisely in these late reflections concerning the polis a genuine mistaking of its essence, namely of the fact that it itself is what is question-worthy and that it must be acknowledged and preserved in such worthiness. If this is the case, then it

---

[15] Heidegger, *"The Ister,"* 80.   [16] Heidegger, *"The Ister,"* 79–80.

A Pure Concept of the Political

seems as though we must think more Greek than the Greeks themselves. It does not merely seem so, it is so.[17]

Any attempt to think through the question of the political, for Heidegger, has to follow a double directive: it must suspend modern preconceptions about the nature of politics and return to a study of the classical polis itself; but it must not assume that classical political theory was able to fully grasp the essence of politics.

Arendt followed this double directive in her thought. To rethink the concept of the political she returned to the Greeks.

> The very word [politics] ... echoes the experiences of the community which first discovered the essence and the realm of the political. It is indeed difficult and even misleading to talk about politics and its innermost principles without drawing to some extent upon the experiences of Greek and Roman antiquity, and this for no other reason than that men have never, either before or after, thought so highly of political activity and bestowed so much dignity on its realm.[18]

But this return was complex. Arendt thought the Greeks first discovered the essence and realm of the political, but their understanding of politics was nontheoretical – they had maxims, notions, and principles, but never an adequate theory of the political.[19] She also claimed that as a political sphere opened up in the *poleis* of ancient Greece, the Greeks had to transform old words and invent new ones in order to talk about this new kind of community; inevitably some of these words led them to think about politics in misleading terms. And finally, she argued that when philosophers began to work out theories of government, they did not fully grasp the specificity of the political realm. Her project was to work out a pure concept of the political by making explicit and articulating in

---

[17] Heidegger, *"The Ister,"* 80–81.   [18] BPF, 154.

[19] Much has been said about this kind of claim. Some thinkers have also claimed the Greeks discovered the political. M. I. Finley wrote: "It was the Greeks, after all, who discovered not only democracy but also politics, the art of reaching decisions by public discussion and then obeying those decisions as a necessary condition of civilized social existence" (M. I. Finley, *Democracy Ancient and Modern* (New Brunswick, NJ: Rutgers University Press, 1937), 14). See also Cynthia Farrar, *The Origins of Democratic Thinking: The Invention of Politics in Classical Athens* (New York: Cambridge University Press, 1988). Others argue it is blindly Eurocentric to locate the origins of politics and democracy in Greece. See Amartya Sen, "Democracy as a Universal Value," *Journal of Democracy*, 10, 3, (1999); B. Isakhan and S. Stockwell, *The Secret History of Democracy* (New York: Palgrave Macmillan, 2011); Kostas Vlassopoulos, *Unthinking the Greek Polis* (New York: Cambridge University Press, 2007); and Jack Goody, *The Theft of History* (New York: Cambridge University Press, 2012).

A Return to Antiquity

concepts the original understanding of politics implicit in the nontheoretical writings of the Greeks.[20]

Why return to the Greeks? Why study the history of the polis if we are looking for the essence of politics? Why start with the historical to find the essential? If a concept of the political is to have universal validity, it should be applicable to political communities in all times and places – why not look at all political communities throughout history and across cultures, and try to isolate the core features they have in common? Isn't it arbitrary and ethnocentric to derive a concept of the political from one culture and one period of time?

Arendt's approach was guided by assumptions implicit in her phenomenology. We cannot find the essence of politics by a comparative study of political communities, because to decide which communities are political we would have to rely on a prior concept of politics; that is, we would have to presuppose what we are trying to find. Instead we have to start with a prime example of political community (a community universally recognized as political), to isolate its distinctive traits (the traits that distinguish it from other kinds of community), to abstract these traits from that specific example, and to articulate them in a general concept that captures the distinctive nature of political communities everywhere. Since the prime example of a political community is the classical polis – the origin of the word "politics" – the test of any concept of the political is how well it grasps its distinctive traits. To work out an adequate concept of the political we have to start from the actual history and language of the polis.

Arendt did not idealize the Greek polis, or hold it up as a model to be emulated. She knew the freedom and equality of its citizens depended on the domination and enslavement of noncitizens.[21] Her aim was not to

---

[20] There has been much debate around the claim that the Greeks had no theory of politics or democracy. Finley agreed that the Greek understanding of politics and democracy was never explicitly articulated: "The Greeks themselves did not develop a theory of democracy. There were notions, maxims, generalities, but these do not add up to a systematic theory. The philosophers attacked democracy; the committed democrats responded by ignoring them, by going about the business of government and politics in a democratic way, without writing treatises on the subject" (Finley, *Democracy Ancient and Modern*, 28). Paul Cartledge concurred: "the ancients did not develop a theory or theories of democracy" (Paul Cartledge, *Democracy: A Life* (New York: Oxford University Press, 2016), 91). Cynthia Farrar, by contrast, argues that the Greeks did theorize about democracy, and that "the failure to observe the existence of democratic theory in ancient Athens rests on a misunderstanding of the nature of democracy and theory" (Farrar, *The Origins of Democratic Thinking*, 5).

[21] HC, 31.

54 A Pure Concept of the Political

glorify the achievements of "Western Civilization," but to grasp the distinctive traits of one exemplary political community – classical Athens – in order to clarify the nature and conditions of politics as such.

To follow Arendt we need a minimal grasp of the history of Athenian politics, the institutions that defined the polis, and the genealogy of key political words.

The basic arc of Athenian political history was a slow and discontinuous movement from monarchy to oligarchy to a relatively inclusive democracy.[22] Pre-classical Athens was apparently ruled by kings until around 700 BC, when the last king was deposed and replaced with a college of nine rulers or *archons* chosen each year by the aristocratic elite. The power structure probably also included a relatively weak Assembly limited to the warrior elite, and an aristocratic Council of the Areopagus that advised the archons and that had the power to veto decisions made in the Assembly. Common Athenians held the status of citizens, but citizenship did not confer political rights or power. In 594 BC an archon named Solon reformed the constitution in a number of ways: he changed the qualifications for office from birth to wealth, so that the archonships were open to rich commoners as well as to the nobility; he outlawed debt-bondage for citizens, so that native-born Athenians could never be enslaved; he instituted a court where citizens could appeal the rulings of the archons; he established a Council of 400; and he opened (or left open) the Assembly to the poorest Athenians. These reforms had the effect of expanding the oligarchy, opening access to power, and elevating the status of citizens. Still, at this point, most citizens could not hold office or speak in the Assembly. In 546 BC, Peisistratos seized power and ruled Athens as a tyrant for the next twenty-one years. After his son was deposed in 510 BC, there was an open struggle for power between two aristocratic factions led by Isagoras and Cleisthenes. Cleisthenes eventually triumphed by proposing a set of constitutional reforms that would create the most democratic polis in Greece. He divided Athens into 139 neighborhoods

[22] My account of Athenian history is indebted to Aristotle, *The Politics and The Constitution of Athens*, ed. and trans. Steven Everson (Cambridge: Cambridge University Press, 1996); Marcel Detienne, *The Masters of Truth in Archaic Greece*, tr. Janet Lloyd (New York: Zone Books, 1996); Herodotus, *The History*, tr. David Grene (Chicago: University of Chicago Press, 1987); Nicole Loraux, *The Invention of Athens*, tr. Alan Sheridan (Cambridge, MA: Harvard University Press, 1986); Josiah Ober, *Mass and Elite in Democratic Athens* (Princeton, NJ: Princeton University Press, 1989); Josiah Ober, *The Rise and Fall of Classical Greece* (Princeton, NJ: Princeton University Press, 2015); Jean-Pierre Vernant, *The Origins of Greek Thought*, anonymous translation (Ithaca, NY: Cornell University Press, 1982).

or *demes*, and instituted deme assemblies that were open to all citizens. Every year each deme sent a fixed number of members to sit on a newly established Council of 500. The Council was in charge of setting the agenda for the citywide assemblies, which were moved to an open space west of the Acropolis called the Pnyx. The foundation of Cleisthenes' reforms was the concept of isonomy (ἰσονομία), the notion that all citizens were equal (ἴσος) by law (νόμος). Isonomy meant that all citizens could participate in the local assemblies, that they were eligible to serve on the Council of 500, and most importantly that all citizens had the right to meet in the Assembly. Assemblies began with the question "What man has good advice to give the polis and wishes to make it known?" Any male citizen could take part in the ensuing deliberations, and all deliberations were decided collectively, one man one vote.

Over the next century, Athens saw a number of constitutional reforms that weakened or dismantled oligarchic institutions and that made it possible for all male citizens to participate in governing the polis. After 487 BC the nine archons were no longer selected by the Areopagus council but chosen by lottery from a pool of citizens preelected by the demes. In 462 BC the Areopagus lost certain key powers, including (probably) the power to review and veto decisions made by the Assembly. A few years later, in 457 BC, the property requirements for the offices of archon and magistrate were lowered, and office holders were for the first time paid for public service. In the 440s Athens began to pay citizens who served as jurors, and around 400 BC it began to provide small payments to citizens who attended the Assembly. By the mid-fourth century, when Aristotle was writing, the Assembly met around forty times a year, and attendance ranged from thousands to tens of thousands of citizens. During the fourth century the constitution went through minor changes until the democratic government was overthrown in 322 BC. Other poleis went through similar developments, and while none became as democratic as Athens, all used various forms of self-government.

By the classical age, the polis was understood as a specific form of community defined by two institutions. The first was citizenship; in every polis the native-born men were all given a certain equality of status and rights. M. I. Finley wrote:

> All the city-states had in common one feature, the incorporation of peasants, craftsmen and shopkeepers into the political community as members, as citizens; even those who had neither the obligation nor the privilege of bearing arms, it is important to underscore. They were not at first (and in some communities never) members with full rights, not citizens in the full

56   A Pure Concept of the Political

sense that the terms acquired in Classical Greece and Rome. But even limited recognition was without precedent in history.[23]

The second institution was collective deliberation and decision-making: every polis had at least one small council and a larger assembly in which qualified citizens could talk about issues facing the community and decide how to deal with them. Finley wrote:

> Every city-state government consisted of at least a larger assembly ... a smaller council or councils and a number of officials rotated among the eligible men, most often on an annual basis. The composition of these bodies, their method of selection, their powers, the names by which they were known, all varied greatly, in place and time, but the tripartite system was so ubiquitous that one may think of it as synonymous with city-state government.[24]

These two institutions let all men of a certain status come together and to have an equal say in decisions affecting the community. This coming together opened up a public space in which citizens could discuss and act on matters of common concern.

The key words of Greek politics took their sense from the experiences proper to this history and these institutions. Arendt's concept of the political is based on her interpretation of these words.

Isonomy (ἰσονομία) did not simply mean equality before the law, according to Arendt, but equal right to take part in the institutions of government – the juries, the offices, the Council, and above all the Assembly:

> we misunderstand the Greek term for a free constitution, *isonomia*, to mean what equality before the law means to us. But *isonomia* does not mean that all men are equal before the law, or that the law is the same for all, but merely that all have the same claim to political activity, and in the polis this activity primarily took the form of speaking with one another. *Isonomia* is therefore essentially the equal right to speak, and as such the same thing as *isegoria*.[25]

Isegoria (ἰσηγορία) meant not simply freedom of speech but the right of all citizens equally (ἴσος) to speak in the Assembly (ἀγορεύω). It did not just mean that citizens were guaranteed a private realm where they could speak without government censorship; it meant that citizens were guaranteed a public sphere in which they could have a voice in collective deliberations.

---

[23] M. I. Finley, *Politics in the Ancient World* (Cambridge: Cambridge University Press, 1983), 15.
[24] Finley, *Politics in the Ancient World*, 57.   [25] PP, 118. WP, 40.

A Return to Antiquity

In other words, *isegoria* did not just limit the power of government over citizens; it gave citizens an equal share of the government's power–an equal right to participate in the debates in the assemblies and to have an equal say (a vote) in their decisions.

The Greek word for "persuasion" – *peitho* (πείθω) – has to be understood in the context of these institutions, where political activity consisted first of all in deliberation. Arendt argued that modern translations fail to do justice to the Greek word, which named not just a power of discourse but also a divinity: "'Persuasion is a very weak and inadequate translation of the ancient *peithein*, the political importance of which is indicated by the fact that Peitho, the goddess of persuasion, had a temple in Athens."[26] We may be tempted to distinguish two senses of *peitho*: first, the power of discourse to change the way we see things, a power that allows us to convey our views to others, to see things from their perspective, to resolve differences without violence, to reach agreement without coercion, and to maintain concord among citizens without force; and second, the proper name of a goddess, *Peitho*, whom the Athenians honored with a temple set up on the south slope of the Acropolis after the unification of Athens. But this distinction is misleading – it divides what for the Greeks was one and the same. There was not persuasion on the one hand and a goddess on the other. Persuasion was a goddess, a force both beneficent and dangerous to which humans were subject and which exceeded their full control and understanding. The supreme importance of persuasion is evident at the end of "The Eumenides," where Athena persuades the Furies to stay and accept a place of honor in Athens, on the condition that they recognize and honor the divinity of *Peitho*.

> But if you honor [ἁγνὸν ἐστὶ σοὶ]
> The divine power of Persuasion [Πειθοῦς σέβας],
> The charm and enchantment of my tongue,
> you might stay with us.[27]

Aeschylus put this praise of Persuasion in a scene that shows her power, since Athena is able to placate the Furies and to reconcile the old and new gods through the power of persuasion alone.

It is also in this context that we should understand the origin of rhetoric, according to Arendt: "To persuade, *peithein*, was the specifically political form of speech, and since the Athenians were proud that they, unlike the

---

[26] PP, 7.

[27] Aeschylus, *Oresteia*, ed. and trans. Alan H. Sommerstein (Cambridge: Harvard University Press, 2008), 465 (lines 885–887). (I have modified the translation.)

58   A Pure Concept of the Political

barbarians, conducted their political affairs in the form of speech and without compulsion, they considered rhetoric, the art of persuasion, the highest, the truly political art."[28] Today the word "rhetoric" has been abstracted from the political context in which it emerged, and this abstraction has both narrowed and expanded its sense: narrowed because rhetoric is often reduced to the study of tropes and of the performative power of language; expanded because any text that contains tropes or performative language is said to have a rhetorical dimension. At the limit, this expansion culminates in the claim that "everything is rhetorical." Arendt by contrast stressed the origin of rhetoric in the development of the polis: "It is characteristic for this development that every politician was called a '*rhetor*' [speaker] and that rhetoric, the art of public speaking, as distinguished from dialectic, the art of philosophic speech, is defined by Aristotle as the art of persuasion."[29] Rhetoric in the original sense was not a dimension of all discourse, but the art of public speech among citizens in the polis.

Arendt argued that the emergence of *isonomia* and *isegoria* in Greece profoundly affected the concept of freedom or *eleutheria* (ἐλευθερία). This originally meant freedom in the basic sense of freedom of movement.

> According to Greek etymology, that is, according to Greek self-interpretation, the root of the word for freedom, *eleutheria*, is *eleuthein hopos ero*, to go as I wish, and there is no doubt that the basic freedom was understood as freedom of movement. A person was free who could move as he wished; the I-can, not the I-will, was the criterion.[30]

But as collective action among the citizens came to depend on collective deliberation, the meaning of freedom came to include prominently the freedom to speak.

> It is only natural that in this authentically political space what one understood by freedom now shifted; the sense of enterprise and adventure faded more and more, and what was as it were merely an indispensable accessory in these adventures – the constant presence of others, the interaction with one's peers in the public space of the agora, *isegoria* in the word of Herodotus – became the authentic content of being-free. At the same time, the most important activity for being free shifted from acting to speaking, from free action to free speech.[31]

As freedom came to be understood as free speech, the absence of free speech came to be equated with slavery. In *The Phoenician Women*, for

---

[28] PP, 7.   [29] HC, 26.
[30] Hannah Arendt, *The Life of the Mind: Willing* (New York: Harcourt Brace, 1978), 19.
[31] PP, 124. WP, 47. [The English is my translation.]

A Return to Antiquity

example, Euripides has Polyneices say that the worst thing about exile is that one does not have the right to speak freely: "One thing is most important: no free speech." Jocasta responds, "That's a slave's life–not to say what one thinks."[32] A free city was one in which citizens enjoy *isegoria*. In *The Suppliant Women*, Euripides has Theseus define freedom with the question that opened the Athenian assemblies: "Freedom is this: 'Who has good counsel to offer the polis?'"[33] By extension, a free city was a city in which the power of government is not concentrated in the hands of a ruler, but in which all the citizens had a share of government power: "Athens is not ruled by one man, but is a free city [ἐλευθέρα πόλις]. Here the people rule, and power is held by yearly turns. They do not give the most to the rich; the poor also have an equal share."[34] Freedom in this sense was not just a matter of freedom from government, and it was not located only in a private sphere beyond government control. *Eleutheria* included above all the right to take part in self-government, and it was realized not outside but within the realm of politics.

The word "citizen" (πολίτης) came to mean not just a native of a polis but one who enjoyed a certain status within it. As citizens won greater access to the spheres of power, citizenship (πολιτεία) was defined by the duty and right to participate in governing the community. Arendt emphasized the esteem the Greeks had for citizenship. The life of the citizen was commonly considered better that of a ruler. In *Ion*, Euripides has the hero extol citizenship over rulership: "Tyranny is foolishly praised; it has a pleasant face, but inside it is painful . . . I would rather live happy as one of the people than as a tyrant."[35] Citizenship made possible a polity not subject to a ruler but governed by equals.

The word "polis" came to mean a specific form of community native to Greece and defined by institutions of citizenship and self-government, according to Arendt: "The polis, properly speaking, is not the city-state in its physical location; it is the organization of the people as it arises out of acting and speaking together, and its true space lies between people living together for this purpose, no matter where they happen to be."[36] The polis

---

[32] Euripides, *Helen; Phoenician Women; Orestes*, ed. and trans. David Kovacs (Cambridge, MA: Harvard University Press, 2002), 249 (lines 390–391).

[33] Euripides, *Suppliant Women; Electra; Heracles*, ed. and trans. David Kovacs (Cambridge, MA: Harvard University Press, 1998), 57 (line 438).

[34] Euripides, *Suppliant Women*, 54 (lines 404–408).

[35] Euripides, *Trojan Women; Iphigenia among the Taurians; Ion*, ed. and trans. David Kovacs (Cambridge, MA: Harvard University Press, 1999), 399 (lines 621–626).

[36] HC, 198.

60 A Pure Concept of the Political

was "different from other settlements (for which the Greeks used another word [*astu*]) because it was built around this public space, the public realm in which those who were free and equal could meet at any time."[37] The polis was considered a distinct form of community because it made possible a kind of freedom that did not exist anywhere else:

> What distinguished human community within the polis from all other forms of human community, which the Greeks knew well, was freedom. But this does not mean that the political, or politics, was understood as a means that made possible human freedom, a free life. To be free and to live in a polis were in a certain sense one and the same thing.[38]

So the verb *politeuo* (πολιτεύω) meant at the same time to live in a polis, to be a free citizen, to have a certain form of government, and to take part in government.

For the Greeks, the polis was distinct from three other kinds of communities, according to Arendt.

First, they distinguished the polis from the household or *oikos* (οἶκος): "According to Greek thought, the human capacity for political organization is not only different from but stands in direct opposition to that natural association whose center is the home (*oikia*) and the family."[39] The *oikos* was grounded in the need to live together in order to master the necessities of life. The management (*nomia*) of the household (*oikos*) was economics (*oikonomia*) – the sphere of activities concerned with survival and prosperity: "The distinctive trait of the household sphere was that in it men lived together because they were driven by their wants and needs. The driving force was life itself . . . which, for its individual maintenance and its survival as the life of the species, needs the company of others."[40] But the polis existed not for the sake of life but for the sake of the freedom opened up by concerted action and self-government. Arendt also stressed that the *oikos* was the sphere of private life, in opposition to the public life of the polis, and that the boundary between public and private was sacrosanct.[41] The power of the polity ended at the threshold of the *oikos*; within his household each male citizen was sovereign. The household was thus a sphere of strict hierarchy; every household was ruled by a master (κύριος) or despot (δεσπότης), who commanded the obedience of his wife, children, servants, and slaves. The community of male citizens, by contrast, was a sphere of equality. Citizens were equal before the law, and no citizen as citizen had the right to tell others what to do.

---

[37] PP, 123. WP, 46. [38] PP, 116. WP, 38. [39] HC, 24. [40] HC, 30. [41] HC, 29.

A Return to Antiquity

The Greeks also distinguished the polis from the empires of the non-Greeks, in whose empires the power to decide and to act was concentrated in the hands of a single ruler, such as the Persian emperor or the Egyptian pharaoh, who commanded the absolute obedience of his subjects and against whose power there was no limit, no appeal, no recourse. To the Greeks, this relation between subject and ruler seemed to be essentially the same as the relation between slaves and their masters or "despots" (δεσπότης), and so they called such government "despotic." In a despotic government there was no place for subjects to do what citizens did in a Greek polis – to come together and to deliberate and act on matters of common concern. For the Greeks there was an essential difference between political and despotic communities, between living in a polis (πολιτεύω) and living under a despotic regime (δεσποτέω). Despotism was not a political system but an anti-political form of government.

Last, the Greeks distinguished the political life from life under a tyranny. The word "tyrant" in Greek (τύραννος) meant a monarch who had not inherited his position but who had seized power. Oedipus was called the tyrant of Thebes, for instance, not because he "tyrannized" the city in the modern sense but because he was not (apparently) the heir to the throne. A tyrant in Greece could be a wise and just ruler, and a tyrannical regime could bring about peace and prosperity. Arendt claimed the Greeks objected to tyranny not because it failed to protect their lives and livelihoods, but because it deprived them of freedom.

> The Greeks knew from their own experience that a reasonable tyrant [*ein vernünftiger Tyrann*] (what we call an enlightened despot) was a great advantage in matters pertaining to the prosperity of the state and the flourishing of the material and intellectual arts. Only freedom disappeared. The citizens were sent back to their homes, and the agora, the space where there could be a free interaction between equals, was deserted. Freedom had no place [under a tyranny], which meant there was no more political freedom.[42]

The Greeks knew that enlightened tyranny might be a good form of government if the end of government were simply security and prosperity, but in general they took it for granted that "politics and freedom are bound to one another, and that tyranny is the worst form of government, indeed the most anti-political."[43]

---

[42] PP, 119. WP, 41. [My translation.]   [43] PP, 120. WP, 42. [My translation.]

62 A Pure Concept of the Political

The word "political" (τὸ πολιτικόν) meant what was proper to a polis. It applied to anything that belonged to a free city, to a body of citizens and, more narrowly, to citizens who took the lead in public affairs and spoke in the assembly: "The word *politikon* was really an adjective for the organization of the polis, and not a designation for any kind of community whatsoever."[44]

Politics (ἡ πολιτική) then was simply what citizens did in a polis.

> The meaning of the political, and not its end, was this: that free men – beyond violence, coercion, and domination – associated with one another as equals, and only when necessary (namely, in wartime) commanded and obeyed one another, all other affairs being governed by discussion and mutual persuasion.[45]

Politics meant the practice of self-government, a way of being together in which citizens governed the city through public deliberation and collective decisions.

Arendt insisted that politics for the Greeks was not a means to an end. Political life had a dignity of its own. "Men have never, either before or after, thought so highly of political activity and bestowed so much dignity upon its realm."[46] The political life – the life of a citizen – was valued for its own sake.

She explained this dignity by pointing to four traits of the classical polis.

First, the polis was a space of freedom, in two distinct senses. In private life, citizens were free in the sense that they were not subject to control or coercion by others. Within the boundaries of the private sphere, inside his own house, in the isolated domain of the *oikos*, each male citizen was sovereign – there were few constraints on what he could say or do. Freedom in this sense is the absence of constraint. But for the Greeks this negative freedom was only of limited value, since the sovereign isolation of private life severely narrows effectiveness of speech and the range of what people can actually do: "Action ... is never possible in isolation; to be isolated is to be deprived of the capacity to act. Action and speech need the surrounding presence of others."[47] The polis was also a space of freedom in the sense that it instituted a public sphere where citizens could speak and act together. By opening a space where citizens could deliberate and decide what to do together, and by enabling citizens to act in concert to execute their decisions, the polis vastly expanded the range of things that Athenian

---

[44] PP, 116. WP, 37. [My translation.]   [45] PP, 117. WP, 39. [My translation.]   [46] BPF, 154.
[47] HC, 188.

citizens could actually do, far beyond what each one could do on his own in the sovereign isolation of private life. Freedom in this sense is positive – it is measured not by the absence of constraints but by the horizon of possibilities that are open to us, the range of things it is actually possible for us to do.

Second, the polis was a space of struggle or *agon*, which the Greeks saw as essential to a good life. A good life was honorable; what they honored was excellence; and excellence was best cultivated and manifested through struggle. Struggle enables men to rise to heights they cannot reach on their own, and the showdown with an opponent is a moment of truth in which men show who they are. It was only in his showdown with Hector, for instance, that Achilles could reach and manifest his true greatness as a warrior. One space of *agon* was the battlefield. Another was the council of warriors in *The Iliad*, where allies sought to outshine each other in speaking and giving advice for the common good. A third space of *agon* was the athletic contest, in which the struggle between opponents was isolated from the life or death fight between enemies and transposed into a competition among friends; the point of the athletic contest was to cultivate and celebrate excellence by opening a space where men could reach and manifest greatness in their struggle to outshine each other. Arendt argued that the polis itself was a space of *agon*, where struggle had been isolated from the life or death violence between enemies and transposed into a competition for distinction among fellow citizens.

> It would appear as if the Greeks separated struggle – without which neither Achilles nor Hector would ever have made his appearance and been able to prove who he was – from the military world of war, in which brute force has its original home, and in doing so turned struggle into an integrating component of the polis and the political sphere.[48]

This is an essential point: Politics was like warfare in the sense that they both involved struggle. But politics was essentially different from warfare. It was not domesticated warfare, or war continued by other means. It was closer to the athletic contest or warrior council, in which *agon* was allowed precisely because the struggle for distinction between friends and allies ultimately contributed to the common good. "The public realm itself, the polis, was permeated by a fiercely agonal spirit, where everybody had constantly to distinguish himself from all others, to show through unique deeds or achievements that he was the best of all."[49] The Greek polis was

---

[48] PP, 171–172. WP, 101.   [49] HC, 41.

64   A Pure Concept of the Political

of course rife with conflict, rivalry, and enmity, but then so is every other form of human community. What was distinctive about the polis was that it made a place for such struggles, not as a domesticated form of warfare but as a competition among citizens, an *agon* that existed for the sake of the common good. Politics for the Greeks was agonistic but not essentially polemical.

Third, the Greeks valued politics because the polis was a space of appearances, in two senses. The first sense has to do with the revelatory power of speech and action – the power of action and speech to reveal the unique character of the one who speaks and acts. This revelation of character is different from the deliberate projection of an image; no matter how carefully we try to control our public image, our words and actions inadvertently reveal who we are. Our character becomes apparent through our words and deeds. "In acting and speaking, men show who they are, reveal actively their unique personal identities and thus make their appearance in the human world."[50] The polis was a space of appearance in this first sense: by clearing a public sphere in which citizens could speak and act together, it gave men the chance to emerge from the obscurity of silence and passivity and to show who they were. "The polis was supposed to multiply occasions to win 'immortal fame,' that is, to multiply the chances for everybody to distinguish himself, to show in deed and word who he was in his unique distinctiveness."[51]

But the polis was also a space of appearance in a second sense. In the sovereign isolation of the private sphere, each individual is condemned not just to obscurity but also to seeing the world from only one perspective – the perspective proper to his place in the world. By instituting a public space where citizens could speak with each other on matters of common concern, the polis opened a place in which citizens could hear different perspectives and start to see the world from several different points of view. Life in the polis was an end in itself for the Greeks, in part because they understood that we are in touch with reality to the extent that we can see it from multiple perspectives. Arendt made this point in four sentences worth quoting at length:

> No one can adequately grasp the objective world in its full reality all on his own, because the world always shows and reveals itself to him from only one perspective, which corresponds to his standpoint in the world and is determined by it. If someone wants to see and experience the world as it 'really' is, he can do so only by understanding it as something that is shared

[50] HC, 179.   [51] HC, 197.

A Return to Antiquity

by many people, lies between them, separates and links them, showing itself differently to each and comprehensible only to the extent that many people can talk about it and exchange their opinions and perspectives with one another, over against one another. Only in the freedom of our speaking with one another does the world, as that about which we speak, emerge into its objectivity and visibility from all sides. Living in a real world and speaking with one another about it are basically one and the same, and to the Greeks, private life seemed "idiotic" because it lacked the diversity that comes with speaking about something and thus the experience of how things really function in the world.[52]

In public life, citizens were forced to confront and respond to perspectives other than their own, and in this multiplicity of perspectives the world revealed itself more clearly and completely than in the sovereign isolation of private life.

Finally, the polis was also a space of memory. Every human community is a site of memory in the sense that its identity depends on stories that make sense of the present in light of the past. But the polis was a site of memory in a more distinctive sense: it not only instituted a public sphere where citizens could speak and act together, it also instituted a cult of remembrance that ensured the greatest speeches and actions would be preserved in memory and recorded for posterity, so that the supreme achievements of its citizens would win immortal fame. This cult of remembrance was in part a way to sustain the ethos of the polis by celebrating the heroes who best exemplified its ideals. But it also provided some consolation for the ultimate futility of human existence, since it promised that, while all mortals are doomed to die, the words and deeds in which they revealed who they were could achieve a kind of immortality.

> [Another] function of the polis ... was to offer a remedy for the futility of action and speech; for the chances that a deed deserving fame would not be forgotten, that it actually would become "immortal," were not very good ... Men's life together in the form of the polis seemed to assure that the most futile of human activities, action and speech, and the least tangible and most ephemeral of man-made "products," the deeds and stories which are their outcome, would become imperishable. The organization of the polis ... is a kind of organized remembrance.[53]

This cult of remembrance was exemplified for Arendt by the funeral oration of Pericles, who promised his fellow citizens that "the admiration

---

[52] PP, 129. WP, 52.   [53] HC, 197–198.

66 A Pure Concept of the Political

of the present and succeeding ages will be ours."[54] It assured citizens that their ephemeral existence would not vanish into oblivion, but achieve the reality that comes from being not just seen and heard but remembered forever.

Arendt insisted on the historical specificity of the polis. The word "polis" did not refer to any community whatsoever, but to a specific kind of community that emerged at a certain time and place: "According to the Greeks, [politics] had only existed in Greece, and even there only for a relatively short time."[55] The word "politics" does not refer to a universal and necessary dimension of human life; it denotes the way of being together proper to this specific kind of community. But she also insisted on the universal significance of the Greek word; it refers to a way of being together that – under certain conditions – is possible in all times and all places: "our very word 'politics' is derived from and indicates this one very specific form of political life, bestowing upon it a kind of universal validity."[56] So a concept of the political must do two things at once. It must do justice to the specificity of the polis – the test of any concept of the political is whether it adequately grasps the distinctive traits of the Greek polis. But it must also have universal validity – it must abstract from these distinctive traits the essential traits of the political itself; that is, the traits that make a community political, and so are common to every political community.

Arendt's project was not just to understand the Greek polis in its particularity. Her aim was to start with a specific example of a polity and to move toward the political in general. She began with a description of politics in the classical polis, and moved toward a reflection on the nature of politics as such.

What then made Greek politics exemplary? What were the conditions and principles of political life in Greece? What are the indispensable conditions and innermost principles of politics in general?

A Pure Concept of the Political

Political life in classical Greece depended on certain conditions from which Arendt tried to isolate the conditions of the political life as such. We can single out four.

---

[54] Thucydides, *The Landmark Thucydides*, ed. Robert B. Strassler, trans. Richard Crawley (New York: Free Press, 1996), 114.
[55] PP, 116. WP, 38.   [56] PP, 45.

A Pure Concept of the Political

First, politics is based on the experience of plurality and commonality. What we have in common with others, according to Arendt, is not a human nature within each individual, but the world in which we live – the horizon of meaning in which things have sense and worth, and the earth that is our common ground: "Politics emerges in the space-between-men, hence in something that is basically exterior to man."[57] Our being in the world is always plural – we live among others who are more or less different from us: "Politics is about the community and reciprocity of beings who are different ... Politics rests on the fact of human plurality."[58] What makes us different is not that we possess different natures but simply that we see the same world from different points of view: "This plurality ... is specifically the condition ... of all political life."[59] The political life is possible because being human means being in the world with others.

Second, politics is made possible by discourse. Our power to see the same world from different points of view is multiplied by our ability to speak: "Men in the plural, that is, men insofar as they live and move and act in this world, can experience meaningfulness only because they can talk with and make sense to each other and to themselves."[60] Humans can be political because they are endowed with speech: "Wherever the relevance of speech is at stake, matters become political by definition, for speech is what makes man a political being."[61]

Third, political life requires a public sphere where people can articulate different points of view on the world they share in common: "The reality of the public realm relies on the simultaneous presence of innumerable perspectives and aspects in which the common world presents itself and for which no common measurement or denominator can ever be devised."[62] Politics is impossible where the public realm is eliminated, since this elimination destroys the sense of belonging to a common world and suppresses the plurality of perspectives on which political life depends. A community in which all share the same point of view, or in which different perspectives are not allowed to appear, is not a political community.

Fourth, politics is possible only when people recognize some common good. Conflicts can be resolved politically when shared interests outweigh particular interests. "Interests constitute, in the word's most literal significance, something which inter-est, which lies between people and therefore can relate and bind them together."[63] There can be no politics where

---

[57] PP, 95. WP, 11.   [58] PP, 93. WP, 9.   [59] HC, 7.   [60] HC, 4.   [61] HC, 3.
[62] HC, 57.   [63] HC, 182.

68   A Pure Concept of the Political

people find themselves together without recognizing any common good.[64] Politics in the strict sense becomes impossible whenever the competition for government power degenerates into a life-or-death struggle for dominance, where each competing group aims to seize and exercise government power for its own good at the expense of all others. The more clearly people recognize a common good, and the more it outweighs what is good for each particular faction, the easier it is to establish a genuinely political community.

These four conditions make political life possible but not inevitable: "A political realm does not automatically come into being wherever men live together."[65] The political realm depends on a space of appearance that is a permanent possibility but not a permanent fact of human existence: "Wherever people gather together, it is potentially there, but only potentially, not necessarily and not forever."[66]

What then is politics?

Arendt singled out seven traits that define the sphere of the political.

1. Political life excludes the rule of some over others. To rule is to have power over people, as a master has power over slaves, or as a despot has power over subjects. It was essential to the polis that relations of rule were banished among male citizens; no citizen as citizen had the power to command other citizens and to demand their obedience. The Greeks prided themselves on this rejection of rulership, according to Arendt. In *The History* Herodotus tells the story of Otanes, a Persian who advocated isonomy and who refused to be either king or subject, saying that he was willing neither to be a ruler nor to submit to the rule of another:[67] "οὔτε γὰρ ἄρχειν οὔτε ἄρχεσθαι ἐθέλω." "I am not willing to rule or to be ruled."[68] For Arendt this rejection of rulership is essential: "Since Herodotus, [the polis] was understood as a form of political organization in which the citizens lived together under conditions of no-rule, without a division between ruler and ruled."[69] The polis let male citizens live in equality rather than in the hierarchy inherent in any form of rule.

2. Political life is based on the principle of equality. Political equality meant equality of rights (*isonomia*), equality of power (*isokratia*), and equal right to speak in the assembly (*isegoria*).[70] The equality among

---

[64] OT, 311.   [65] OR, 19.   [66] HC, 199.   [67] HC, 32.

[68] Herodotus, *The Persian Wars, vol. II*, trans. A. D. Godley (Cambridge MA: Harvard University Press, 1921), 110 (Book III, chapter 83). (I have modified the translation.)

[69] OR, 30.   [70] See M. I. Finley, *Politics in the Ancient World*, 139.

A Pure Concept of the Political

enfranchised citizens of a polis stood in sharp contrast to the inequality among members of a household: "The polis was distinguished from the household in that it knew only 'equals,' whereas the household was the center of the strictest inequality."[71] Each citizen had an equal part in the polis, and none had authority over the others.

3. Political life excludes violence: "In Greek self-understanding, to force people by violence, to command rather than to persuade, were pre-political ways to deal with people characteristic of life outside the polis, of home and family life, where the household head ruled with uncontested, despotic powers, or of life in the barbarian empires of Asia, whose despotism was frequently likened to the organization of the household."[72] To use any kind of force on citizens was to treat them as inferiors and thus to violate their status as equals. Arendt noted that this exclusion of violence was the basis for "the Athenian custom of 'persuading' those who had been condemned to death to commit suicide by drinking the hemlock cup, thus sparing the Athenian citizen under all circumstances the indignity of physical violation."[73] To say that political life excludes violence does not mean that violence is absent from political communities; Arendt knew of course that the freedom in the Greek polis depended on slavery and domination within the household. Violence was the prepolitical condition of possibility of politics: "Coercion and violence have always been the means to found and enlarge or secure the space of politics, but they are not in themselves political."[74] Matters that naturally involve violence (such as war and slavery) are objects of political concern, but take place outside the political realm and are not in themselves political.

4. In political life, violence and coercion are replaced by speech: "To be political, to live in a polis, meant that everything was decided through words and persuasion and not through force and violence."[75] The mode of speech proper to political life is persuasion, since in persuasion I speak to others as people who are capable of making up their own minds, and who are free to accept or reject my point of view. The centrality of speech in the life of the polis is suggested by the fact that the Athenians had a temple on the Acropolis dedicated to the goddess persuasion, *Peitho* (Πείθω). Speech makes possible a noncoercive and nonviolent way of living together.

5. The primary form of political action is common deliberation. Deliberation concerns questions of ends – practical questions of how we should live together and what we should do in the concrete situations in which we find ourselves. Political life first consists in "speechmaking and

---

[71] HC, 32.   [72] HC, 27.   [73] OR, 12.   [74] PP, 130. WP, 53.   [75] HC, 26.

decision-taking, the oratory and the business, the thinking and the per-suading" that precedes effective action.[76] To participate in the life of a polity means to engage in this common deliberation over communal ends: "Debate constitutes the very essence of political life."[77]

6. The political realm is delimited by the distinction between public and private. Politics has to do with public matters – matters that can and should appear in the common world, and that are legitimately matters of common concern. What is political is whatever is properly of common interest to the polity as a whole. Whatever is deemed private, by contrast, is not properly a matter of political concern or subject to political power. The private realm is the sphere of what is our own (τὸ ἴδιον) as opposed to what is common (τὸ κοινόν) – what we cannot or need not share with others, that to which the polity has no claim and which is properly free of political control. What is private is also what is properly hidden from others and has to be protected from the visibility of the public realm.[78]

7. Politics exists for the sake of freedom: "The realm of the polis was the sphere of freedom."[79] In Greek thought, freedom meant not being ruled by any compulsion, neither the will of others, nor the impulses of one's passions, nor the activities that are necessary to survival. But to be free also meant not to rule others. Aristotle said explicitly that "the life of a free man is better than the life of a despot."[80] For Herodotus, the only Persians who were free were the descendants of Otanes: "till this day his house continues as the only free one in Persia."[81] Arendt insisted that neither those who rule nor those who are ruled are really free: "To be free meant both not to be subject to the necessity of life or to the command of another and not to be in command oneself. It meant neither to rule nor to be ruled."[82] "To be free meant to be free from the inequality present in rulership and to move in a sphere where neither rule nor being ruled existed."[83] Since the political realm excludes any form of rule, it is above all the space in which freedom is possible: "The raison d'être of politics is freedom."[84]

These seven traits can be articulated in a pure concept of the political: *politics is a way of being together, based on principles of equality and nonviolence, in which people decide what to do and how to live together through mutual persuasion and common deliberation on matters of public concern.*

---

[76] OR, 34.   [77] BPF, 241.   [78] HC, 72.   [79]. HC, 30.

[80] Aristotle, *Politics*, trans. H. Rackham (Cambridge, MA: Harvard University Press, 1998), 549 (1325a24).

[81] Herodotus, *The History*, 250.   [82] HC, 32.   [83] HC, 33.   [84] BPF, 146.

Distinctions

This concept of the political implies four distinctions.

1. The distinction between "what is essential to politics" and "what belongs in the political sphere." The word "political" is ambiguous. When we say something is political, we sometimes mean it is an essential part of politics, in the sense that politics cannot exist without it. In this sense Arendt spoke of mutual persuasion and common deliberation as political modes of discourse – they are political in the sense that they are necessary parts of political life: "debate constitutes the very essence of political life."[85] At other times, when we say that something is political, we mean that it is properly a matter of political concern and debate. In this sense we speak of war and violence as political matters – they are political in that they are issues that concern the community as a whole and therefore deserve to be debated and decided in the political sphere. We have to keep these two senses distinct. When Arendt said that politics excludes violence and that violence is not political, for example, she meant that while violence is of course a matter of political concern, it does not belong in the political realm.

So there are two senses of the question, "What is political?" In one sense it asks, "What kinds of things are essential to politics?" This is a theoretical question, and Arendt tried to answer it with her concept of the political. In another sense the question asks, "What matters should be politicized?" that is, "What questions legitimately concern a community and should be resolved through public debate and collective deliberation?" This is a political question that cannot be decided in theory, but has to be endlessly open to public debate. On this second question Arendt had her own opinions, which were informed but not dictated by her understanding of politics. We have to distinguish two facets of Arendt's work: her concept of the political and her opinions on what matters should be politicized. Politics is a universal possibility of human existence for Arendt, but what counts as properly political is a matter of opinion that varies across histories and cultures: "At all times people living together will have affairs that belong in the realm of the public – 'are worthy to be talked about in public.' What these matters are at any historical moment is probably utterly different."[86] Private matters can always be made public, and public matters can always be privatized, and the distinction between

---

[85] BPF, 241.   [86] HA, 316.

72   A Pure Concept of the Political

what is properly public and what is properly private is always open to political debate.[87]

2. The distinction between politics and rule. The strangest part of Arendt's concept of the political is her exclusion of rule from politics. We are so used to thinking of politics in terms of rule that this exclusion seems absurd. But for Arendt it was the confusion of politics with rule that most obscured the specificity of the political.

The difference between rule and politics is clearest in oligarchies, where the power to decide and act is concentrated in the hands of a few people. These few may gather on occasion as equals to discuss matters of common concern and to decide them through mutual persuasion and common deliberation. Once decisions are reached, however, the oligarchs may then impose their will unilaterally on the other members of the community, who have no choice but to obey. In Arendt's terms, in such an oligarchy the political realm is restricted to the few who have power, while most people are powerless and excluded from politics. The (horizontal) relations among such oligarchs are political relations, that is, relations of equality and nonviolence; within the circle of oligarchs there is no division between ruler and ruled. However, the (vertical) relation between the oligarchs and the rest of the community is a relation of rule, that is, a relation of hierarchy and force; the few are able to command and the many are forced to obey. Rule is power over others. Politics is the self-government of equals.

The distinction between politics and rule was essential to the difference between the political realm and the realm of the household. Rulership belonged in the household, not in the body politic: "The whole concept of rule and being ruled, of government and power as we understand them as well as the regulated order attending them, was felt to be pre-political and to belong to the private rather than the public sphere."[88] The body politic proper was defined by the principle that all male citizens were equal and that there was no division between rulers and ruled. (In Athens there were still archons selected by lot every year who administered public affairs, but

---

[87] Arendt would agree with Bonnie Honig's thesis that "A reading of Arendt that grounds itself in the agonistic and performative impulse of her politics must, for the sake of that politics, resist the a priori determination of a public/private distinction that is beyond contestation and amendment." Bonnie Honig, "'Toward an Agonistic Feminism': Hannah Arendt and the Politics of Identity," in *Feminists Theorize the Political*, ed. Judith Butler and Joan W. Scott (New York: Routledge, 1992), 215.

[88] HC, 32.

they were not rulers strictly speaking since – at least in Athens after 462 BC – the ultimate power to decide did not belong to them but to the citizens as a whole.) Each male citizen, however, was the ruler of a household over which he had absolute power.

The distinction between politics and rule was also essential to the difference between political communities and communities ruled by one man. Such monarchies seemed to the Greeks essentially similar to a household ruled by a sovereign master, so they were named and understood in terms derived from the realm of the household. "All Greek and Latin words which express some rulership over others, such as *rex, pater, anax, basileus,* refer originally to household relationships and were names the slaves gave to their master."[89]

3. The distinction between politics and rule implies a distinction between politics and government: we recognize forms of government that have no place for politics (such as totalitarian dictatorships), just as we recognize forms of politics that take place outside the institutions of government (such as movements of nonviolent resistance). The distinction between politics and government allows us to distinguish formal politics (debate and action within institutions that have the power to make decisions binding on the polity as a whole) from informal politics (the activities of those who come together outside of government institutions for the sake of common deliberation and collective action on matters of public concern). It also lets us distinguish de jure political power (the right to make decisions and to direct the actions of institutions) from de facto political power (the support of citizens and the capacity to direct their power to act).

4. Arendt also distinguished political from technical questions. Political debate is appropriate only for questions of opinion – questions to which there can be no one right answer but only incommensurable perspectives: "Public debate can only deal with things which – if we want to put it negatively – we cannot figure out with certainty. Otherwise, if we can figure it out with certainty, why do we all need to get together?"[90] Such questions are political in the sense that they should be resolved by common deliberation. On the other hand, there are questions with one right answer – questions of fact, technique, or expertise: "There are things where the right measures can be figured out. These things can really be

---

[89] HC, 32.   [90] HA, 317.

74 A Pure Concept of the Political

administered and are not then subject to public debate."[91] Such questions are essentially technical and can be delegated to experts.

Arendt knew that few questions are purely technical or purely political. Most questions in the public sphere have a technical side and a side that is properly political. The distinction is not meant to exclude certain issues from the political realm, but only to distinguish two sides within matters of public concern – a side that should be politicized and a side that can be left to experts: "With every one of these questions there is a double face. And one of these faces should not be subject to debate."[92]

Other Views of Arendt's Concept of the Political

Arendt's concept of the political is commonly misunderstood in several ways.

Readers of Arendt have long recognized she had a distinctive understanding of politics, but they have generally viewed the question of the political as one topic among others in her work. This view overlooks the central place in her work of the question of the political, and misses the way her understanding of the political informed her views of the basic realities of political life (power, force, authority, violence, government, contract, law, and freedom). The question of the political is central to her work. It is not one topic among others, but a focal point around which the disparate elements of her thought cohere. (I will try to show this in Chapter 5.)

Many readers of Arendt have overlooked the historical dimension of her thought, and interpreted the political in Arendt as a timeless and universal reality of human life. Margaret Betz Hull has argued, for example, that the political is an intrinsic dimension of subjectivity: "Arendt herself adds yet another dimension to the concept of the subject, namely the political. Her subject is primarily a political subject ..."[93] This oversimplifies Arendt's thought. It is true that humans always have the *potential* to live in political communities, according to Arendt: "Whenever people gather together, [the space of politics] is potentially there, but only potentially, not necessarily and not forever."[94] But this potential has rarely been *realized*: "Politics as such has existed so rarely and in so few places that, historically

---

[91] HA, 317.   [92] HA, 318.
[93] Margaret Betz Hull, *The Hidden Philosophy of Hannah Arendt* (New York: RoutledgeCurzon, 2002), 87.
[94] HC, 199.

Other Views of Arendt's Concept of the Political

speaking, only a few great epochs have known it and turned it into a reality."[95] Politics has been rare because, while humans always have the potential to live politically, it is possible to realize that potential only when the conditions of political life are recognized and affirmed. Politics depends on the conditions of plurality and commonality, on our capacity for speech, on a public sphere where speech is free, and on the recognition of a common good that outweighs particular interests. Where these conditions are denied or suppressed, as in totalitarian regimes, political life is practically impossible. "A political realm does not automatically come into being wherever men live together."[96] This is why politics has existed only in certain times and places: "the notion that politics exists always and everywhere human beings exist is a prejudice."[97] Politics is not a universal and timeless reality of human life, but a historically contingent possibility of human existence.

Commentators on Arendt have also not laid out her concept of the political at an adequate level of precision. When they attempt to define her understanding of politics, their definitions tend to be so broad that they could easily include various nonpolitical forms of activity and community. In *Hannah Arendt and the Meaning of Politics* (1997), for example, John McGowan wrote that for Arendt, "politics has to be, among other things, a realm of self-creation through free, voluntary action undertaken in consort with and in relation to other people."[98] In *Hannah Arendt* (1998), McGowan specified further that in her view "the political is the realm of 'acting in concert' and, as such, the world in which a public, shared world, is created."[99] In "Political Action: Its Nature and Advantages" (2000), George Kateb wrote that for Arendt "politics is action and . . . action is speech in public about public affairs."[100] In *The Reluctant Modernism of Hannah Arendt* (2000), Seyla Benhabib defined "the normative core of the Arendtian conception of the political" as "the creation of a common world through the capacity to make and keep promises among a plurality of humans who mutually respect each other."[101] In *Why Arendt Matters* (2006), Elisabeth Young-Bruehl wrote that "The word *politics* . . . for

---

[95] PP, 119.   [96] OR, 19.   [97] PP, 153; WP, 79.

[98] John McGowan and Craig Calhoun, *Hannah Arendt and the Meaning of Politics* (Minneapolis: University of Minnesota Press, 1997), 9.

[99] John McGowan, *Hannah Arendt: An Introduction* (Minneapolis: University of Minnesota Press, 1998), 29.

[100] George Kateb, *The Cambridge Companion to Hannah Arendt*, ed. Dana Villa (New York: Cambridge University Press, 2000), 132.

[101] Seyla Benhabib, *The Reluctant Modernism of Hannah Arendt* (Walnut Creek, CA: Alta Mira Press, 2000), 166.

76 A Pure Concept of the Political

Arendt refers to human beings acting – discoursing, persuading, deciding on specific deeds, doing them – in the public realm."[102] Bhikhu Parekh argued in *Hannah Arendt and the Search for a New Political Philosophy* (1981) that "For Arendt . . . politics is the activity of conducting the affairs of the community by means of speech."[103] In *Hannah Arendt and Human Rights* (2006), Peg Birmingham claims that for Arendt "the political [is] the realm of representation and the process of signification wherein identities of the 'who' (and these are always both unique and plural) are reinscribed and re-presented within the web of relationships that constitute the *inter-esse* of public spaces."[104] These accounts are too imprecise to fully do justice Arendt's understanding of politics. They fail to grasp the historical distinctiveness of political communities, and they fail to clearly delineate the differences Arendt saw between politics and other forms of community and concerted action.

This imprecision has led to a fourth misunderstanding. Arendt distinguished two senses of the word "political," as we saw: in one sense it means "what is essential to politics"; in another sense it means "what belongs in the political sphere." Many of Arendt's readers have failed to see this distinction. This failure is especially clear in John McGowan, who argues that "*Pace* Arendt, the definition of the political is not and cannot be stable. The definition of what is 'properly' political cannot be grounded on anything except human agreements and conventions . . ."[105] These two sentences confuse the essential difference between "the definition of the political" (what defines the political realm) and "the definition of what is 'properly' political" (what topics ought to be subject to political debate and decision-making).

This confusion has led to a common misunderstanding of Arendt: that because she tried to rigorously distinguish *in principle* between the sphere of politics and other spheres of human existence, she also believed that matters proper to other spheres ought to be excluded from political debate.

One version of this misunderstanding concerns violence. Since Arendt excluded violence in principle from the sphere of politics, it is argued, she also excludes potentially violent conflicts from political debate. In *Hannah Arendt and the Meaning of Politics*, for example, McGowan wrote that

---

[102] Elisabeth Young-Bruehl, *Why Arendt Matters* (New Haven, CT: Yale University Press, 2006), 83.

[103] Bhikhu Parekh, *Hannah Arendt and the Search for a New Political Philosophy* (London: Macmillan, 1981).

[104] Peg Birmingham, *Hannah Arendt and Human Rights* (Bloomington: Indiana University Press, 2006), 27.

[105] McGowan, *Hannah Arendt*, 76.

Other Views of Arendt's Concept of the Political   77

Arendt "exiles the potentially violent conflicts from politics."[106] This is a misreading. Arendt exiles violence from the political realm, in the sense that politics is a way to deal with conflicts nonviolently. But politics does not exclude violence in the sense of exiling potentially violent conflicts from political debate and action. One of the main points of politics is to try to manage nonviolently conflicts that are "potentially violent."

Another version of this misunderstanding concerns economics. In *The Political Philosophy of Hannah Arendt,* Maurizio Passerin d'Entrèves wrote Arendt "maintains that all questions pertaining to the economy are prepolitical."[107] Since Arendt sharply distinguished the sphere of politics from economics, the argument goes, she must have also thought economic questions were not properly a matter of political debate. This is also a misreading. Arendt did argue that economic questions should not be subject to political debate *insofar as* they are purely technical or factual questions. But the logic of her position implies that economic questions should be subject to political debate *to the extent that* they are not purely technical or factual, but touch on questions of justice and the common good, which are obviously matters of political concern.

A third version of this misunderstanding concerns social questions. Arendt sharply distinguished the political from the social. In her view, it was a dangerous confusion to conceive political communities on the model of social communities, to impose on citizens of a polity the norms and relations proper to members of a society, or to conflate political revolution with social transformation. These confusions were central to the antipolitics of National Socialism, and for that reason Arendt was of the opinion that most social matters should not be subject to political power. But her theory of politics does not necessarily exclude social questions from political debate. The logic of her thought implies that social questions may properly be politicized *to the extent that* they are implicated in questions of the common good. Since legal and political equality are essential to political communities, social equality may be an aim of political action *insofar as* social equality is an essential precondition of legal and political equality. While the social and political spheres are *in principle* distinct, it does not follow that social questions are *in fact* necessarily excluded from politics altogether.

---

[106] McGowan and Calhoun, *Hannah Arendt and the Meaning of Politics,* 267.
[107] Maurizio Passerin d'Entrèves, *The Political Philosophy of Hannah Arendt* (New York: Routledge, 1994), 8.

78   A Pure Concept of the Political

The result of these misreadings is a common and misguided critique of Arendt. Critics mistakenly assume that Arendt meant to exclude from politics questions about phenomena proper to nonpolitical spheres of life – as if she wanted political debate to ignore economic questions, social questions, and questions about potentially violent conflicts. It is often said that Arendt's view of politics is narrow, rigid, and nearly empty. Hanna Pitkin spoke of "the curious emptiness of content characterizing Arendt's image of the public sphere."[108] George Kateb argued that for Arendt the content of political discourse must only concern phenomena essential to politics: "political action is talk about politics."[109] Dana Villa claimed that Arendt wanted a "self-contained" politics in which the only proper content of political discourse was politics itself: "the content of political action must be politics."[110] In *The Political Thought of Hannah Arendt*, Michael Gottsegen spoke for many critics when he concluded, "Arendt has excluded too much from politics."[111] This criticism is based on a failure to distinguish two senses of the word "political," which can apply to phenomena essential to politics, but also apply to nonpolitical matters that are subject to political debate. Critics have failed to adequately distinguish Arendt's *theory* of what is essential to politics from her *opinions* on what topics ought to be politicized, and this failure is based on an insufficiently precise understanding of her concept of the political.

Other Concepts of the Political

Other thinkers have conceived politics differently, as we have seen. For Carl Schmitt, politics was the sphere of radical antagonism: "The specific political distinction to which political actions and motives can be reduced is that between friend and enemy."[112] For Emmanuel Lévinas, it was "the art of foreseeing war and of winning it by every means."[113] For Michel Foucault, it was "the set of relations of force in a given society."[114]

---

[108] Hanna Pitkin, *Hanna Fenichel Pitkin: Politics, Justice, Action*, ed. Dean Mathiowetz (New York: Routledge, 2016), 152.
[109] George Kateb, *Hannah Arendt: Politics, Conscience, Evil* (Totowa, NJ: Rowman and Allanheld, 1984), 17.
[110] Dana Villa, *Arendt and Heidegger: The Fate of the Political* (Princeton: Princeton Press, 1996), 37.
[111] Michael Gottsegen, *The Political Thought of Hannah Arendt* (Albany: SUNY Press, 1994), 70.
[112] Carl Schmitt, *The Concept of the Political*, ed. and trans. George Schwab (Chicago: Chicago University of Chicago Press, 1996), 26.
[113] Emmanuel Lévinas, *Totality and Infinity*, tr. Alphonso Lingis (Pittsburgh: Duquesne University, 1969), 21.
[114] Foucault, *Power/Knowledge*, ed. Colin Gordon (New York: Pantheon, 1980), 189.

Other Concepts of the Political

For Michael Oakeshott, it was "the activity of attending to the general arrangements of a set of people whom chance or choice has brought together."[115] For Moses Finley, it was "the art of reaching decisions by public discussion and then of obeying those decisions as a necessary condition of civilized life."[116]

Heidegger also understood the polis differently from Arendt. In his view, the political is not a particular way of being together belonging to a specific kind of community, but rather a fundamental structure of being-together that allows humans to share a common world. In a 1942 lecture he wrote: "In the midst of beings, the polis is the open site of all beings, which are here gathered into their unity because the polis is the ground of such unity and reaches back into that ground. The polis is not some special or isolated region of human activity."[117] The political, in this view, is a universal and necessary dimension of human existence.

Why then single out Arendt's concept of the political? How can we say one concept of the political is better than others? On what basis can we argue that different concepts of the political are more or less adequate? What reasons did Arendt have for rejecting other concepts of the political?

There are four reasons: (1) Any concept of the political must comprehend the prime example of a political community – the Greek polis. (2) Other concepts of the political fail to grasp the distinctive character of the polis. (3) These concepts fail to adequately distinguish politics from other spheres of human existence. (4) These failures have led thinkers to misconceive basic realities of political life. Let us go through these reasons one at a time.

1. One task of thinking, for Arendt, is "to discover the real origins of traditional concepts in order to distill from them anew their original spirit which has so sadly evaporated from the very key words of political language ... leaving behind empty shells with which to settle almost all accounts, regardless of their underlying phenomenal reality."[118] To work out a theoretical concept of a political phenomenon, in this view, we have to start with a prime example and to single out the distinctive traits that make it what it is. One test of a concept is whether it adequately grasps the specificity of that prime example. Take the concept of fascism: there are many different concepts of fascism today, which are applied with more or

---

[115] Oakeshott, *Philosophy, Politics, and Society*, ed. P. Laslett (Oxford: Oxford University Press, 1956), 2.
[116] Finley, *Democracy Ancient and Modern*, 13.   [117] Heidegger, *"The Ister,"* 94.   [118] BPF, 15.

80 A Pure Concept of the Political

less precision to many different phenomena. But the prime example of fascism is still the Italian Fascist movement of the early twentieth century, the original source of the word "fascist." One test of any concept of fascism is whether it grasps the distinctive nature of the original Fascist movement. A concept of fascism is inadequate if it only grasps the traits that the original Fascists share with all other right-wing ideologies; that is, if it applies equally well to all right-wing ideologies and fails to grasp what was distinctive about the original Fascists.

In the same way, any concept of the political is inadequate if it fails to grasp what was distinctive about the Greek polis – the original source of the word "politics." This does not mean the word had a single original sense, or that this original sense is the definitive meaning of the word. It means we have to work towards a general concept of politics starting from an actual example of a political community, and the prime example of a political community is the one first named by the word "politics."

2. Other concepts of the political fail to grasp the distinctive character of the polis. Instead, they define the political in terms of traits proper to all human communities, and so obscure the specificity of the polis. It is correct that the polis was characterized by "extreme antagonism" (Schmitt),[119] "relations of force" (Foucault),[120] "the art of foreseeing war and winning it by any means" (Lévinas),[121] "the art of attending to the general arrangements of a set of people" (Oakeshott),[122] "the open site of all beings" (Heidegger).[123] But these traits also characterize most other forms of human community. To define the political in terms of traits proper to all communities is like trying to define what makes us human in terms of traits we share with all other living beings. Other concepts of the political take for granted "the modern prejudice according to which politics would be an absolute necessity that has existed always and everywhere."[124] By defining the political in terms of traits proper to all human communities, they efface the differences between political and nonpolitical forms of community.[125]

3. These concepts of the political fail to distinguish politics from other spheres of human existence, in several different ways.

---

[119] Schmitt, *The Concept of the Political*, 29. [120] Foucault, *Power/Knowledge*, 189.
[121] Lévinas, *Totality and Infinity*, 21. [122] Oakeshott, *Philosophy, Politics, and Society*, 2.
[123] Heidegger, "*The Ister*," 94. [124] PP, 119. WP, 41.
[125] The exception here is Finley's concept of politics, which is grounded in his study of the polis and derived from the original senses of the word.

Other Concepts of the Political

First, they efface the difference between the polis and the family, and this effacement lends credence to a number of dubious analogies: political authority is modeled on paternal authority; citizenship is modeled on kinship; the bonds between citizens are modeled on the bonds of brotherhood; and political community is understood in terms of the family.

They also efface the distinction between the polis and the *oikos* (the household), an effacement that leads to three confusions. It suggests that politics is merely a means to an end, and that the end of the polis is essentially the same as that of the *oikos* – namely, the survival and prosperity of its members. This makes it seem reasonable to sacrifice the freedom possible in a political community for the safety and prosperity of a well-administered state – its effect is to obscure the essential link between politics and freedom. And it makes it seem reasonable to think of political power on the model of the sovereign power exercised by the master of a house – to conceive all political power in terms of rule and domination.

These concepts of politics also confuse the distinction between political communities and communities governed by a sovereign ruler (monarchy, tyranny, despotism, dictatorship). This confusion goes all the way back to the classical polis, where innovations in the practice of politics were not always matched by innovations in language and thought. In practice, Athenian isonomy dissolved the distinction between rulers and ruled among male citizens after decades of tyrannical rule. But in their thinking, the Greeks continued to understand power in terms of rulership. This is explicit in the words of Theseus we have already cited from *The Suppliant Women*:

> [Athens] is not ruled by one man, but is a free city. Here the people rule [ἀνάσσει], and power is held by yearly turns. They do not give the most to the rich; the poor also have an equal share.[126]

The logic is clear: the people have taken the place of the king, and they continue to do what kings do. The verb here for what the people do (ἀνάσσει) means to be the ruler (ἄναξ), to be the master of a house, to be the king of a people, to be sovereign. This word really does describe the relation between male Athenian citizens and the disenfranchised groups in Athens (foreigners, slaves, women, and children). In this sense it is possible to speak of the male citizens as a ruling class. But it does not make sense to use the concept of rule to describe power relations among enfranchised citizens within the political sphere itself. When citizens gathered in the

---

[126] Euripides, *Suppliant Women*, 55.

82 A Pure Concept of the Political

Assembly to decide on matters of common concern, who was ruling whom? The question makes no sense because, insofar as politics requires genuine equality, the concept of rule strictly speaking is out of place in the political sphere. But the Greeks transposed the language of rule into the political sphere and tried to understand political power in its terms.[127] And the inheritors of Greek thought continued to understand political power in terms derived from nonpolitical domains – sovereignty, dominion, domination, rule.

4. These failures have led thinkers to misconceive the realities of political life. Since common concepts of the political fail to grasp the specificity of the polis, they fail to distinguish between political and nonpolitical forms of community, and these failures have led thinkers to understand political phenomena in terms proper to other spheres of human existence (the family, the household, the rule of a sovereign), terms that distort the distinctive nature of political phenomena. The result of these failures, according to Arendt, is that – across the whole tradition of political theory since the Greeks – the basic realities of political life have been systematically misconceived.

At the core of these misconceptions is the confusion of politics with rule: "our whole tradition of political thought has concluded . . . that the essence of politics is rulership and that the dominant political passion is the passion to rule or govern. This, I propose, is profoundly untrue."[128]

> The greater part of political philosophy since Plato could easily be interpreted as various attempts to find theoretical foundations and practical ways for an escape from politics altogether. The hallmark of all such escapes is the concept of rule, that is, the notion that men can lawfully and politically live together only when some are entitled to command and others are forced to obey.[129]

The confusion of politics with rule leads us to think of political power as analogous to the power of a sovereign ruler; that is, it leads one to think of the (horizontal) power relations within the community of citizens in terms proper to the (vertical) relations of power between the ruling class and the politically disenfranchised. It leads one to think of democratic politics, for example, in terms of "self-rule," "the rule of the people," "majority rule," and "popular sovereignty." The confusion of politics and rule supports a simple-minded equation of power with domination. And this equation

---

[127] PP, 37. [128] OR, 276. [129] HC, 222.

Other Concepts of the Political 83

supports the modern prejudices about politics with which we began: that politics is a universal and necessary part of human life; that politics is a means to an end; and that politics in the narrow sense is ultimately a struggle for power.

Since philosophers have traditionally failed to distinguish politics and rule, according to Arendt, they have failed to adequately distinguish the basic realities of political life. In her book *On Violence*, Arendt singled out the confusion of power, strength, force, authority, and violence. Her words are worth quoting at length.

> It is, I think, a rather sad reflection on the present state of political science that our terminology does not distinguish among such key words as power, strength, force, authority, and, finally, violence – all of which refer to distinct, different phenomena and would hardly exist unless they did … To use them as synonyms not only indicates a certain deafness to linguistic meanings, which would be serious enough, but it has also resulted in a kind of blindness to the realities they correspond to. In such a situation it is always tempting to introduce new definitions, but – though I shall briefly yield to temptation – what is involved is not simply a matter of careless speech. Behind the apparent confusion is a firm conviction in whose light all distinctions would be, at best, of minor importance: the conviction that the most crucial political issue is, and always has been, the question of *Who rules Whom?* Power, strength, force, authority, violence – these are but words to indicate the means by which man rules over man; they are held to be synonyms because they have the same function. It is only after one ceases to reduce public affairs to the business of domination that the original data in the realm of human affairs will appear, or, rather, reappear, in their authentic diversity.[130]

The equation of politics and rule has led political philosophers to misconceive many phenomena essential to politics: not just power, strength, force, authority, and violence, but also opinion, judgment, imagination, rhetoric, persuasion, deliberation, action, government, contract, law, principle, and freedom.

How have these phenomena been misconceived? What are the sources of these misconceptions? And how did Arendt conceive the basic realities of political life?

---

[130] OV, 43–44.

CHAPTER 4

Thinking before Theory

Since Arendt thought that Western philosophy had never had a pure concept of the political, in her attempt to work out her own concept of politics she looked not just to the theories of classical philosophers but also to the *nontheoretical* insights of classical historians and poets

This distinction may seem naïve. The ubiquity of theory is now a cliché. Theory is supposed to be inescapable. People who think they are free of theory, it is said, are under the influence of theories of which they are unaware. This cliché has a grain of truth: every way of thought is guided or misguided by prior assumptions. But to call all such assumptions "theoretical" is to expand the concept of theory to the point where it loses any precise meaning. If we want to understand the heterogeneity of different ways of thought, we have to distinguish what is traditionally called "theory" – the kind of thought that philosophers have aimed at since Plato – from nontheoretical forms of thought. This distinction is essential to understanding the differences between the kinds of thinking central to politics and philosophy.

What then are the differences between political and philosophical thought?

Philosophers have traditionally understood these differences in terms of simple oppositions: the philosophical life is contemplative; the political life is active. Philosophy is theoretical in the sense that it is concerned with the eternal, necessary, and general; political thought is nontheoretical in that it is concerned with the ephemeral, contingent, and singular. Philosophy is the realm of truth, while politics is the realm of appearance. Philosophy is a matter of knowledge and wisdom, while political thought is a matter of opinion, imagination, and judgment.

The differences between political and philosophical discourse are commonly understood in these same oppositions. The philosopher tries to clarify and to show, while the citizen tries to convince; philosophical differences are resolved through logic and evidence, while political differences are resolved through persuasion. Philosophers reject the kinds of

Faculties of Political Thought

arguments (appeals to emotion, to authority, and to common sense) that prevail in political debate. The art of philosophical speech is dialectic, while the art of political speech is rhetoric. Political discourse is a matter of deliberation rather than dialogue; it ultimately aims not at acquiring wisdom but at making decisions. Dialogue is endless, since philosophical questions are never definitively closed, while deliberation is finite, in that it is bound to the time frames of specific situations.

Arendt made a simple point: these oppositions belong to the philosophical tradition – we understand political thought and discourse in philosophical terms and from a philosophical perspective. Politicians and activists tend to think and speak in nontheoretical ways, and so have never articulated in theory their experiences of thought and discourse. Political thought and discourse have been understood not in light of their role and their powers in the political realm, but in light of their weakness and inadequacy in the realm of philosophy. Philosophers have measured political thought and discourse against philosophical standards, and so have tended to think of them as merely crude or defective forms of philosophical discourse and thought. Precisely because philosophers view politics from a philosophical perspective, they have conceived political thought and discourse in a distorted way.

Arendt tried to rethink the nature of political thought and discourse from a nonphilosophical point of view: "I want to look at politics, so to speak, with eyes unclouded by philosophy."[1]

At the center of this task are a few essential questions: What is opinion? What is judgment? What is persuasion? What is rhetoric? What are the nontheoretical forms of thought that prevail in politics?

Faculties of Political Thought

The central faculties of thought in politics are opinion, judgment, and imagination, according to Arendt. But because they are not theoretical, she thought, philosophers have tended to neglect them or to see them as crude forms of theory. "Opinion and judgment obviously belong to the faculties of reason, but the point of the matter is that these two, politically most important, rational faculties had been almost entirely neglected by the tradition of political as well as philosophical thought."[2] To rethink the nature of political thought, we have to reconceive the faculties on which it relies.

[1] EU, 2.   [2] OR, 229.

86   Thinking before Theory

Opinion

Arendt's view of political thought drew on her understanding of appearance. Philosophers have traditionally juxtaposed appearance to being. The way things *appear* is opposed to the way they really *are*. Appearance in this sense is secondary and derivative – a mere seeming or semblance that conceals beings themselves. Arendt argued that appearance in this sense depends on appearance in a more basic sense – appearing in the sense of beings showing themselves as such, as when something "appears" over the horizon, or when actors are said to "appear" on stage. Mere appearances, in the sense of seeming or semblance, depend on this originary level of appearing, in the sense of *the self-showing of beings themselves*:

> Living things *make their appearance* like actors on a stage set for them. The stage is common to all who are alive, but it *seems* different to each species, different also to each individual specimen. Seeming – the it-seems-to-me, *dokei moi* – is the mode, perhaps the only possible one in which an appearing world is acknowledged and perceived. To appear always means to seem to others, and this seeming varies according to the standpoint and the perspective of the spectators.[3]

This passage distinguishes several senses of appearance. Like actors on a stage, beings may *seem* to be something they are not, and they may *seem* different to different points of view. But both kinds of seeming depend on beings making an appearance in the world and showing themselves as such. This basic sense of appearing is implicit in the word "phenomenology." The word "phenomenon" comes from the middle-voice present participle of the verb φαίνειν, which means "to come to light," "to enter the world," "to reveal oneself," "to show oneself," "to shine," and "to appear," as when a new person comes into being and appears in the world. Phenomena in this sense are not mere appearances; they are beings themselves as they appear in experience. To be a phenomenon means to appear as such. The being of phenomena is precisely their appearing. In this basic sense of the word, Arendt argued, *to be* means *to appear*. "In this world which we enter, appearing from a nowhere, and from which we disappear into a nowhere, *Being and Appearing coincide.*"[4]

---

[3] LMT, 21.

[4] LMT, 19. Heidegger makes this point in his *Introduction to Metaphysics*, trans. Gregory Fried and Richard Polt (New Haven: Yale University Press, 2000), 197: "Being means appearing. Appearing does not mean something derivative, which from time to time meets up with Being. Being essentially unfolds *as* appearing." He most clearly lays out the different senses of "appearance" in section 7a of *Being and Time*, trans. Joan Stambaugh (Albany: SUNY Press, 1996), 25–28.

Faculties of Political Thought

This concept of appearance enabled Arendt to rethink the nature of opinion, which is commonly understood in four senses. In one sense, opinion is belief based on second-hand reputation rather than first-hand experience. In another sense, it is belief based on surface appearances rather than underlying realities. In a third sense, opinion is belief based on the limited and distorted appearances beings offer to particular points of view. And lastly, it can mean belief about beings that is devoid of any true understanding of what they are in essence. In each sense, opinion is opposed to true knowledge, as appearance is opposed to true being. Opinion is seen as a defective or inferior form of understanding, rather than a distinctive way of accessing truth. The task of theory has traditionally been to leave behind the sphere of opinion in order to move towards truth.

As Arendt expanded the concept of appearing, she also expanded the concept of opinion. Opinion can give us access not just to mere appearances, she argued; it can let us see beings as they appear in the world and show themselves in actual experience. This understanding of opinion is implicit in the Greek language, she suggested, where the word for "opinion" and "appearance" are the same – *doxa* (δόξα). My opinions (δόξαι) about phenomena are based on the way they appear to me (δοκέουσιν μοί).

> To Socrates, as to his fellow citizens, *doxa* was the formulation in speech of what *dokei moi*, that is, "of what appears to me." This *doxa* had as its topic not what Aristotle called the *eikos*, the probable ... but comprehension of the world "as it opens itself to me." It was not, therefore, subjective fantasy and arbitrariness, but it was also not something absolute and valid for all. The assumption was that the world opens up differently to every man according to his position in it ...[5]

Our opinions are grounded in the way things appear to us, where appearance means not just semblance or mere appearance but the self-showing of beings themselves. So opinion is not just a kind of pseudo-knowledge that must be left behind in order to move towards truth. Truth is not necessarily opposed to opinion. Opinion *in this sense* may be a source of truth. Socratic dialectic may bring to light the grains of truth implicit in unexamined opinions: "dialectic brings forth truth *not* by destroying *doxa* or opinion, but on the contrary by revealing *doxa* in its own truthfulness."[6]

Here we have to be careful. Arendt insisted opinion is different from factual or mathematical truth: "The blurring of the dividing line between factual truth and opinion belongs among the many forms that

---

[5] PP, 14.   [6] PP, 15.

88   Thinking before Theory

lying can assume."[7] But she also insisted that opinion is not simply opposed to truth. She understood the truth of opinion *in the most basic sense* – opinion as openness to the appearing of phenomena – as a matter of truth in the sense of disclosure or unhiddenness: "This truth – *a-letheia*, that which is disclosed (Heidegger) – can be conceived only as another 'appearance,' another phenomenon originally hidden."[8] Everything depends on understanding how different *kinds* of opinion are opposed to or compatible with different *kinds* of truth.

Opinion in this basic sense is a matter of perspective. The way things appear to us depends in part on the stance we take and the place we occupy in relation to them. We see different aspects of the same things depending on our different degrees of involvement or detachment, distance or proximity, pathos or apathy, concern or indifference, experience or naïveté. Our perspective depends on the standpoint proper to our place in the world – the groups to which we belong, the traditions we have inherited, the languages in which we think, the criteria by which we judge, the standards by which we measure things. It is only within a free and open public realm that a plurality of perspectives can appear.

> The reality of the public realm relies on the simultaneous presence of innumerable perspectives and aspects in which the common world presents itself and for which *no common measure* or denominator can ever be devised. For though the common world is the common meeting ground of all, those who are present have different locations within it, and the locations of one can no more coincide with the location of another than the location of two objects. Being seen and being heard by others derive their significance from the fact that everybody sees and hears from a different position.[9]

No "common measure" can be devised that would let us transcend the play of perspectives. Her claim is not that we cannot in fact try to devise such common measures, but simply that any such measure will itself always constitute one perspective, whose limitations will be apparent only from a different point of view. Philosophy and political thought are both caught in this play of perspectives.

Judgment

The traditional aim of philosophy is to move from opinion to knowledge. To know something philosophically means to grasp what it is by

---

[7] BPF, 250.   [8] LMT, 24.   [9] HC, 57 (italics added).

Faculties of Political Thought

subsuming it under a precise and definite concept, a concept that captures the essence of what it conceives. The formulation of definitive concepts is a traditional task of theory. While theory has a long and complex genealogy, for much of the tradition it meant to contemplate the eternal and necessary essences of things, and to try to construct general forms or formulae that gather and articulate their essential traits. Political thought is nontheoretical in this sense. For the most part it does not focus on what is general, necessary, and timeless, but deals with what is ephemeral, contingent, and unique – it aims to illuminate the nature of singular situations and to understand the course of action they demand. Theoretical knowledge is of limited use in the political realm since (as Aristotle said) the singular and contingent are beyond the scope of theory (ἔξο τοῦ θεωρεῖν γένηται); that is, since theory cannot grasp what is singular except insofar as the singular can be subsumed under a general form.[10] So thought in the political realm has to rely on a faculty of reason other than theoretical knowledge.

This other faculty is judgment or *phronesis* (φρόνησις), according to Arendt: "Political thought is essentially founded on the faculty of judgment."[11] She followed Kant in distinguishing two kinds of judgment: determinant and reflective.[12] In a determinant judgment we start with a general rule or concept and apply it to a particular case. In a reflective judgment we start with a particular case, and try to find the general rule or concept under which it may be properly subsumed. In both cases, Arendt argued, judgment is a matter of fitting something particular into a general form.

> [Judgment] designates first and foremost the act of subsumption by which we place the individual and the particular under something general and universal; the act of following a rule and applying criteria by which the concrete is recognized or justified, and on whose basis it will be possible to make a decision.[13]

Both forms of judgment let us see things as examples of a type, as instances of something general. Both determinant and reflective judgments are compatible with theory, in the sense that they rely on universally applicable concepts.

---

[10] Arendt follows Aristotle here. See *Nicomachean Ethics*, trans. H. Rackham (Cambridge, MA: Harvard University Press, 1994), 333 (line 1139b21).
[11] PP, 101. WP, 19.
[12] Kant lays out the difference between determinant and reflective judgment in the Third Critique. Immanuel Kant, *Critique of Judgment*, trans. J. H. Bernard (New York: Hafner, 1951), 15–16.
[13] PP, 102. WP, 20.

Thinking before Theory

But Arendt argued there is a third kind of judgment, through which we see things in their singularity without relying on general concepts or rules.

> But to judge can also signify something altogether different, and it is always this judgment we must use when we are confronted with something that we have never seen before and for which we have no available criteria. This judgment, which is without criteria, cannot be based on anything other than the evidence of the object itself, and it has no presupposition other than the aptitude of this human capacity to judge which is much closer to the capacity to decide than to the capacity to place and to subsume ... We experience this kind of judgment in everyday life each time that, confronted with an unknown situation, we deem that somebody has judged the situation well or poorly.[14]

A situation is never just a particular example of a general phenomenon. Every situation is singular and has to be judged in its singularity. To be judicious in this sense is to respond appropriately to what is unique without relying on general forms or rules.[15] Political judgment is for the most part not theoretical in the sense that it is not based on a general knowledge that can be applied indifferently to many different things; it is the ability to understand each thing in its singularity.[16]

Imagination

In addition to opinion and judgment, political thought relies on imagination, which lets us remove ourselves from our immediate situation and enables us to put ourselves in the place of others. Imagination allows a certain distance and perspective on our own affairs, and helps us sense the gravity and magnitude of situations that otherwise would seem remote and unreal.

> Imagination alone enables us to see things in their proper perspective, to be strong enough to put that which is too close at a certain distance so that we can see and understand it without bias or prejudice, to be generous enough to bridge abysses of remoteness until we can see and understand everything that is too far away from us as though it were our own affair. This distancing of some things and bridging the abysses to others is part of the dialogue of understanding, for whose purposes direct experience establishes too close a contact and mere knowledge erects artificial barriers.[17]

---

[14] PP, 102. WP, 20–21.   [15] RJ, 188–189.

[16] For an in-depth account of Arendt's concept of judgment, see Max Deutscher, *Judgment after Arendt* (New York: Routledge, 2016).

[17] EU, 323.

Imagination is not the same as empathy: empathy lets us sense what others are feeling, but it does not necessarily let us see things from their perspective. Imagination allows us to detach ourselves from our situation and to try to put ourselves in the place of others, to see the world from other points of view.

Forms of Political Thought

If political thought differs from philosophy in the faculties of reason it uses (opinion, judgment, imagination), it also differs from philosophy in the forms it takes. Arendt focused on three forms of thought – usually ignored by philosophers – that predominate in the sphere of politics: thinking in examples; thinking in stories; and what she called "representative" thought.

Thinking in Examples

Examples do menial work in philosophy. At its best, philosophy starts by reflecting on concrete examples, but this reflection is merely a preliminary step on the way to theoretical knowledge. In Plato's dialogues, for example, when Socrates asks essential questions he always rejects as inadequate answers that merely give examples. Our ability to give apt examples shows that unexamined opinions already contain a degree of insight into the essential. But this insight is indefinite. The task of theory is to move beyond examples to a precise and definite comprehension of a general essence.

Examples play a different role in political thought, according to Arendt. In political life we are to a large extent concerned with judging singularities (persons, events, situations), and to that extent our judgments cannot rely for guidance only on general concepts and theories. In politics, general concepts tend to be less illuminating than singular examples. In Arendt's view, most political and moral thought is less a matter of theory than a matter of "thinking in examples."[18]

> Most political virtues and vices are thought of in terms of exemplary individuals: Achilles for courage, Solon for insight (wisdom) etc ... We judge and tell right from wrong by having present in our mind some incident and some person, absent in time or space, that have become examples.[19]

---

[18] RJ, 146.   [19] RJ, 144–145.

92 Thinking before Theory

Such examples are singular. They do not exemplify general rules. Nor are they models to be imitated or standards by which to measure our own lives. Nor do they have value merely as instances of more general phenomena. Instead, the works and lives of exemplary individuals illuminate the possibilities of human existence and function as points of reference that allow us to orient ourselves in the darkness of human affairs.

The role of examples in political thought was essential to two of Arendt's books, *Men in Dark Times* and *Eichmann in Jerusalem*. Both contained profiles of singular individuals, and these profiles were exercises in judgment in the sense that their first aim was to do justice to each person in his or her singularity. Arendt emphasized this singularity in her report on the trial of Eichmann: "The focus of every trial is upon the person of the defendant, a man of flesh and blood with an individual history, with an always unique set of qualities, peculiarities, behavior patterns, and circumstances."[20] Her profiles had two aims. They could serve as a starting point for theoretical reflection. *Eichmann in Jerusalem* was a profile of a single man rather than a theory of evil, and yet in Arendt's view any theory of evil would have to come to terms with Eichmann in his singularity. But she also thought her profiles could serve as portraits of exemplary lives. In *Men in Dark Times* she wrote: "Even in the darkest of times we have the right to expect some illumination, and . . . such illumination may well come less from theories and concepts than from the uncertain, flickering, and often weak light that some men and women, in their lives and works, will kindle under almost all circumstances and will shed over the time span that was given them on earth."[21]

Thinking in Stories

Exemplary thought is related to thinking in narrative. Arendt stressed that narrative is a way to think about what is singular – what eludes the generality of conceptual thought precisely because it is unique.[22] Thinking in narrative is a way to grasp the singular essence of persons or events.

By "person," Arendt meant not *what* we are but *who* we are. *What* we are is a question of the roles we play or the traits we share with others; *who* we are is a question of our irreplaceable singularity. We can describe what we are in general terms – the qualities we possess, the groups to which we

[20] EJ, 285.   [21] Arendt, *Men in Dark Times* (New York: Harcourt Brace, 1993), ix.
[22] For a more extended discussion of Arendt's thoughts on narrative, see Lisa Jane Disch, *Hannah Arendt and the Limits of Philosophy* (Ithaca: Cornell University Press, 1994).

Forms of Political Thought 93

belong, the roles we have chosen or into which we were born. But general terms cannot capture who we are as persons. "The moment we want to say who somebody is, our very vocabulary leads us astray into saying what he is; we get entangled in a description of qualities he necessarily shares with others like him; we begin to describe a type or a 'character' in the old meaning of the word, with the result that his specific uniqueness escapes us."[23] General descriptions fail to do justice to who we are, even when we try to describe ourselves.

But if we only grasp *what* we are in general terms, we show *who* we are in our actions and words. Whenever we act or speak we risk revealing what matters to us, what we really think, what we do and do not know, what we are made of – everything that makes us the person we are. "In acting and speaking, men show who they are, reveal their unique personal identities and thus make their appearance in the human world."[24] The revelatory power of actions and words is not something we can fully control. I can of course try to control the image I show the world by carefully choosing what I say and do, but whenever I have to speak and act spontaneously my improvised words and bungled actions reveal who I am more clearly than the most carefully crafted persona. Words and actions are meaningful in ways we don't intend. This is the insight implicit in the clichés that "action reveals character" and that "nothing reveals a person more than her words." We understand *what* people are in general terms; but we understand *who* they are in light of their actions and words.

A human life is a sequence of more or less meaningful actions and words that, for Arendt, between birth and death make up a more or less coherent story. A life story is meaningful, not because it expresses our intentions but because it reveals who we are. "Nobody is the author or producer of his own life story. In other words, the stories, the results of action and speech, reveal an agent, but this agent is not an author or producer."[25] If we want to understand who someone is we have to know her life story. "Who somebody is or was we can know only by knowing the story of which he is himself the hero."[26]

To think of a person in narrative is to construct a story that aims to illuminate who she is. Thinking in narrative is obviously a form of construction – a storyteller tries to select the hero's most revealing words and actions and to arrange them in a sequence that brings out their inner connections and contradictions. But this kind of narrative thinking at its best does not aim to impose meaning on meaningless raw material, but

[23] HC, 181.   [24] HC, 179.   [25] HC, 184.   [26] HC, 186.

94   Thinking before Theory

aims to make explicit the meaning of the hero's own actions and words, to
gather and multiply their revelatory power. When we try to tell someone's
life story, our aim is not just to produce a well-made narrative but to grasp
and illuminate a "human essence – not human nature in general (which
does not exist) nor the sum total of qualities and shortcomings in the
individual, but the essence of who somebody is."[27] Narrative thought in
this case aims at a kind of essential truth.

Just as narrative lets us think of people in their singularity, for Arendt it
is also a way to think the singularity of events.

An "event" is not just anything that happens, in her view, but a
happening that interrupts the usual course of things and that exceeds the
possibilities we can foresee and imagine. A revolution is an event in this
sense, while the rising and setting of the sun is not. A real event is not a
link in a calculable chain of causes and effects, but an occurrence that
transcends the intentions and expectations of those who live through it. An
occurrence is not an event if it happens repeatedly or if can be produced
and reproduced at will. Every event is unique.

On this point Arendt was critical of three common assumptions of
modern philosophies of history.

First, the assumption that history is not a series of events but a process.
Conceiving history as a process assumes that "nothing is meaningful in and
by itself," and that events have meaning only as part of a larger whole.[28]
Historical processes are supposed to be the contexts within which events
are significant, so that to understand the historical significance of an event
is to understand its place within a whole process. In this regard, Arendt
criticized Kant and others for whom "the process as a whole appears to be
guided by an 'intention of nature' unknown to acting men but comprehensible to those who come after them."[29] In this conception of history,
the task of the thinker is to focus not on singular events – which by
themselves are historically meaningless – but on the processes (development, evolution, progress, or regress) within which they take place. "What
the concept of process implies is that the concrete and the general, the
single thing or event and the universal meaning, have parted company.
The process, which alone makes meaningful whatever it happens to carry
along, has thus acquired a monopoly of universality and significance."[30]
The concept of process effaces the meaning of events in their singularity.

A second assumption is that human history is meaningful to the extent
that it is causally determined, so that to understand events is to explain

[27] HC, 193.   [28] BPF, 63.   [29] BPF, 82.   [30] BPF, 64.

Forms of Political Thought

them in causal terms. These causes may be of two kinds: history may be seen as a progression governed by a final cause or *telos* (such as freedom); or historical events may be seen as links in a chain of causes and effects governed by laws of efficient causality. But Arendt argued that to think of human history in causal terms is to efface the distinctive nature of events, which is precisely to break unforeseeably and unpredictably with what has come before: "Causality . . . is an altogether alien and falsifying category in the historical sciences."[31]

> Whoever in the historical sciences honestly believes in causality actually denies the subject matter of his own science. He denies by the same token the very existence of events which, always suddenly and unpredictably, change the whole physiognomy of a given era. Belief in causality, in other words, is the historian's way of denying human freedom which, in terms of the political and historical sciences, is the human capacity for making a new beginning.[32]

The concept of causality distorts our understanding of human history because it effaces the novelty and singularity of events.

A third assumption is that humans "make" their own history. This assumption draws on the insight that human history is the result of action, but it misconceives action on the model of production or making. In Marx's thought, this misconception leads to the idea that the *telos* of history, which for Kant and Hegel was revealed only in retrospect to the contemplative gaze of the philosopher, can become the ultimate aim of human activity, revealed to the visionary foresight of the revolutionary. Arendt thought this misconception – which conceives events as means to an end – distorts our understanding of history in several ways: it denies the inherent unpredictability of human action; it generates the illusion that we can understand events in light of a historical process whose end is known in advance; and it leads to the delusion that we can control our historical destiny.[33] Above all, by subsuming events within a process subject to human control, it effaces both the radical novelty of events and their singular significance: "Single events and deeds and sufferings have no more meaning here than hammer and nails have with respect to the finished table."[34]

These three assumptions are grounded in a contemplative stance toward history: the stance of one who sees through the flux of singular, contingent, ephemeral events to an underlying ground of eternal, necessary, and

---

[31] EU, 319.   [32] EU, 319.   [33] BPF, 84.   [34] BPF, 80.

Thinking before Theory

general essences. This "essentially contemplative philosophy," according to Arendt, has led thinkers to conceive of history in categories foreign to the experience of action. This is true even of Marx, who, despite inverting the traditional hierarchy of contemplation over action, drew his basic terms from the experience not of action but of fabrication: "the age-old identification of action with making and fabricating was supplemented and perfected, as it were, through identifying the contemplative gaze of the historian with the contemplation of the model (the *eidos* or 'shape' from which Plato had derived his 'ideas') that guides the craftsman and precedes all making."[35] Precisely because they are not derived from the experience of action and historical change, these general categories dictate an approach to history that allows only a limited and distorted view.

> Such generalizations and categorizations extinguish the "natural" light history itself offers, and by the same token, destroy the actual story, with its unique distinction and its eternal meaning, that each historical period has to tell us. Within the framework of preconceived categories, the crudest of which is causality, events in the sense of something irrevocably *new* can never happen.[36]

Once historical questions are framed in these terms (process, cause, means, end), it is hard even to ask about the meaning of events in their singularity. Instead of focusing on words and actions and asking what they reveal about a situation and about the people involved, we are led to focus on the underlying causes of a process and to ask about the significance of actions and words within this process as a whole. This focus on historical significance is liable to blind us to the revelatory power of what was actually said and done. "The historian, by gazing backward into the historical process, has been so accustomed to discovering an 'objective' meaning, independent of the aims and awareness of the actors, that he is liable to overlook what actually happened in his attempt to discern some objective trend."[37] The result is that modern philosophies of history tend to de-emphasize or neglect the words, actions, and events that constitute the sphere of politics: "the single deeds and acts constituting the realm of politics, properly speaking, were left in limbo."[38]

In her own thought, Arendt looked to the example of classical historians, who focused on events, and the words and deeds of those who lived through them. "What is difficult for us to realize is that [in classical historiography] the great deeds and works of which mortals are capable,

---

[35] BPF, 78.   [36] EU, 319–320 (italics added).   [37] BPF, 88.   [38] BPF, 85.

Forms of Political Thought

and which become the topic of historical narrative, are not seen as parts of either an encompassing whole or a process; on the contrary, the stress is always on single instances and single gestures."[39] This focus on the singular, contingent, and ephemeral was guided by the assumption that events could be meaningful in themselves, in the sense that they had the power to reveal the situations in which they occurred and to show what human beings were capable of.

> Greek and Roman historiography, much as they differ from each other, both take it for granted that the meaning or, as the Romans would say, the lesson of each event, deed, or occurrence is revealed in and by itself . . . Everything that was done or happened contained and disclosed its share of "general" meaning within the confines of its individual shape and did not need a developing and engulfing process to become significant.[40]

If classical historians focused on events and actions, it was not because they were unaware of historical causality and context. The task of the historian was not to explain events in light of their causes and context, but to understand their causes and context in light of the events: "causality and context were seen in a light provided by the event itself, illuminating a specific segment of human affairs; they were not envisaged as having an independent existence of which the event would be only the more or less accidental though adequate expression."[41] This approach to history, for Arendt, was born of the experience of action and of involvement in human affairs. Among its key assumptions is that events themselves have an illuminating power, the power to illuminate not just the time in which they occur but the possibilities of human existence. We allude to this power when we say that something has become clear "in light of" recent events. This idiom implies that the events can reveal what was not apparent before they took place. At the same time, events have the power to confront us with something that exceeds established forms of understanding, surpasses our power of imagination, and transcends the horizon of what we had believed possible, either because it is radically new or else because it has long been distorted or concealed. The task of the historian is precisely to understand the singular essence of the event – what happened – and to grasp what it reveals.

> Just as in our personal lives our worst fears and best hopes will never adequately prepare us for what actually happens . . . so each event in human history reveals an unexpected landscape of human deeds, sufferings, and

---

[39] BPF, 42–43.   [40] BPF, 64.   [41] BPF, 64.

new possibilities which together transcend the sum total of all willed intentions and the significance of all origins. It is the task of the historian to detect this unexpected *new* with all its implications in any given period and to bring out the full power of its significance.[42]

To think of an event in narrative is to construct a story that illuminates what happened. Narrative thought is a form of construction – one tries to select the most illuminating facts and to arrange them in a sequence that brings out their inner connections and contradictions. But at its best narrative thought does not just impose order on chaos, but brings out the meaning (the revelatory character) of events themselves. Historical narrative aims to construct stories that not only fit the facts but that let us see "the inner truth of the event."[43] Thinking in stories aims at a kind of essential truth.

So historical truth is complex. Narratives may be true in the sense that they are factually correct, but untrue in a deeper sense if they lay out facts in a way that distorts or conceals the nature of what happened. Historical thought must aim not just to get the facts right, but also to reveal the nature of situations and the meaning of events. The most revealing events may be minor incidents that are utterly insignificant from a causal point of view. In a 1966 report on the trial of Nazis charged with murder at Auschwitz, for example, Arendt emphasized that the most illuminating moments in the trial often took the form of anecdotes: "Instead of the truth, however, the reader will find moments of truth, and these moments are actually the only means of articulating this chaos of viciousness and evil. The moments arise unexpectedly, like oases in the desert. They are anecdotes, and they tell in utter brevity what it was all about."[44] To understand the truth of historical narratives we have to conceive truth not only as factual correctness but also as disclosure or unconcealment of the meaning of the past.

Arendt's historical studies are exercises in this kind of thought. They aimed not just to present facts but to answer essential questions: What is totalitarianism? What is revolution? What does revolution reveal about the nature of power? Who was Adolph Eichmann? What does Eichmann's life show about the nature of evil? Stories may answer such questions without trying to grasp the essential in precise and definite concepts: "storytelling reveals meaning without committing the error of defining it."[45] Narrative thought illuminates the darkness of human affairs, but in a light more

---

[42] EU, 320.   [43] MDT, 20.   [44] RJ, 255.   [45] MDT, 105.

Forms of Political Thought 99

intense and revealing than the clarity of conceptual thought: "No philosophy, no analysis, no aphorism, be it ever so profound, can compare in intensity and richness of meaning with a properly narrated story."[46]

Representative Thought

Opinion, imagination, and judgment make possible another way of thinking. Opinion is perspectival, in the sense that my unexamined opinions are simply the way things appear to me from my own standpoint. But we are not bound to our standpoint and the limited view it allows. We are able to refine our opinions by imagining the world from other points of view, and this ability strengthens our powers of judgment. Arendt followed Kant in calling this mode of thought an "enlarged way of thinking" (*eine erweiterte Denkungsart*),[47] or more simply "*representative thought.*"[48] This enlarged way of thinking is central to political thought.

> Political thought is representative. I form an opinion by considering a given issue from a number of different viewpoints, by making present to my mind the standpoints of those who are absent; that is, I represent them. This process of representation does not blindly adopt the actual views of those who stand somewhere else, and hence look upon the world from a different perspective; this is a question neither of empathy, as though I tried to be or to feel like somebody else, nor of counting noses and joining a majority, but of being and thinking in my own identity where actually I am not. The more people's standpoints I have present in my mind while I am pondering a given issue, and the better I can imagine how I would feel and think if I were in their place, the stronger will be my capacity for representative thinking and the more valid my final conclusions, my opinion.[49]

Thinking in politics is primarily a matter of forming judicious opinions by considering many different viewpoints.

We cannot think this way on our own, according to Arendt. To transcend the limits of our unexamined opinions we have to expose our views to others and to be exposed to other points of view. This need for others helps explain the power of common deliberation. People who know how to deliberate together can reach more judicious decisions than any one of them could reach in isolation.

> Since opinions are formed and tested in the process of exchange of opinion against opinion, their differences can be mediated only by passing them

[46] MDT, 22.   [47] See §40 of Kant, *Critique of Judgment*, 137.   [48] BPF, 220.
[49] BPF, 241.

Thinking before Theory

> through the medium of a body of men, chosen for the purpose; these men, taken by themselves, are not wise, and yet their common purpose is wisdom – wisdom under the conditions of the fallibility and frailty of the human mind.[50]

To deliberate together is to weigh different opinions in order to work toward insights that no one possesses in advance. This means to articulate my views in order to persuade others, but also to expose my views to criticism in order to see their limitations. It means to consider other opinions in order to expose their weaknesses or errors, but also to see the grains of truth in other points of view.

We can see things from other perspectives only if we detach ourselves from our given point of view, and this detachment from our own standpoint is possible only if we are impartial. So an essential virtue of political thought is impartiality.

> The very process of opinion formation is determined by those in whose places somebody thinks and uses his own mind, and the only condition for the exertion of the imagination is disinterestedness, the liberation from one's own private interests. Hence even if I shun all company or am completely isolated while forming an opinion, I am not simply together only with myself in the solitude of philosophical thought; I remain in this world of universal interdependence, where I can make myself the representative of everybody else. Of course, I can refuse to do this and form an opinion that takes only my interests, or the interests of the group to which I belong, into account; nothing, indeed, is more common, even among highly sophisticated people, than the blind obstinacy that becomes manifest in lack of imagination and failure to judge. But the very quality of an opinion, as of a judgment, depends on the degree of its impartiality.[51]

To be partial is to identify with one party and so to confine oneself to one particular point of view. Partisanship is rarely a matter of consciously elevating party over country, or particular interests over the common good. More often it comes from an inability to acknowledge that our views are partial rather than comprehensive, that our vision of the common good is framed by our place in the community. The hallmark of partisans is typically not the naked assertion of particular interests over the common good, but the inability to see any difference between the good of their party and the good of the community as a whole. For the true partisan, other parties are not parts of the whole but enemies of the whole, not partners in the political process but traitors or subversives who must be defeated at all costs.

---

[50] OR, 227.   [51] BPF, 241–242.

Forms of Political Thought   101

Hence the rhetoric of partisanship: only our faction are true believers; only our party are true patriots; only our country represents the interests of humanity as a whole. To be impartial is not to stand outside the play of perspectives, but to detach ourselves from our place in the world and so to free ourselves from the limitations of any one point of view: "Impartiality is obtained by taking the viewpoints of others into account; impartiality is not the result of some higher standpoint that would then actually settle the dispute by being above the melée."[52] For Arendt the exemplar of impartiality is Homer, who praised both the Trojans and Achaeans without taking sides, and who told the story of the Trojan War without confining himself to the perspective of either camp.[53]

Impartiality makes possible a kind of objectivity. But the objectivity of political thought is not the same as the objectivity of modern science. In both cases the basic meaning of objectivity is the same: to be objective is to see things for what they are. In modern science this means to see things as they are in themselves, independent of the human mind and apart from human opinions and judgments. Modern science objectifies the world in the sense that it subtracts from things the meaning they have for us and reduces them to the bare elements that are clear and distinct to everyone. This objectification is achieved largely through the use of measure; by devising common measures and by focusing only on what is measurable, we can achieve a knowledge of the world that is the same for everyone and that transcends the differences of judgment and opinion tied to different perspectives. But this objectification also entails a reduction of meaning: modern science aims to master a world that it empties of meaning and value.

For Arendt, this reduction of meaning differentiates scientific objectivity from the objectivity of political thought. Political thought deals with human action, and human action is irreducibly meaningful. We do not see actions for what they are if we bracket their human meanings and reduce them to elements that are clear and distinct to everyone; to objectify human actions in this way does not let us see them as they are in themselves – intrinsically meaningful – but instead impoverishes and distorts our understanding of them. To understand human actions is to understand their meaning, and meaning cannot be objectified – it cannot be made so clearly and distinctly present to thought that it appears the

---

[52] Hannah Arendt, *Lectures on Kant's Political Philosophy*, ed. Ronald Beiner (Chicago: University of Chicago Press, 1982), 42.
[53] BPF, 51.

Thinking before Theory

same to everyone. This is why Arendt said the realities of political life can only appear from the vantage of "innumerable perspectives ... for which no common measure or denominator can ever be devised."[54]

But if political thought is necessarily caught in a play of perspectives, this does not mean that our understanding of political matters is necessarily "subjective" or that we cannot aspire to a kind of objectivity. To judge a situation well, we have to move beyond the limited perspective afforded by our own subjective perceptions and to learn to see things from different points of view. The more perspectives we can understand the more comprehensive will be our grasp of reality, and the more "objective" will be our opinion. (Arendt here is close to Nietzsche.)[55] Objectivity in political thought is not a matter of transcending the play of perspectives altogether, but of seeing things from many different points of view. For Arendt, the exemplar of this kind of objectivity is Thucydides, who in his history of the Peloponnesian War was able to articulate the standpoints and interests of all the different warring parties.[56]

So political thought is different from philosophy. Philosophy has traditionally tried to illuminate the nature of what is general, necessary, and eternal; it has aspired to truths that are universal and timeless. Political thought is largely nontheoretical in that it tends to focus on what is unique and contingent, and it aims at truths that are limited and ephemeral. So political thought tends to rely on rational faculties (opinion, judgment, imagination) that are different from those central to philosophy.

Political Discourse

Just as political thought differs from philosophy, so political discourse differs from philosophical discourse. Philosophers have tended to see political discourse as simply a debased or defective version of philosophical discourse. But Arendt's reflections on political thought help to clarify the distinctive nature of discourse in politics.

---

[54] HC, 57.

[55] Objectivity for Nietzsche is not a matter of transcending the play of perspectives, but the ability to invert perspectives and to see things from many points of view. Dana Villa puts this well: "Arendt ingeniously adapts Nietzsche's perspectivism to the needs of the public realm, using it to show how human plurality supports the reality of a common public world." See Dana Villa, *Socratic Citizenship* (Princeton: Princeton University Press, 2001), 255–256. For Nietzsche's view of objectivity, see Friedrich Nietzsche, *On the Genealogy of Morality*, ed. Keith Ansell-Pearson, trans. Carol Diethe (New York: Cambridge University Press, 1994), 92.

[56] BPF, 52.

Political Discourse 103

For Arendt, the specifically political form of discourse is persuasion. Persuasive discourse conveys not just ideas, but an attunement to and understanding of the world. When we speak we do more than communicate meanings; we also reveal (whether we intend to or not) our outlook, our disposition, our character, our stance toward others, the assumptions we take for granted, and the standpoint from which we see the world. When we listen to others we initially have to accept the terms in which they think, to attune ourselves to how they feel, to see things in light of their concerns, to expose ourselves to the force of their convictions, to understand where they are coming from, to follow their approach to a topic, and open ourselves to their point of view. Listening does not give us access to the mind of the speaker, but it does sometimes let us see things from the speaker's perspective. We can never know for sure what others think of us, for example, but we can hear words that inadvertently show that the speaker sees us differently from the way we see ourselves, so that through the power of words we are suddenly able to see ourselves as though from the outside and, as it were, through the eyes of the other. This experience is just one example of what we go through every day. To listen to others is to open ourselves to their point of view, so that under the influence of their words reality appears differently to us. Words have the power to alter the way the world appears. The Greeks called this power *peitho*, persuasion.

To persuade someone in this sense is to change their opinion by changing the way things actually appear to them. I am open to persuasion when I am willing to listen, to be moved, to acquiesce to a movement that removes me from my previous point of view and makes visible aspects of a topic that were invisible to me before. This movement is unsettling. In the course of being persuaded I have to waver between two incompatible but plausible versions of reality. I am persuaded not when I agree to believe what someone says, but when under the influence of someone's discourse reality actually appears to me to be what it is said to be, and when I relinquish my old perspective and accept this appearance as closer to the truth.

Persuasion is distinct from other forms of discourse. It is not a matter of coercion, since it is not possible to force others to see how things appear from a different point of view. It is not a matter of command, since we rely on persuasion precisely when we have no right to demand obedience. It is not a matter of proof, since it pertains to matters of opinion and not to matters that can be proved and known for sure.

Arendt's reflections on political thought help to clarify the importance of free discourse in political life. Political thought is primarily concerned

Thinking before Theory

with what is unique, contingent, and ephemeral – singular individuals, shifting situations, unprecedented events – and so relies less on theory than on the faculties of opinion, imagination, and reflective judgment. These faculties do not work well in isolation. In order to refine our opinions and to make responsible judgments, we have to open ourselves to other points of view. For Arendt, the significance of public discourse lies in its power to free us from the limitations of a single perspective. "This is the meaning of public life ... Only where things can be seen by many in a variety of aspects without changing their identity, so that those who are gathered around them know they see sameness in utter diversity, can worldly reality truly and reliably appear."[57] Our grasp of reality depends on our ability to see the same world from different points of view, according to Arendt. Her words are worth quoting again in full:

> No one by himself and without his fellow man can grasp what objectively exists in an adequate way and in all its reality, because what exists does not show itself and appear to him except within a perspective that is relative to the position that he occupies and which belongs to him. If he wants to see the world, to experience it as it "really" is, he cannot do so unless he grasps it as something that is common to many people, which exists between them, which both separates and links them, which shows itself differently to each and which can only be understood to the extent that many people talk about it and mutually exchange their opinions and their perspectives. It is only through freedom of discussion that the world appears ... in its objectivity, visible in all its aspects. To-live-in-a-real-world and to-discuss-it-with-others are at bottom one and the same thing, and if private life seemed "idiotic" to the Greeks it was because private life was deprived of the many-sidedness that comes out in talking-about-things, and so was deprived of the experience of how things truly happen in the world.[58]

Our grip on reality is weakened when we are deprived of other perspectives, either when we are isolated from others or when all others share our point of view. The privation of private life is just this deprivation of others who, because they view things from a different angle, allow us to see aspects of the world that are hidden from our given point of view.

Discourse does not just express representative thinking; according to Arendt, it makes representative thinking possible. Our capacity for representative thought – our ability to look at things from many sides in order to more clearly see them for what they are – depends on our ability to talk with others.

---

[57] HC, 57.   [58] PP, 128–129. WP, 52 (my translation).

Political Discourse

> This enlarged way of thinking, which as judgment knows how to transcend its own individual limitations ... cannot function in strict isolation or solitude; it needs the presence of others "in whose place" it must think, whose perspectives it must take into consideration, and without whom it never has the opportunity to operate at all.[59]

Thinking requires a public realm in which we can expose our thoughts to the test of free and open examination. This is especially clear in the case of representative thought. In order to be able to consider things from a number of different points of view, there has to be a public realm in which we can freely exchange opinions.

Kant's notion of representative thought thus led Arendt to rethink common notions of free speech. Free speech is commonly understood as a way to let people advocate their particular points of view. Arendt argued that free speech is better understood as a way to let us transcend our particular points of view. Freedom of speech makes possible freedom of thought.

> Freedom of speech and thought, as *we* understand it, is the right of an individual to express himself and his opinion in order to be able to persuade others to share his viewpoint. This presupposes that I am capable of making up my mind all by myself and that the claim I have on the government is to permit me to propagandize whatever I have already fixed in my mind. *Kant's* view of this matter is very different. He believes that the very faculty of thinking depends on its public use; without the "test of free and open examination," no thinking and no opinion-forming are possible.[60]

The principle of free speech does not just delimit a private sphere where we can say whatever we want; it also institutes a public sphere in which we can air and refine our views. Without free speech, the right to freedom of thought is meaningless. Free and open debate is the condition of judicious political thought.

As it first emerged in the Greek polis, political speech at its best is simply the forceful exchange of views necessary for citizens to be able to see their situation from many different perspectives and so to come to judicious decisions on how to act.

> Polis-life ... to an incredibly large extent consisted of citizens talking with one another. In this incessant talk the Greeks discovered that the world we have in common is usually regarded from an infinite number of different

[59] BPF, 220–221.   [60] KPP, 40 (italics added).

Thinking before Theory

> standpoints, to which correspond the most diverse points of view. In a sheer inexhaustible flow of arguments . . . the Greek learned to exchange his own view point, his own 'opinion'–the way the world appeared and opened up to him (*dokei moi*, "it appears to me," from which comes *doxa*, or "opinion") – with those of his fellow citizens. Greeks learned to *understand* – not to understand one another as individual persons, but to look upon the same world from one another's standpoint, to see the same in very different and frequently opposing aspects.[61]

For this to happen, citizens have to transcend their personal interests and their unformed opinions – to recognize a common or overlapping interest that outweighs their private interests, and not only to try to persuade others to share their point of view but also to be willing to be persuaded by others. The Greek estimation of the political life was based in part on the belief that, for questions about how to live together, the opinions of any one ruler are bound to be limited and one-sided, and that through common deliberation a group of thoughtful and judicious citizens will reliably make better decisions than any one person could on his own.[62]

One might object that this account of political speech is utterly unrealistic. Anyone who has spent time in politics knows that, for the most part, political discourse is a miasma of platitudes, clichés, distortions, spin, propaganda, demagoguery, polemic, ad hominem attacks, bullshit, and outright lies. This was as true in classical Athens as it is true today. Why did Arendt insist that "debate constitutes the very essence of political life" when real debate is actually so rare?

Arendt assumed that to understand the nature of political discourse we have to focus on what distinguishes public discourse in political and nonpolitical communities. While real debate is rare in political life, it is nonexistent in nonpolitical regimes. Anyone who has lived under a nonpolitical form of government – where public discourse is dominated by official propaganda, sermons from leaders, masses chanting slogans, and where expressing the wrong opinion in public can lead to prison, abduction, or assassination – knows that real debate in such conditions is

---

[61] BPF, 51.

[62] Aristotle makes this point in the *Politics*: "For it is possible that the many, though not individually good men, yet when they come together may be better, not individually but collectively, than those who are so." "For although each individual separately will be a worse judge than the experts, the whole of them assembled together will be better or at least as good judges." Aristotle, *Politics*, 221–223 and 227 (1281b1–4 and 1282a16–18).

Political Discourse

practically impossible. Public discourse in political and nonpolitical regimes are both afflicted by platitudes, spin, polemics, bullshit, and lies. What distinguishes political discourse is the *possibility* of open debate and common deliberation. We recognize this possibility when we complain that it is so rarely realized. This complaint is based on the insight that political discourse has the potential to be more than the debased sophistries of politicians in their endless struggle for power – that at its best political discourse is a way for citizens to talk things through in order to reach considered decisions about what to do and how to live together.

CHAPTER 5

Classical Political Philosophy

The Greeks originally understood politics in light of their active engagement in the life of the polis, according to Arendt, but this original understanding was distorted by the philosophical tradition begun by Plato and Aristotle and passed down by Roman and Christian thinkers: "the original Greek understanding of politics [has] been lost."[1] Philosophers in this tradition have seen philosophy and politics as mutually exclusive ways of life, and they have theorized politics in light of philosophical interests rather than working out their concepts on the basis of actual political experiences.

> Our tradition of political thought . . . far from comprehending and conceptualizing all the political experiences of Western mankind, grew out of a specific historical constellation: the trial of Socrates and the conflict between the philosopher and the polis. It eliminated many experiences of an earlier past that were irrelevant to its immediate political purposes and proceeded until its end . . . in a highly selective manner.[2]

Both Plato and Aristotle considered the philosophical life superior to political life. Both saw political thought and discourse as inferior to the kind of thought and discourse proper to philosophy. Both claimed to have reached a wisdom superior to the political opinions of their fellow citizens. Arendt argued that they founded a tradition of political theory that is implicitly hostile to democratic politics – a tradition in which the task of a political theorist is to withdraw from political life, to find philosophical answers to political questions, and to return to the political sphere not as a citizen among citizens but as a teacher, umpire, judge, or ruler. The role of political philosophy for them is to transcend rather than participate in political discourse.

But Arendt saw in Socrates a different relation between philosophy and politics. Socrates did not aim to rule the polis, but neither did he simply

[1] HC, 23.   [2] HC, 12.

withdraw from political life altogether. Instead he brought into the life of the polis an endless dialogue on essential questions, by speaking as a citizen to his fellow citizens in the agora. In her view, this dialogical style of thought is more hospitable to democratic politics, in that it aims not to transcend but to refine political discourse.

So her stance toward philosophy was complex. She tried to critically dismantle the tradition inaugurated by Plato and Aristotle. But she also looked back to Socrates for the model of a politically engaged thinker.[3] To understand her critique of classical political philosophy we have to understand her interpretations of Socrates, Plato, and Aristotle.

Socrates

Arendt distinguished Socratic from Platonic thought. Her distinction is obviously uncertain; Socrates did not write, and we have access to his thought primarily through the testimony of Plato. But Plato's work is divided against itself. The way of thought articulated in the later works is different from, even inimical to, the way of thought implicit in the works written close to the death of Socrates. Arendt explained this division by assuming Plato's early works were influenced by Socrates, while in his later works Plato worked out a way of thought more fully his own.[4] "There exists a sharp dividing line between what is authentically Socratic and the philosophy taught by Plato. The stumbling block here is the fact that Plato used Socrates as the philosopher, not only in the early and clearly 'Socratic' dialogues but also later, when he often made him the spokesman for theories and doctrines that were entirely un-Socratic."[5] The difference between Socrates and Plato was not that they held different theories. It was that Plato eventually founded a school and taught a kind of doctrine, while Socrates had no school and claimed he never taught anything, but only asked questions and engaged in dialogue. Socrates and Plato differed not just in what they thought but in their ways of thinking.

Socratic thought starts with the experience of wonder, according to Arendt. It was said that Socrates would sometimes stop and think for hours, struck with wonder and lost in thought. This is a recognizable

---

[3] LMT, 167–169.
[4] The distinction between Socratic and Platonic thought goes back at least to Diogenes Laertes, who wrote that "Plato ... treats for his own part themes which Socrates disowned, although he puts everything in the mouth of Socrates." Diogenes Laertes, *Lives of Eminent Philosophers*, vol. 1, trans. R. D. Hicks (Cambridge, MA: Harvard University Press, 2006), 175.
[5] LMT, 168.

experience – it sometimes happens that we find ourselves in the presence of something obscure, and this obscurity is not simply a region of the unknown but the depth of the incomprehensible. It is not that we encounter something unfamiliar, but that within what is familiar we sense a side of things that is turned away from us and beyond our grasp. We may still recognize each thing for what it is, but this "what it is" no longer seems entirely clear. If we attend to this obscurity something happens – the strangeness of things becomes apparent and, if we let this strangeness overwhelm us, we are struck by a sense of wonder. To wonder is to be open to the mystery of things.

Socrates is an exemplary thinker for Arendt because of his aptitude for wonder, because he did not claim to know anything noble and good, and because he did not present his opinion (*doxa*) as doctrine or dogma. What set Socrates apart from other thinkers was his ability to endure perplexity and his willingness to acknowledge his lack of understanding: "His distinction from his fellow citizens is not that he possesses any special truth from which the multitude is excluded, but that he remains always ready to endure the pathos of wonder and thereby avoids the dogmatism of mere opinion holders."[6] Socrates' profession of ignorance, his claim that he had nothing to teach, was based on this experience of wonder. Instead of imparting knowledge to others, Socrates imparted his perplexity.[7]

This perplexity is speechless, according to Arendt – words fail us when we are overcome with wonder, and when we do begin to speak we articulate our wonder in the form of questions.

> As soon as the speechless state of wonder translates itself into words, it will not begin with statements but will formulate in unending variations what we call the ultimate questions – What is being? Who is man? What meaning has life? What is death …? It is from the actual experience of not-knowing, in which one of the basic aspects of the human condition on earth reveals itself, that the ultimate questions arise.[8]

The ultimate questions emerge from the experience of wonder, and they remain genuine questions as long as they are rooted in that experience.

These questions ask of each being what it is: "What is X?" This "what it is" we traditionally call an "essence." Socrates saw that, to be able to see things for what they are, we have to already have some prior understanding of their essence. His questions aim to explicate, clarify, and refine this prior understanding. Essential questions require a kind of inner conversion – to

---

[6] Hannah Arendt, "Philosophy and Politics," in *Social Research* 57, 1 (1990), 101.   [7] RJ, 173.
[8] Arendt, "Philosophy and Politics," 98.

respond to them we have to suspend our usual relation to the world and turn our attention away from particular beings towards the mystery of their nature. The attempt to answer such questions requires a kind of withdrawal from the world, a movement in thought away from beings back towards what allows us to recognize them as such. This effort to grasp and illuminate the essence of things is what Arendt called "thinking."

> Thinking always deals with absences and removes itself from what is present and close at hand. This, of course, does not prove the existence of a world other than the one we are part of in ordinary life, but it means that reality and existence ... can be temporarily suspended, lose their weight and, together with this weight, their meaning for the thinking ego. What now, during the thinking activity, become meaningful are distillations, products of de-sensing, and such distillations are not mere abstract concepts; they were once called "essences."[9]

In her view, the essences of things never stand fully revealed – it is never entirely clear to us what things are.

> Whenever we talk of the "nature" or the "essence" of a thing, we actually mean this innermost kernel of whose existence we can never be so sure as we are of darkness and density. True understanding does not tire of interminable dialogue and "vicious circles" because it trusts that imagination eventually will catch at least a glimpse of the always frightening light of truth.[10]

We tend to grasp the essence of things most readily through language, by putting our thoughts into words. The activity of thinking is for the most part a kind of inner speech, a silent dialogue with myself. As long as thinking is rooted in wonder – as long as it is attuned to the essential obscurity of things and is aware of its own limitations – it constantly renews itself and so remains interminable.

Arendt explained the nature of thinking with a simple example. A meditation on housing and dwelling can help us to clarify the meaning of the word "house," she argued, and this clarification can help us to better understand what a house is. (Plato and Aristotle also used the example of a house to illustrate their concepts of essence.) Her discussion is worth quoting at length.

---

[9] LMT, 199. Arendt's thought has been distorted by debates over "essentialism" and "anti-essentialism." Arendt asked essential questions, but she critically dismantled the inherited concepts of essence such questions have traditionally presupposed.

[10] EU, 322.

Classical Political Philosophy

> The house in and by itself, *auto kath'auto*, that which makes us use the word for all these particular and very different buildings, is never seen, neither by the eyes of the body nor by the eyes of the mind; every imagined house, be it ever so abstract, having the bare minimum to make it recognizable, is already a particular house. This house as such, of which we must have a notion in order to recognize particular buildings as houses, has been explained in different ways and called by different names in the history of philosophy ... The point here is that it implies something considerably less tangible than the structure perceived by our eyes. It implies "housing somebody" and being "dwelt in" as no tent could house or serve as a dwelling place which is put up today and taken down tomorrow. The word "house" is the "unseen measure," "holds the limits of all things" pertaining to dwelling; it is a word that could not exist unless one presupposes thinking about being housed, dwelling, having a home. As a word, "house" is shorthand for all these things, the kind of shorthand without which thinking ... would not be possible at all. The word "house" is something like a frozen thought that thinking must unfreeze whenever it wants to find out the original meaning. In medieval philosophy, this kind of thinking was called "meditation," and the word should be heard as different from, even opposed to, contemplation. At all events, this kind of pondering reflection does not produce definitions and in that sense is entirely without results, though someone who had pondered the meaning of "house" might make his own look better.[11]

A few points. First, Arendt retained the traditional commitment to essential questions, but interpreted the meaning of essence in an untraditional way. The essence of house is not an ideal form seen with the eyes of the mind as the physical house is seen with the eyes of the body. Nor can a house be defined by isolating a core set of objective properties or functional predicates common to all houses. The essence of house becomes clearer to us only when we clarify the meaning of housing, dwelling, being at home. Arendt implies this understanding of essence is implicit in Socratic thought. Socratic thought does not fix a general definition against which particular houses can be measured; it has instead the effect of dissolving every fixed definition and measure. For Arendt it is in the nature of thought "to undo, unfreeze, as it were, what language, the medium of thinking, has frozen into thought-words (concepts, sentences, definitions, doctrines) ... The consequence is that thinking inevitably has a destructive, undermining effect on all established criteria, values, measurements of good and evil, in short, on those customs and rules of conduct we treat of

---

[11] LMT, 71. RJ, 172–173.

in morals and ethics."[12] Because Socratic thought calls into question the concepts and standards that usually guide our approach to things, Arendt called it "thinking without a bannister."[13]

Arendt also tried to clarify the nature of Socratic thought by contrasting it with what it is not. It is not cognition, since it does not subsume particular beings under general concepts. It is not representative thinking, since it is not a matter of seeing beings from many different points of view. It is not a matter of deliberation, since it does not aim at a decision to act.[14] It is not a matter of judgment, since it deals with the nature of things in general rather than with singularities.[15]

But she insisted Socratic thinking can help other modes of thought. Socratic thought can initially paralyze cognition, since it tends to undo the concepts that we usually take for granted; but it can ultimately strengthen our powers of cognition, since it allows us to transform and refine the terms in which we think. The critical power of Socratic thought can also strengthen our capacity for representative thought, since it attunes us to the limitations of our own views and so helps us to be open to the views of others. Socratic thinking can also paralyze deliberation, since it calls into question the values and criteria that usually guide our decisions; and yet it also allows us to reflect on these criteria and to consider our decisions more carefully. To make this point she returned to the example of housing and dwelling.

> If your action consisted of applying general rules of conduct to particular cases as they arise in ordinary life, then you will find yourself paralyzed because no such rules can withstand the winds of thought. To use once more the example of the frozen thought inherent in the word "house," once you have thought about its implied meaning – dwelling, having a home, being housed – you are no longer likely to accept for your own home whatever the fashion of the time may prescribe; but this by no means guarantees that you will be able to come up with an acceptable solution for your own housing problems.[16]

Finally, Socratic thought can strengthen our powers of judgment. Thinking gives us a critical distance from the terms in which we usually recognize and evaluate things, and so it helps us see each thing for what it is rather than thoughtlessly measuring it against a general standard.

---

[12] LMT, 75.

[13] HA, 336. For a deep discussion of this point, see Tracy Strong, *Politics Without Vision: Thinking without a Banister in the Twentieth Century* (Chicago: University of Chicago Press, 2012), 325–369.

[14] RJ, 173.   [15] RJ, 189.   [16] RJ, 176.

> The faculty of judging particulars (as Kant discovered it); the ability to say, "This is wrong," "This is beautiful," etc., is not the same as the faculty of thinking. Thinking deals with invisibles, with representations of things that are absent; judging always concerns particulars and things close at hand. But the two are interrelated in a way similar to the way consciousness and conscience are interconnected. If thinking, the two-in-one of the soundless dialogue, actualizes the difference within our identity as given in consciousness and thereby results in conscience as its byproduct, then judging, the byproduct of the liberating effect of thinking, realizes thinking, makes it manifest in the world of appearances, where I am never alone and always much too busy to be able to think. The manifestation of the wind of thought is no knowledge; it is the ability to tell right from wrong, beautiful from ugly. And this may indeed prevent catastrophes, at least for myself, in the rare moments when the chips are down.[17]

Socratic thinking is not the same as cognition, representative thought, deliberation, or judgment, and yet indirectly it has the power to refine these other modes of thought.

Socratic thinking has its dangers, according to Arendt. One danger is paralysis: since thinking tends to "unfreeze" the assumptions "frozen" into concepts and doctrines, it "inevitably has a destructive, undermining effect on all established criteria, values, measurements for good and evil."[18] If we are used to following rules and applying set standards, rather than relying on our own judgment, the destructive effect of thinking may leave us paralyzed. Another danger is a kind of nihilism, a rejection of all standards and the unthinking refusal to judge. Arendt thought this danger was exemplified by certain followers of Socrates, who "changed the nonresults of Socratic thinking into negative results," who mistook the endless questioning of doctrines and standards for a doctrine that rejected all standards, and who concluded that without definitive standards it was impossible to make meaningful judgments. These followers turned out to be a very real threat to the polis, according to Arendt, but that threat did not come from their thinking but from their desire for a doctrine that would relieve them of the need to think.[19]

But if Socratic thought is dangerous, Arendt argued, thoughtlessness is worse. Evil is often the result not of wickedness but of thoughtlessness, not of the deliberate transgression of common values but of thoughtless adherence to them. (The most significant characteristic of Adolf Eichmann, in her view, was "not stupidity but a curious, quite authentic

---

[17] LMT, 93. RJ, 189.   [18] RJ, 176.   [19] RJ, 177–178.

Socrates 115

inability to think.")[20] Whenever we simply apply inherited concepts and fulfill conventional responsibilities, we abdicate a deeper responsibility to see things for what they are and to decide on our own what to do. This abdication of responsibility allows us to do evil with a good conscience, since we are secure in the knowledge that our intentions are good and that we are doing what everyone does. Thinking disturbs this good conscience when it calls all values into question and confronts us with the responsibility to judge for ourselves. But the destructive effect of thinking is not simply negative since it allows us to refine our powers of cognition, deliberation, and judgment. "Socrates ... seems indeed to have held that talking and thinking about piety, justice, courage, and the rest were liable to make men more pious, more just, more courageous, even though they were not given either definitions or further 'values' to direct their further conduct."[21]

Arendt's reflections on thinking and judging are incomplete. She never explained precisely how thinking liberates the faculty of judgment; nor did she explain what it means to judge something right or wrong; nor did she explain how or why it is that, in moments of crisis, some people are able to judge right from wrong even in that absence of unequivocal standards of conduct.[22] But this incompleteness is less a flaw in her work than a reticence that leaves open essential questions: What was the connection between Eichmann's evil and his thoughtlessness? Was there a connection between Socrates' thoughtfulness and his refusal to obey the dictates of the Thirty Tyrants? What do these examples show about the connection of thought to judgment?

Since deliberation and judgment are central to politics, Arendt argued, Socratic thought has a certain relevance to political life. Socrates himself highlighted this relevance at his trial when he claimed that his public philosophizing was the greatest boon ever bestowed on the city of Athens. He saw himself not as an architect, umpire, or teacher, but as a midwife and a gadfly. His political role as a thinker was neither to design the city, nor to rule it, nor to teach his fellow citizens, but to wake his fellow citizens from the slumber of thoughtlessness.[23]

---

[20] RJ, 159.   [21] RJ, 173.

[22] Here I am indebted to Richard Bernstein's essay, "'The Banality of Evil' Reconsidered," in Craig Calhoun and John McGowan, *Hannah Arendt and the Meaning of Politics* (Minneapolis: University of Minnesota Press, 1997), 297–322.

[23] RJ, 174–176.

> The role of the philosopher, then, is not to rule the city but to be its "gadfly," not to tell philosophical truths but to make citizens more truthful ... Socrates did not want to educate the citizens so much as he wanted to improve their *doxai* [opinions], which constituted the political life in which he too took part.[24]

Socrates played this role through dialogue. Dialogue was a way to infect his fellow citizens with wonder, to bring to light the truths and errors implicit in their opinions, and so to rouse them into thoughtfulness. The aim of dialogue was not to introduce into the polis truths that would supersede political debate; in Arendt's view, Socrates "probably did not look upon [dialectic] as the opposite or even the counterpart to persuasion, and it is certain that he did not oppose the results of this dialectic to *doxa*, opinion."[25] His aim was to introduce into political life the art of thinking—the "interminable dialogue between [the mind] and the essence of everything that is."[26]

Arendt saw Socrates not as a potential ruler who claimed to have returned to the cave of public life from the heights of solitary contemplation, but as a thinker who introduced pure thinking into public life by speaking informally as a citizen to other citizens on essential questions relevant to matters of public concern:

> A man who counted himself neither among the many nor among the few; who did not aspire to being a ruler of cities or claim to know how to improve and take care of the citizens' souls; who did not believe that men could be wise and did not envy the gods their divine wisdom in case they should possess it; and who therefore had never even tried his hand at formulating a doctrine that could be taught and learned.[27]

Socrates showed that it is possible to be a politically engaged thinker who reflects on the nature of political things in light of experiences proper to the political realm. Arendt returned to Socrates to retrieve a possible way of doing of political theory – a possibility largely implicit and unrealized in the tradition of Western philosophy.

Plato

For Arendt, the Western tradition of political philosophy began with Plato. The trial of Socrates led Plato to think of the relation of politics and philosophy in a deeply unsocratic way. "Our tradition of political

---

[24] Arendt, "Philosophy and Politics," 81. [25] Arendt, "Philosophy and Politics," 80.
[26] EU, 322. [27] RJ, 168–169.

Plato 117

thought began when the death of Socrates made Plato despair of polis life and, at the same time, doubt certain fundamentals of Socrates' teachings."[28] How did Plato depart from Socrates's way of thought?

Socrates had tried to introduce dialectic into the political discourse of Athens, and his fellow citizens had responded by putting him to death. Plato in turn proposed to use philosophy to transcend political discourse altogether, Arendt argued, and this proposal eventually led him to abandon Socrates' stance towards politics. But Plato misunderstood the nature of political thought, she argued, so that his political philosophy covered over the original Greek understanding of politics.

The trial of Socrates revealed the weakness of philosophy in the political realm. It showed that in the public realm philosophical truth becomes simply one opinion among others;[29] that truth could be less persuasive than idle talk and slander; and that credulous and ignorant citizens could be persuaded to do terrible injustices. Plato saw that politics is a matter of appearances, that things appear differently to people in different situations, that differences of opinion can never be definitively resolved through persuasion, and that in politics there is never a firm basis for making reliable decisions. He apparently concluded that a just and thriving city could not be reached through political means—through public debate and common deliberation among citizens. In his *Seventh Letter* he wrote:

> I was driven to assert, in praise of true philosophy, that nothing else can enable one to see what is right for states and for individuals, and that the troubles of mankind will never cease until either true and genuine philosophers attain political power or the rulers of states by some dispensation of providence become genuine philosophers.[30]

Politics was ruled by persuasion, but persuasion had failed to prevent injustice. There had to be a better way.

Arendt thought that Plato was guided by the experience not of thought but of measure. Measure is a way to transcend the distortions of appearance. We know things do not appear to our senses as they really are, but that their appearance depends on the perspective from which we see them, so that what is far from us seems small while what is close to us looms large. These distortions of perspective generate differences of opinion. But it is possible to move beyond appearances and to resolve differences of opinion through the use of measure. The size of an object may seem

---

[28] Arendt, "Philosophy and Politics," 73.   [29] BPF, 238.
[30] Plato, *Phaedrus and Letters VII and VIII*, trans. Walter Hamilton (New York: Penguin, 1985), 114.

Classical Political Philosophy

different to us depending on the points of view from which we see it, but we can know its size for sure by measuring it against a constant standard such as a yardstick. Or we might have different opinions about the mass of a piece of gold, but we can resolve those differences by weighing it against a standard unit. Measure lets us transcend the distortions of appearance and to definitively resolve certain differences of opinion.[31]

Plato transposed the notion of measure into the realm of thought. This transposition was based on an analogy: just as appearances can mislead our perceptions of particular beings, so too can appearances mislead our understanding of what beings are. And just as we can resolve different opinions about the size or weight of things by measuring them against a fixed standard, so too can we resolve differences of opinions about what things are by measuring them against their essence. If we want to know the relative purity of a piece of gold, for example, it may be impossible to tell on the basis of mere appearance. But since we know that gold in general has certain objective traits, we can test the genuineness of any piece of gold by measuring it against a fixed standard. If we can define the general nature of gold, we can use this general definition as an absolute standard against which we can measure the purity of any particular piece of gold. Essence can be a kind of measure.

Plato extended this notion of measure to all things. Just as we distinguish between genuine gold and fool's gold, so we also distinguish true friends from false friends, real science from pseudoscience, real virtue from the semblance of virtue, genuine justice from travesties of justice. People have different opinions about what is genuine and what is not – my actions tend to seem especially virtuous to me, while the actions of my enemies tend to seem especially vile and disgraceful. Plato saw that if we could truly define what justice is in essence, we could use this definition as an absolute standard against which to measure the relative justice of any particular act.

Plato introduced this notion of measure into the sphere of politics. The problem of political thought, in Arendt's words, is that it "relies on the simultaneous presence of innumerable perspectives and aspects in which the common world presents itself and for which [there is] *no common measure*."[32] Without definite measures, we can deliberate endlessly without really knowing what we are talking about. As long as we don't know what justice really is, we have no certain criteria by which to make political

---

[31] See Plato, *The Republic*, trans. Paul Shorey (Cambridge, MA: Harvard University Press, 1990), 602c–d.

[32] HC, 57 (italics added).

Plato 119

decisions. But if we could grasp the essence of political things, we could devise general definitions that would enable us to definitively resolve political differences and to build a just community. Rather than dealing with political differences through the endless exchange of opinions, we could definitively resolve political differences by transcending opinions altogether. If philosophy could find measures grounded in the essence of things – standards that transcend the political realm – then politics itself would be superfluous. The endless debates essential to political life could be replaced by philosophical understanding.

In a lecture course in 1927, Heidegger tried to critically dismantle the Platonic notion that essences can serve as a kind of measure. He argued that this notion depends on interpreting essences as ideal forms on which actual beings are more or less perfectly modeled, and that this interpretation of essence is not based in the experience of thinking but in the experience of making.

> The potter forms a vase out of clay. All forming of shaped products is effected by using an image, in the sense of a model, as a guide or standard. The thing is produced by looking to the anticipated look of what is to be produced by shaping, forming. It is this anticipated look of the thing, sighted beforehand, that the Greeks mean ontologically by *eidos, idea*.[33]

Heidegger argued that Plato conceived of essence as measure through a threefold operation: first he abstracted the words *eidos* and *idea* from the sphere of production; then he transposed the words to a philosophical level of thought, so that they named not an aspect of particular beings but their essential nature; and then he applied this expanded sense of *eidos* and *idea* to all beings. So Plato conceived of essence in terms derived not from the experience of thinking but from the experience of making: "the chief ancient determinations for the thingness or reality of a being originate in productive activity, the comprehension of being by way of production."[34] By tracing the lineage of Plato's concept of essence back to the experiences from which it was born, Heidegger tried to deprive it of its seeming self-evidence, to clarify its original sense, and to alert us to the ways in which it both guides and misguides thought. This way of thinking – which tries to free thought of inherited prejudices by tracing metaphysical concepts back to the experiences from which they

---

[33] Martin Heidegger, *Basic Problems of Phenomenology*, trans. Albert Hofstadter (Indianapolis: Indiana University Press, 1988), 106.
[34] Heidegger, *Basic Problems of Phenomenology*, 105.

were derived – he called the phenomenological *"Destruktion"* or "critical dismantling" of the metaphysical tradition.

Arendt appropriated this form of phenomenology in her critique of Plato's philosophy of politics. She argued that Plato's interpretation of essence as measure was not grounded in the experience of thought but in the experience of making or *poiesis*. Plato often used examples drawn from the experience of making to explain the notion of ideas. Implicit in these examples is a simple analogy. Craftsmen understand what their products are, and this understanding guides the design of their products and determines how they will look. Before an architect starts to make a house, for example, she will foresee its final look, and this foresight will guide the actual construction of the house, so that the actual house itself will in some sense be merely the imitation of the foreseen look. In Greek, the word for "look" is *idea* (ἰδέα or εἶδος). Since the essence of a product (what it is) is manifest in its general *idea* (look), Plato used the word to name the essence of products in general. An ideal house, in this sense, is one that perfectly embodies what a house really is. The task of the architect is to understand what houses are in essence, to imagine a house that instantiates this ideal, and to use this ideal image as a model to guide the construction of an actual house. The task of the philosopher is simply to make explicit and to refine the kind of knowledge possessed by craftsmen. The ideal is the measure of the actual.

Arendt concluded that a key part of Plato's conception of thought – the interpretation of essence as *idea* – is not actually grounded in the experience of thinking, but is derived from the experience of measure and making.

> This quality of permanence in the model or image, of being there before fabrication starts and remaining after it has come to an end, surviving all the possible use objects it continues to help into existence, had a powerful influence on Plato's doctrine of eternal ideas. Insofar as his teaching was inspired by the word idea or *eidos* ("shape" or "form"), which he used for the first time in a philosophical context, it rested on experiences in *poiesis* or fabrication, and although Plato used his theory to express quite different and perhaps much more "philosophical" experiences, he never failed to draw his examples from the field of making when he wanted to demonstrate the plausibility of what he was saying. The one eternal idea presiding over a multitude of perishable things derives its plausibility in Plato's teachings from the permanence and oneness of the model according to which many and perishable objects can be made.[35]

[35] HC, 142–143.

Plato 121

In this argument Arendt followed Heidegger's attempt to critically dismantle the metaphysical tradition.

But Arendt saw what Heidegger failed to see: the implications for political theory of this *Destruktion* of the Platonic notion of essence. The interpretation of essence as idea sets the task of the political philosopher, which Plato laid out most clearly in the allegory of the cave. The philosopher should not waste time in the darkness of the political realm arguing with fellow citizens over what is singular, ephemeral, and contingent. He should turn away from the world of becoming and turn towards the realm of Being. Only by leaving the ephemera of political life and ascending in thought to the ideas will he be able to see what things really are. Once he has seen what political things are – once he knows what justice is, what man is, what the polis is – he has to return to the cave, not in order to engage in political debate with his fellow citizens, but to educate them through reasoned argument; that is, to turn them away from worldly things, to guide them up out of the cave, and to let them see the ideas for themselves.

The task of the political philosopher is analogous to the task of the architect: to understand what a city is; to design an ideal city on the basis of this understanding; to measure the actual polis against this ideal; and to use this ideal as a model to guide the remaking of the polis. Political philosophy is a matter of finding absolute standards grounded in the essences of things, and translating these standards into principles, laws, and blueprints for institutions that could ensure justice in the polis. Arendt argued that this view has influenced the whole tradition of political philosophy.

> To the philosopher, politics – if he did not regard this whole realm as beneath his dignity – became the field in which the elementary necessities of human life are taken care of and to which absolute philosophical standards are applied ... Because Plato in a sense deformed philosophy for political purposes, philosophy continued to provide standards and rules, yardsticks and measurements with which the human mind could at least attempt to understand what was happening in the realm of human affairs.[36]

The task of the political philosopher for Plato is not to be a gadfly, like Socrates, but to be the teacher, umpire, architect, or even ruler of the polity.

---

[36] Arendt, "Philosophy and Politics," 102.

Classical Political Philosophy

The notion of essence as idea led Plato to mistake the nature of political thought, according to Arendt. If we interpret essences simply as what beings are, we can look for the essences of things in the flux of the political realm – a politician grasps the essential when he understands the nature of a singular and ephemeral event, just as the philosopher grasps the essential when he understands the nature of a general phenomenon. But if we interpret essences in Platonic terms as eternal and general ideas, then political thought only touches on the essential to the extent that it discovers the eternal and the necessary beneath the ephemeral contingencies of politics. To focus on the ephemera of political life, for Plato, is to focus on the inessential.

The interpretation of essence as idea also distorted Plato's view of truth. On this point Arendt acknowledged a debt to Heidegger, who argued that Plato's thought had obscured an authentic understanding of truth implicit in the Greek word *aletheia*. In his view, *aletheia* meant not just a correspondence of thought to reality, but in a deeper sense meant the illumination of beings that first makes such correspondence possible. But since Plato thought of essences as ideal forms, to which particular beings corresponded and against which they could be measured, Plato foregrounded the sense of truth as correspondence and obscured the more basic sense of truth as illumination. Arendt noted her debt to Heidegger in an essay on political authority:

> This presentation is indebted to Martin Heidegger's great interpretation of the cave parable in *Platons Lehre von der Wahrheit*, Bern 1947. Heidegger demonstrates how Plato transformed the concept of truth (*aletheia*) until it became identical with correct statements (*orthotes*). Correctness indeed, and not truth, would be required if the philosopher's knowledge is the ability to measure.[37]

But Arendt again saw what Heidegger failed to see: the implications of Plato's notion of truth for political philosophy. If truth is a matter of illumination or unconcealment (ἀλήθεια), the nontheoretical insights of political thought can lay claim to truth. One can look for truth in the ephemera of human affairs, since there is truth in an opinion that sheds light on a specific situation, or a judgment that illuminates the nature of a singular act, just as there is truth in a definition that clarifies the nature of a general phenomenon. But if truth is a matter of correspondence, and if beings are true only insofar as they correspond to their ideal form, then

---

[37] BPF, 291.

Plato   123

only theory can lay claim to truth. Theory is true insofar as it is informed by and corresponds to these eternal forms, while political thought is concerned with semblances of the forms rather than the forms themselves. In Platonic terms, political thought is true only to the extent that it recognizes in the ephemera of politics the generality and eternity of the ideas.

Arendt's critique of Plato implies a stark conclusion: Plato's interpretation of essence, and his notion of truth, led him to systematically distort the phenomena of political life and the faculties of political thought. Four distortions stand out:

1. The notion of truth as correctness entailed a simplified notion of *appearance*. In the allegory of the cave, essences do not appear in the outward look of particular beings; beings are merely semblances of the ideas. So appearance is interpreted not as the self-showing of beings themselves, but as mere semblance or illusion.

2. This Platonic notion of appearance implied a demotion of *opinion*. Opinion is seen not as a faculty of reason but as an inferior form of philosophical theory. Just as the craftsman uses weights and measures to move beyond appearance to an objective knowledge of the mass and size of things, so the philosopher should use the ideas to move beyond opinions about things to an objective knowledge of what they are. The task of the political philosopher is to replace opinion with knowledge.

3. The demotion of opinion goes with a simplified notion of *judgment*. Judgment is interpreted not as the ability to see and evaluate beings as singularities, but as the ability to apply the general to the particular, or to subsume the particular under the general (determinant or reflective judgment). Plato assumed all judgment requires a reference to a general standard, without which judgment becomes either arbitrary guesswork or subjective preference. To judge correctly one must know the true standards, and the true standards are those grounded in the essence of things. To judge is to measure the actual against the ideal, so that the ability to judge is ultimately based on a knowledge of the ideas.[38] In this way Plato confused impartial judgment with objective knowledge. Objectivity for

---

[38] This view of judgment was articulated by Leo Strauss: "To judge soundly one must know the true standards. If political philosophy wishes to do justice to its subject matter, it must strive for genuine knowledge of these standards. Political philosophy is the attempt to truly know the nature of political things and the right, or good, political order" Leo Strauss, *What Is Political Philosophy?* (Chicago: University of Chicago Press, 1988), 11–12. Arendt agreed that political theory aims to understand the essences of political phenomena, but she questioned the Platonic interpretation of essence as a kind of standard or measure.

him was not a matter of seeing things from many perspectives, but of moving beyond the distortions of perspective to a comprehensive grasp of reality, a view from nowhere. Judgments should be based not on weighing many opinions, but on a knowledge that transcends the realm of opinion altogether.

4. The attempt to replace opinion with philosophical knowledge also entailed a demotion of *deliberation*. For Plato, the ends of communal life are not a matter of incommensurable perspectives and opinions; they are a matter of definite philosophical knowledge. Deliberation is no longer understood as debate over the ends of communal life, but merely as debate over the best way to achieve the ends that can be known through philosophical contemplation. The most basic level of political debate is largely superfluous. The polity should ultimately be ruled not by the opinions of citizens but by the wisdom of philosophers.

In short, Plato interpreted political thought as a defective form of philosophy. His philosophy of politics aimed to replace opinion with truth, judgment with knowledge, rhetoric with dialectic. It aimed to transcend the public debate that is the essence of politics, and to replace the plurality of opinions with single truth that is valid for all. The ultimate aim of his political philosophy was to replace politics with philosophy.

For Arendt this is the decisive point: Plato founded a tradition of political philosophy that is basically anti-political.[39] He derived basic concepts from nonpolitical experiences; he interpreted political phenomena in nonpolitical terms; and he sketched a form of government that dispensed with politics altogether. So Plato's view of politics distorted and concealed the original Greek understanding of the political.

The key to this distortion for Arendt was the concept of rule. Politics in the original sense excluded any form of rule; the polis "was understood as a form of political organization in which the citizens lived together under conditions of no-rule, without a division between ruler and ruled."[40] Plato assumed politics was a matter of rule, and this assumption obscured the absence of rulership essential to political life.

> The greater part of political philosophy since Plato could easily be interpreted as various attempts to find theoretical foundations and practical ways for an escape from politics altogether. The hallmark of such escapes is the

---

[39] Alan Ryan made this point in his book *On Politics*: "Plato's political thought is antipolitical . . . The founder of European political thought is the founder of antipolitical thinking." Alan Ryan, *On Politics* (New York: W. W. Norton, 2012), 111.

[40] OR, 30.

Plato   125

concept of rule, that is, the notion that men can lawfully and politically live together only when some are entitled to command and others forced to obey.[41]

The assumption that politics is a matter of rule (*archein*) is still implicit in common definitions of different forms of government: monarchy (rule by one), oligarchy (rule by a few), theocracy (rule by God) and democracy (defined as the rule of the people).

Arendt argued that for the Greeks rulership was prepolitical and belonged to the private sphere of the household or *oikos* rather than to the public sphere of the polis. "All Greek and Latin words which express some rulership over others, such as *rex, pater, anax, basileus*, refer originally to household relationships and were names slaves gave to their masters."[42] To introduce the concept of rule into political thought was thus to confuse the polis and the *oikos*:

> It is the decisive contention of the Statesman that no difference existed between the constitution of a large household and that of the polis ... so that the same science would cover political and 'economic' or household matters.[43]

This confusion effaced the differences between leadership and rulership, and obscured the distinction between political and nonpolitical forms of power: "According to Greek understanding, the relationship between ruling and being ruled, between command and obedience, was by definition identical with the relationship between master and slaves."[44] So the introduction of the concept of rule into political thought had the effect of effacing the specificity of the polis in particular and the political realm as such.

While Plato took the concept of rule from the realm of the household, Arendt argued, he generalized it to encompass any relation of power.

> Historically, the concept of rule, though originating in the household and family realm, has played its most decisive part in the organization of public matters and is for us invariably connected with politics. This should not make us overlook the fact that for Plato it was a much more general category. He saw in it the chief device for ordering and judging human affairs in every respect.[45]

What Plato wanted for the polis was a form of rule that relied on free obedience rather than on persuasion or threats of violence. He saw that

[41] HC, 222.   [42] HC, 32.   [43] HC, 223.   [44] HC, 224.   [45] HC, 224.

Classical Political Philosophy

free obedience was proper to any power relation in which followers recognize that a leader has superior expertise. Patients freely obey doctors, just as sailors freely obey a captain in whom they recognize superior seamanship, and as apprentices freely obey the orders of a master-craftsman. In the ideal city, Plato thought, the citizens would recognize the political expertise of the philosopher-king and would freely obey his laws:

> Plato was originally guided by a great number of models of existing relations, such as that between the shepherd and his sheep, between the helmsman of a ship and the passengers, between the physician and the patient, or between the master and the slave. In all these instances either expert knowledge commands confidence so that neither force nor persuasion are necessary to obtain compliance, or the ruler and the ruled belong to two altogether different categories of beings, one of which is already by implication subject to the other ... Although it is obvious that Plato himself was not satisfied with these models, for his purpose, to establish the 'authority' of the philosopher over the polis, he returned to them time and again, because only in these instances of glaring inequality could rule be exerted without seizure of power and the possession of the means of violence.[46]

The argument that philosophers were naturally fit to rule the polis derived its plausibility especially from the analogy between the philosopher and the craftsman.

Arendt argued this analogy took its plausibility from the interpretation of essence as idea, which itself was derived from the experience of making. Once the wisdom of the philosopher-king was interpreted as analogous to the technical expertise of the craftsman, the relation of ruler to citizens could be likened to the relation between a master craftsmen who gives commands and the workers who carry them out. The interpretation of essence as idea thus supported the analogy between governing and making, and this analogy reinforced the interpretation of politics as a matter of rule.

> By sheer force of conceptualization and philosophical clarification, the Platonic identification of knowledge with command and rulership, and of action with obedience and execution, overruled all earlier experiences and articulations in the political realm and became authoritative for the whole tradition of political thought, even after the roots of experience from which Plato derived his concepts had long been forgotten. Apart from the unique Platonic mixture of depth and beauty, whose weight was bound to carry his

---

[46] BPF, 108–109.

Plato

thoughts through the centuries, the reason for the longevity of this particular part of his work is that he strengthened his substitution of rulership for action through an even more plausible interpretation in terms of making and fabrication. It is indeed true ... that the division between knowing and doing, so alien to the realm of action, whose validity and meaningfulness are destroyed the moment thought and action part company, is an everyday experience in fabrication, whose processes obviously fall into two parts: first, perceiving the image or shape (*eidos*) of the product-to-be, and then organizing the means and starting the execution.[47]

To equate politics and rule, and to understand the ruler as a master craftsman, is to see politics as a matter of technical expertise and management rather than of considered opinion and common deliberation.

The analogy of the philosopher and the craftsman distorted the nature of political action, according to Arendt. Since Plato thought of the essence of the polis as an ideal city of which actual cities were merely imperfect copies, this ideal could serve as a model to guide the philosopher's effort to remake the city, just as the idea of the house guides the architect's effort to build any particular home.

In the *Republic*, the philosopher-king applies the ideas as the craftsman applies his rules and standards; he "makes" his City as the sculptor makes a statue; and in the final Platonic work these same ideas have even become laws which need only be executed ... The point is that Plato and, to a lesser degree, Aristotle, who thought craftsmen not even worthy of full-fledged citizenship, were the first to propose handling political matters and ruling political bodies in the mode of fabrication.[48]

The analogy between philosopher and craftsman led Plato to confuse action with making, and to think of political action on the model of production.

The confusion of action with making degraded politics into a means to higher ends. Making is usually merely a means to an end, while action is an end in itself. This is an essential difference between political action (debating what to do and how to live together) and production (working to realize ends given in advance), between the deliberation essential to politics and the instrumental reasoning essential to production. With Plato, however, political action was understood not as the act of deliberation over final ends, but as the attempt to realize an end discovered in advance by philosophical knowledge. Arendt argued this

---

[47] HC, 225.   [48] HC, 227 and 230.

128   Classical Political Philosophy

instrumental conception of political action has dominated the whole tradition of political philosophy.

> The substitution of making for acting and the concomitant degradation of politics into a means to obtain an allegedly "higher" end ... is as old as the tradition of political philosophy ... How persistent and successful the transformation of action into a mode of making has been is easily attested by the whole terminology of political theory and political thought, which indeed makes it almost impossible to discuss these matters without using the categories of means and end and thinking in terms of instrumentality.[49]

In Plato, political life was no longer an end in itself, but simply a means to an end.[50]

The confusion of acting and making also made it possible to justify violence in politics, according to Arendt. Plato himself never condoned violence, but once politics is subordinated to a higher end it is always possible to justify violence as a means to that end. "Violence, without which no fabrication could ever come to pass, has always played an important role in political schemes and thinking based upon an interpretation of action in terms of making."[51] The interpretation of politics as a means to an end outlived Plato, and this interpretation made it possible for later thinkers to justify and glorify violence. "Only the modern age ... brought forth the much older implications of violence inherent in all interpretations of human affairs as a sphere of making ... As long as we believe that we deal with ends and means in the political realm, we shall not be able to prevent anybody's using all means to pursue recognized ends."[52] Justifications for violence in the political realm today still rely on the confusion of acting and making ("If you want to make an omelet, you have to break some eggs.").

The confusion of acting with making, Arendt argued, also separated knowing from doing. In the act of deliberation, thought and action are indissociable. But in the process of making something, there is an obvious gap between formulating a project and carrying it out. The one who knows what to do does not have to do it herself, and the ones who follow her instructions do not have to know what they are doing.

---

[49] HC, 229.
[50] Leo Strauss held this view: "Political life derives its dignity from something which transcends political life." Leo Strauss, *The Rebirth of Classical Political Rationalism* (Chicago: University of Chicago Press, 1989), 161.
[51] HC, 228.   [52] HC, 228–229.

Plato was the first to introduce the division between those who know and do not act and those who act and do not know, instead of the old articulation of action into beginning and achieving, so that knowing what to do and doing it became two altogether different performances.[53]

The separation of knowing and doing makes plausible a hierarchy between ruler and ruled. Once insight into political matters is understood as analogous to technical expertise, it follows that experts should direct the actions of the others. The dissociation of knowing and doing thus undermines the principle of political equality. The equality of citizens is replaced by a hierarchy in which those who are capable of philosophical insight are naturally fit to rule, and those who are incapable of rational discourse are naturally fit to be ruled.

Arendt concluded that Plato's political philosophy was essentially anti-political. Plato's aim was not to introduce essential questions into political discourse, as Socrates had done, but to replace political discourse with philosophical knowledge. Plato thought of politics in terms of experiences proper to nonpolitical spheres of life. The effect of his thought was to efface the original understanding of politics, and the result of this effacement was that politics was reduced to a matter of rule, so that the basic question of political philosophy became "Who rules whom?" This question is central to the *Republic*: "τὸ δὴ μετὰ τοῦτο τί ἂν ἡμῖν διαιρετέον εἴη; ἆρ'οὐκ αὐτῶν τούτων οἵτινες ἄρξοθσί τε καὶ ἄρξονται; What would it be that we must determine? Isn't it who among these men will rule and who will be ruled?"[54] This tradition of political philosophy still persists today, most clearly in the work of Leo Strauss:

> All political conflicts that arise within the community are at least related to, if they do not proceed from, the most fundamental political controversy: the controversy as to what type of man should rule the community.[55]

Arendt suggests that this question is not a fundamental problem of political life, that it does not belong to a "permanent" and "natural horizon of human thought," but that it belongs to a specific tradition of political philosophy, and that this tradition has misunderstood the nature of politics from the ground up.

---

[53] HC, 223.   [54] Plato, *The Republic*, 412b.   [55] Strauss, *Classical Political Rationalism*, 54.

130　　　　　　　Classical Political Philosophy

Aristotle

Arendt's relation to Aristotle was complex. In her view, Aristotle's political philosophy is internally divided: he was guided in part by the nontheoretical understanding of politics implicit in the language of Athens; but he was misguided by the metaphysical concepts with which he tried to grasp political phenomena. There is a tension in Aristotle's work between an authentic understanding of politics, and the metaphysical framework in which he worked out his practical philosophy. This tension is the source of blind spots, incongruities, and contradictions in his thought.[56] Arendt's work on Aristotle is thus guided by a few key questions: What are the terms in which Aristotle conceives the nature of politics? What was the original provenance of these terms? How do his concepts illuminate or obscure the nature of political action? How well do they capture the essence of politics?

Aristotle divided knowledge into three branches: productive, practical, and theoretical. Productive knowledge deals with making; practical knowledge deals with ethics and politics; theoretical knowledge deals with math, physics, and metaphysics. In his metaphysics Aristotle laid out his understanding of essence, and tried to define in precise and definite terms what we are asking for when we ask of something what it is. Metaphysics in this sense has a certain priority over the other sciences, since our approach to beings is always guided in advance by a prior understanding of what they are, and any attempt to grasp what beings are is always guided in advance by a prior interpretation of the meaning of essence. To study democracies, for example, we have to have some prior understanding of what democracy is; and any attempt to say what democracy is will be guided by a prior understanding of this essential "what-it-is." Questions of political philosophy are in this way implicated in questions of metaphysics. What then are the basic concepts of Aristotle's metaphysics?

Metaphysics for Aristotle is the science that contemplates Being as Being (ἐπιστήμη τις ἣ θεωρεῖ τὸ ὂν ἦ ὄν).[57] In his view, every being is essentially a substance (οὐσία) with essential and accidental properties (συμβεβηκός).[58] The word "substance" has four meanings: (a) the essence of a thing, "the what it is" (τὸ τί ἦν εἶναι); (b) the universal, what belongs to all such things

---

[56] BPF, 118.

[57] Aristotle, *Metaphysics*, trans. Hugh Tredennick (Cambridge, MA: Harvard University Press, 1989), 147 (1003a).

[58] Aristotle, *Metaphysics*, 313 (1028b4).

Aristotle 131

(τὸ καθόλου); (c) the genus to which such things belong (τὸ γένος); and (d) the underlying ground that precedes the appearance and survives the destruction of actual beings (τὸ ὑποκείμενον).[59] These four meanings converge not on the *idea* (εἶδος) of things, but on their principles and causes (ἡ οὐσία ἀρχὴ καὶ αἰτία τις ἐστίν).[60] The word "principle" or *arche* (ἀρχή) comes from the verb *archein* (ἄρχειν), which means "to begin," "to lead," and "to rule." Aristotle combined these meanings in his concept of *arche*: the *arche* of something is both the origin from which it begins and the underlying ground that governs the way it is. The *arche* of philosophy is wonder, for example, since wonder is both the origin of questioning and the underlying pathos that grounds and guides philosophical thought. The word "cause" (αἰτία) means what is responsible for something being the way it is; for Aristotle every being has four causes: its form (τὸ εἶδος καὶ παράδειγμα); its matter (ἡ ὕλη); its source of motion (ὅθεν ἡ ἀρχὴ τῆς μεταβολῆς); and its end or *telos* (τὸ τέλος).[61] The telos of a being is that for whose sake it exists, the work or *ergon* (ἔργον) towards which it moves or is moved. When things reach their *telos* – when they achieve their end (ὅις ὑπάρχει τὸ τέλος) – they are perfect or *teleion* (τέλειον).[62] As long as something has not reached its *telos* it exists in the mode of potentiality or *dunamis* (δύναμις); when it reaches its end and performs its proper work or activity, it exists in the mode of working, actuality or *energeia* (ἐνέργεια).[63]

Aristotle often used two kinds of examples to explain these basic concepts.

The first example is building a house.[64] To truly know what a house is we must know not only its form but also its matter, its source of motion,

---

[59] Aristotle, *Metaphysics*, 315–317 (1028b33–6).   [60] Aristotle, *Metaphysics*, 395 (1041a10).

[61] Aristotle, *Metaphysics*, 211 (1013a24–1013b).   [62] Aristotle, *Metaphysics*, 267 (1021b23).

[63] Aristotle explicitly derived his concept of actuality (ἐνέργεια) from work or activity (ἔργον): "The term 'actuality'(ἐνέργεια), with its implications of 'complete reality,' has been extended from motions, to which it properly belongs, to other things" (Aristotle, *Metaphysics*, 439 (1047a30)). "For the activity (*ergon*) is the end (*telos*), and the actuality (*energeia*) is the activity (*ergon*). Hence the term 'actuality' is derived from 'activity' and tends to mean 'perfection'" (τὸ γὰρ ἔργον τέλος, ἡ δὲ ἐνέργεια τὸ ἔργον. διὸ καὶ τοὔνομα ἐνέργεια λέγεται κατὰ τὸ ἔργον, καὶ συντείνει πρὸς τὴν ἐντελέχειαν.) (Aristotle, *Metaphysics*, 459) (1050a23).

[64] Aristotle often used examples of houses and architecture to illustrate his basic metaphysical concepts:

    (a) The concept of principle (ἀρχή) (Aristotle, *Metaphysics*, 209) (1013a5 and 1013a14).

    (b) The concept of cause (αἰτία) (Aristotle, *Metaphysics*, 215 and 217) (1014a9 and 1014a25).

    (c) The concept of potentiality (δύναμις) (Aristotle, *Metaphysics*, 251) (1019a16).

    (d) The concept of coming from something (τὸ ἔκ τινος εἶναι) (Aristotle, *Metaphysics*, 277) (1023a34).

    (e) The concept of accident (κατὰ συμβεβηκὸς) (Aristotle, *Metaphysics*, 299) (1026b8).

    (f) The concept of form (εἶδος) (Aristotle, *Metaphysics*, 339) (1032b14).

    (g) The relation of matter to form (ὕλη and εἶδος) (Aristotle, *Metaphysics*, 347) (1033b21).

132   Classical Political Philosophy

its end, and its principle. The principle of a house is the human need for dwelling; its matter is the stuff from which it is made; its source of motion is the architects and the builders; and its *telos* is the house's work or function. When the house is being designed and constructed it is merely potential, in the sense that it is moving towards its final form. It becomes actual when it reaches its final form and fulfills its function. A perfect (*teleion*) house is one that fully achieves its end (*telos*).

Aristotle also explained these concepts using the example of living beings. What is essential to an acorn, for example, is not its properties but its underlying causes: the matter of which it is made; the form of the mature tree it contains; the source of its growth; and the end towards which it grows. The oak exists potentially in the acorn, and it exists actually when the movement of growth has reached its end.

Where do these concepts come from? To what region of beings did they originally belong? In light of what experience does Aristotle understand all beings in these terms?

Arendt argued that Aristotle's examples point to the provenance of his concepts. The examples of living things suggest that Aristotle worked out his metaphysics by generalizing concepts that originally belonged to the sphere of animal and plant life. In *The Life of the Mind*, she claimed the concepts of actuality and potentiality were derived from the experience of living things and then transposed into the sphere of production:

> The human product, this "compound of matter and form" – for instance, a house made of wood according to a form preexisting in the craftsman's mind (*nous*) – clearly was not made out of nothing, and so was understood by Aristotle to preexist "potentially" before it was actualized by human hands. This notion was derived from the mode of being peculiar to living things, where everything that appears grows out of something that contains the finished product potentially, as the oak exists potentially in the acorn and the animal in the semen.[65]

It would seem Aristotle derived his categories from the experience of living things.

But this derivation is incomplete. In *The Human Condition*, Arendt argued that the word "form" or *eidos* originally belonged to the sphere of making, and this implies that Aristotle conceived of living beings

---

(h) The difference of natural and artificial generation (γίγνεται) (Aristotle, *Metaphysics*, 349) (1034a12).
(i) The concept of substance (οὐσία) (Aristotle, *Metaphysics*, 385) (1039b26).
(j) The concept of essence (τὸ τι ἦν εἶναι) (Aristotle, *Metaphysics*, 397) (1041a27 and 1041b7).

[65] LMW, 15.

Aristotle

themselves in terms that are ultimately derived from the experience of production.[66] The development of living beings is understood in terms of the making of products. This analogy is explicit in the *Metaphysics*: "It is the same with natural formations as it is with the products of art. For the seed produces [ποιεῖ] just as those things that come from art [τὰ ἀπο τέχνης]. It contains the form potentially [ἔχει γὰρ δυνάμει τὸ εἶδος]."[67] Both natural and artificial things are products; the difference between the natural and the artificial is simply that what is natural has its *eidos* and its source of motion within itself, while the *eidos* and source of motion of artificial things lie outside themselves in the one who makes them.

The basic terms of Aristotle's metaphysics ultimately come from the experience of making, Arendt argued. His concepts are derived from terms most appropriate to one sphere of beings – products. Although Aristotle carefully distinguishes between nature and art, his basic concepts lead him to conceive all beings on the model of products.

How did Aristotle use these metaphysical concepts in his practical philosophy?

The concepts of the *Metaphysics* provide the framework of Aristotle's ethics, since he understood human existence in the same terms with which he understood everything else. To grasp what it is to be human is to grasp the substance of "man" – his form, his matter, his source of motion, and above all his *telos*.[68] The *telos* of human life is happiness, and the highest happiness depends on the highest work of human beings.[69] Since Aristotle articulated his metaphysical concepts in terms derived from the sphere of making, the basic terms of his metaphysics led him to think of "man" on the model of the artist and craftsman. This model is explicit in the *Nicomachean Ethics*:

> Perhaps we shall find the best good if we first find the work of man [τὸ ἔργον τοῦ ἀνθρώπου]. For just as the good, i.e. doing well, for a flautist, a sculptor, and every craftsman, and in general, for everything that has a work and action, seems to depend on its work, the same seems to be true of man, if there is a work proper to him. So then do the carpenter and leatherworker have their proper work and action, while man has none and is by nature without any work [ἀργον]?[70]

---

[66] HC, 142.   [67] Aristotle, *Metaphysics*, 351 (1034a34).

[68] I translate ἀνθρώπος as "man" to capture the masculine singular form of the word in Aristotle's Greek.

[69] Aristotle, *Nicomachean Ethics*, trans. H. Rackham (Cambridge, MA: Harvard University Press, 1994), 31 (1097b20–1). See *Nicomachean Ethics*, 607 and 613 (1176a31–32 and 1177a12–21).

[70] Aristotle, *Nicomachean Ethics*, 31 (1097b25).

134   Classical Political Philosophy

The work of man turns out to be a way of life (ζωήν τινα) in which, through the practice of the virtues, he actualizes his nature as man.[71] Man becomes what he is by doing the work proper to man.

The concepts of the *Metaphysics* also provided the framework for Aristotle's political thought. In the *Politics*, Aristotle conceived the polis in the same metaphysical terms. The material of the polis is its population and its territory.[72] The form of the polis is its constitution. Its sources of motion are the statesman and the natural impulse of human beings to live together.[73] And the *telos* of the polis is living well, the happiness of its citizens.[74] In other words, the *telos* of the polis is to allow men to reach their *telos*, to become what they are, to live the best life, to achieve the highest happiness.

Aristotle's most basic ethical and political question is the question of human nature: What is man? What is his *telos*? What is his proper work? What is the best life?

Aristotle answered these questions in the *Nicomachean Ethics*. In his view, the highest work of man is philosophical contemplation, since contemplation provides the highest happiness available to man. So the best life is the life devoted to philosophy. Ethics and politics have their *raison d'être* in something that transcends the ethical and political sphere. The political life ultimately aims at something beyond politics – the contemplative life of the philosopher.[75]

How did Aristotle's metaphysical thought guide or misguide his view of politics?

Arendt objected not just to Aristotle's answer to the question of human nature, but to the terms in which the question was framed: What are the *eidos* and *telos* of man? In her view, these concepts fail to grasp what is distinctive to human beings. She did not say Aristotle misunderstood human nature, or that man has no distinctive way of being. Her argument was that Aristotle's concept of essence cannot fully grasp what is proper to human beings. While his concepts may allow us to grasp the essence of nonhuman beings, they can only distort our understanding of ourselves when they are applied to human existence.

---

[71] Aristotle, *Nicomachean Ethics*, 33 (1098a-13-19).
[72] Aristotle, *Politics*, trans. H. Rackham (Cambridge, MA: Harvard University Press, 1998), 553 (1326a1–5).
[73] Aristotle, *Politics*, 9 (1253a).   [74] Aristotle, *Politics*, 218 and 571 (1280b39–40 and 1328a).
[75] Aristotle, *Nicomachean Ethics*, 615 and 623 (1177b1–4 and 1178a22–26).

Aristotle 135

It is highly unlikely that we, who can know, determine, and define the natural essences of all things surrounding us, which we are not, should ever be able to do the same for ourselves ... Nothing entitles us to assume that man has a nature or essence *in the same sense* as other things ... The perplexity is that the modes of human cognition applicable to things with "natural" qualities, including ourselves to the limited extent that we are specimens of the most highly developed species of organic life, fail us when we raise the question: And who are we?[76]

Arendt did not deny there are universal and necessary structures of human existence. She only doubted we have an essence "in the same sense as other things." We cannot assume that humans can be understood with concepts proper to nonhuman beings. Nor can we assume that humans have a specific work and *telos* in the same sense that other things do. Aristotle's teleological view of man does *to some extent* illuminate the basic structures of human existence, but it distorts our existence by interpreting it in terms of concepts derived from other kinds of beings. It is not that Aristotle has the wrong answer to the question of human nature, but that the question itself implies a misconception of human being. To ask about the natural ends of human life, Arendt thought, is "to speak about a 'who' as though it were a 'what.'"[77]

Aristotle's teleology thus led him to misconceive the nature of political action, Arendt argued. In the *Nicomachean Ethics*, Aristotle drew a clear distinction between action and production, doing and making, *praxis* and *poiesis*. *Poiesis* is any activity that is not done for its own sake, but that has its end beyond itself in the product to be made. *Praxis* is any activity that has its end in itself in the sense that it is done for its own sake.[78] *Poiesis* is a means to an end, whereas *praxis* is beyond the means/end schema in the sense that acting well (εὐπραχία) is its own end. For most of the *Nicomachean Ethics* it seems that the work of man is to excel in politics and ethics, since excellence in the political and ethical spheres is an end in itself.[79] But at the end of the book it turns out that the happiness of the

---

[76] HC, 10–11 (italics added).

[77] HC, 10. Giorgio Agamben followed Arendt in arguing that we cannot understand the political in terms of Aristotle's metaphysics. Agamben actually defined the political in terms of our lack of any proper work or *telos*: "Politics is that which corresponds to the essential inoperability of humankind, to the radical being-without-work of human communities. There is politics because human beings are *argos* – beings who cannot be defined by any proper operation – that is, beings of pure potentiality that no identity or vocation can possibly exhaust." Giorgio Agamben, *Means without End: Notes on Politics* (Minneapolis: Minnesota University Press, 2000), 140.

[78] Aristotle, *Nicomachean Ethics*, 337 (1140b4).

[79] HC, 206. See Aristotle, *Nicomachean Ethics*, 609 (1176b6–9).

136 Classical Political Philosophy

political life is only a second-rate happiness, and that the highest happiness is achievable only in the philosophical life. The *telos* of man can only be reached outside the ethical and political sphere. Philosophical contemplation is the only activity loved wholly for its own sake, whereas all *praxis* aims at something beyond the action itself.[80] So political action can no longer be understood as having its end in itself; it has to be understood as ultimately a means to a higher end.

Aristotle's metaphysical concepts led him to think of political action on the model of production, and to think of the polis as a kind of product: politicians are like manual workmen (χειροτέχναι) who do the labor of forming the polis;[81] while the philosopher is like the architect (ἀρχιτέκτων) who understands the essence of the city and who is therefore fit to design its form.[82] This technical analogy is explicit in the *Politics*:

> Just as a weaver or a shipbuilder or any other craftsman must have the material proper to their craft ... so too the statesman or legislator must have the materials proper to him.[83]

Just as, for the architect, the form of a house follows from its work, which is to shelter and sustain the way of life proper to its inhabitants, so too, for the political theorist, the form of best city will follow from its work, which is to make possible for its citizens the best way of life – the life of contemplation.[84]

Aristotle's metaphysics reinforced the confusion of *praxis* and *poiesis* already implicit in Plato, Arendt thought, and this confusion led him to accept some of the assumptions underlying Plato's philosophy of politics. Like Plato, Aristotle saw politics as a means to an end. Like Plato, he separated knowing and doing. And this separation of knowing and doing led him, like Plato, to think of politics as a matter of rule.

But the attempt to understand politics in terms of his metaphysics had several other consequences for his political philosophy, according to Arendt.

1. Aristotle reduced deliberation to instrumental thinking. Arendt noted that for Aristotle, "we deliberate only about means to an end that we take

---

[80] Aristotle, *Nicomachean Ethics*, 615–617 (1177b1–18).
[81] Aristotle, *Nicomachean Ethics*, 347 (1141b27).
[82] Aristotle, *Nicomachean Ethics*, 429 (1152b1–4).
[83] Aristotle, *Politics*, 553 (1325b41–1326a6). (I have modified the translation.)
[84] LMW, 62. This analogy – between the statesman and the architect – was central to the work of Leo Strauss: "The legislative skill is, therefore, the most 'architectonic' political skill that is known to political life." (Strauss, *Classical Political Rationalism*, 53.)

Aristotle

for granted, that we cannot choose ... ends are inherent in human nature and the same for all."[85] The ends of political life should not be endlessly debated but determined once and for all by philosophical knowledge; political deliberation should only concern the best way to achieve ends given in advance by philosophy.

2. Aristotle dissociated political action from happiness, and located the highest happiness outside the sphere of politics: "From practical pursuits we look to secure some advantage, greater or smaller, beyond the action itself ... The activity of the politician is unleisured, and aims at securing something beyond the mere participation in politics – positions of authority and honor, or, if the happiness of the politician himself and of his fellow-citizens, this happiness is conceived as something distinct from political activity."[86] Even when philosophers discarded Aristotle's teleology, Arendt argued, they generally retained the assumption that we engage in politics only to secure happiness outside political life.

3. Aristotle's metaphysics obscured the specific temporality of human existence. Arendt argued that the concepts of actuality and potentiality were drawn from the sphere of organic growth rather than from the experience of action. "When Aristotle holds that 'coming-into-being necessarily implies the pre-existence of something which is potentially but not actually,' he is applying the cyclical movement in which everything that is alive swings ... to the realm of human affairs."[87] But the concepts of actuality and potentiality fail to grasp the radical openness of free action. What exists "potentially" always moves towards an end given in advance, so that the future it aims at is in some sense already present, according to Arendt: "The view that everything real must be preceded by a potentiality as one of its causes implicitly denies the future as an authentic tense: the future is nothing but a consequence of the past."[88] Aristotle's metaphysics effaces the possibility of radical novelty – of actions or events that bring about something unprecedented, something that was not foreseen or even imagined.[89]

4. Aristotle's philosophy devalues the whole realm of action, since his understanding of essence consigns all action to the realm of the inessential. For Aristotle, what is essential is what is necessarily the way it is – the unchanging and underlying ground (ὑποκείμενον). Whatever could be

---

[85] See Aristotle, *Eudemian Ethics*, trans. H. Rackham (Cambridge, MA: Harvard University Press, 1971), 1226b10, and *Nicomachean Ethics*, 1112b12.

[86] Aristotle, *Nicomachean Ethics*, 615 (1177b3–15).   [87] LMW, 16.   [88] LMW, 15.

[89] Agamben extended Arendt's critique of Aristotle's concept of potentiality. See Giorgio Agamben, *Homo Sacer: Sovereign Power and Bare Life* (Stanford: Stanford University Press, 1998), 39–48.

138   Classical Political Philosophy

otherwise is not essential but accidental or contingent (συμβηβεκός). Arendt noted that since any free action is something that could be other than it is, the whole sphere of action is not essential.

> In the framework of these categories, everything that happens in the realm of human affairs is accidental or contingent ("πρακτὸν δ'ἐστὶ τὸ ἐνδεξόμε-νον καὶ ἄλλος ἔχειν" "what is brought into being by action is that which could also be otherwise"): Aristotle's very words already indicate the realm's low ontological status.[90]

This is why poetry is more serious than history for Aristotle: poetry deals with the universal (τὰ καθόλου) – what is likely or necessary (τὸ εἰκὸς ἢ τὸ ἀναγκαῖον) – while history deals only with particulars (τὰ καθ'ἕκαστον).[91]

5. This devaluation of the sphere of action entails a demotion of political thought. Since deliberation and judgment deal with what is contingent and therefore inessential, they occupy the lowest rung in the hierarchy of different kinds of thought, Arendt argued: "Thus Aristotle, in a discussion of the different kinds of cognition in his *Metaphysics*, places *dianoia* and *episteme praktike*, practical insight and political science, at the lowest rank of his order, and puts above them the sciences of fabrication, *episteme poietike*, which immediately precedes and leads to *theoria*, the contemplation of truth."[92]

In short, Aristotle's political philosophy distorts and debases political life, according to Arendt. The decisive point is not that Aristotle valued the contemplative life above the active life; nor that he tried to understand politics in teleological terms. What is decisive for Arendt is the task that Aristotle set for political philosophy: to derive the goals and standards of political life from a knowledge of human nature. This task outlasted Aristotle's teleological approach to politics and his evaluation of the contemplative life. Any attempt to derive the aims and standards of political life from a knowledge of human nature is ultimately an attempt to replace politics with philosophy. It assumes that the question of how to live together is not a matter of opinion but of knowledge; it is not to be addressed through the endless deliberation of politics, but to be answered

---

[90] Arendt quotes from *De Anima*, 433a30. LMW, 15.
[91] Aristotle, *Poetics*, trans. Stephen Halliwell (Cambridge, MA: Harvard University Press, 1995), 59 (1451b5–8).
[92] HC, 301.

Later Political Theory

through philosophical argument. Aristotle's political philosophy is ultimately an attempt to replace politics with philosophy.[93]

Later Political Theory

Classical political theory is silent on matters that now seem essential to politics, according to Arendt. While the first philosophers spoke of freedom, for example, they never really asked what it is: "There is no preoccupation with freedom in the whole history of great philosophy from the pre-Socratics up to Plotinus."[94] Nor did they ask about the nature of authority: "Neither the Greek language nor the varied political experiences of Greek history shows any knowledge of authority and the kind of rule it implies."[95] Nor did they look for a transcendent source to sanction human law: "Neither the Greek *nomos* nor the Roman *lex* was of divine origin, [and] neither the Greek nor the Roman concept of legislation needed divine inspiration."[96] Why were these questions ignored by the first philosophers? How were they introduced into political theory?

The answer for Arendt lies in the distance between ancient philosophy and politics. The citizens who led a political life didn't need a theory of politics, and so never fully articulated their understanding in theoretical terms. The philosophers, who had withdrawn from politics, tried to grasp the nature of the polis in theory, not by working out concepts on the basis of their own political experience, but by drawing on terms and models from other spheres of life. Classical political philosophy thus obscured the nature of politics in two ways: it transposed into political theory models and concepts foreign to politics, which could grasp political realities in only a crude and misleading way; and it ignored political phenomena that resisted its concepts and that were foreign to its concerns.

In her approach to ancient political philosophy, Arendt set herself three tasks: to explicate the nontheoretical understanding of political phenomena neglected by philosophers; to show how this understanding was distorted by later concepts; and to trace these concepts back to the original experiences from which they emerged.

---

[93] Here I am indebted to Dana Villa's discussion of Arendt and Aristotle in *Arendt and Heidegger: The Fate of the Political* (Princeton: Princeton University Press, 1996).

[94] BPF, 145. In *The Life of the Mind* she cites a number of scholars who agree on this point: Thomas Hobbes; Etienne Gilson; and Henry Herbert Williams. Williams, for example, writes that it cannot be "seriously maintained that the problem of freedom ever became a subject of debate in the philosophy of Socrates, Plato, and Aristotle" (LMW, 16).

[95] BPF, 104. [96] OR, 186.

140 Classical Political Philosophy

Freedom

Arendt's approach to the question of freedom was guided by a few assumptions: that we already have a nontheoretical understanding of freedom rooted in lived experience; that we primarily experience freedom in action; that the point of politics is to make free action possible; and that "the *raison d'être* of politics is freedom." If traditional concepts of freedom are grounded in nonpolitical experiences, these concepts can only distort our understanding of political freedom.

These assumptions underlie three arguments.

First, Arendt argued we cannot understand freedom in the prevailing terms of modern political theory. Modern theory has been dominated by two concepts of freedom, which Isaiah Berlin has called "positive" and "negative" freedom. Positive freedom is the right to take part in democratic self-government, "to participate in the process by which my life is to be controlled."[97] Negative freedom is the right to be free from control, to have an inviolable space of private life "within which a man can act unobstructed by others."[98] While these two concepts are often opposed, modern philosophers conceive both kinds of freedom in terms of sovereignty and will. Positive freedom is understood in terms of the sovereignty of the people and the popular will. Negative freedom is understood in terms of the sovereignty of the individual and personal autonomy. Arendt argued the concepts of sovereignty and will are not derived from the experience of politics, and that to think of political freedom in terms of sovereignty and will is to think of politics in nonpolitical terms. She began her reflections on freedom by suspending trust in modern concepts of freedom.

Second, she argued that we cannot understand freedom by returning to classical political philosophy: "It does not follow that we need only revert to older, pre-modern traditions and theories. Indeed, the greatest difficulty in reaching an understanding of what freedom is arises from the fact that a simple return to tradition, and especially to what we are wont to call the great tradition, does not help us."[99] The limits of ancient political philosophy are ultimately based on the withdrawal of philosophers from politics and the traditional opposition between the active and the contemplative life.

---

[97] Isaiah Berlin, *Four Essays on Liberty* (Oxford: Oxford University Press, 1969), 131.
[98] Berlin, *Four Essays on Liberty*, 122.   [99] BPF, 156–157.

Later Political Theory

Our philosophical tradition of political thought, beginning with Parmenides and Plato, was founded explicitly in opposition to this polis and its citizenship. The way of life chosen by the philosopher was understood in opposition to the *bios politikos*, the political way of life. Freedom, therefore, the very center of politics as the Greeks understood it, was an idea which almost by definition could not enter the framework of Greek philosophy.[100]

For Arendt, human freedom first appears in the experience of action rather than thought. But since philosophers valued the life of thought over the life of action, they were not concerned with freedom as it actually appeared in the political realm. Since they were intensely concerned with the virtue of self-control, they abstracted the word "freedom" from the worldly sphere and interpreted it in light of the inner experience of self-mastery. This abstraction has obscured and distorted the essence of freedom.

> It is the contention of the following considerations that the reason for this obscurity is that the phenomenon of freedom does not appear in the realm of thought at all, that neither freedom nor its opposite is experienced in the dialogue between me and myself in the course of which the great philosophic and metaphysical questions arise, and that the philosophical tradition ... had distorted, instead of clarifying, the very idea of freedom such as it is given in human experience by transposing it from its original field, the realm of politics and human affairs in general, to an inward domain, the will, where it would be open to self-inspection.[101]

By transposing the question of freedom from a worldly to an inner realm, philosophers detached the word from the original experiences from which it was born.

Third, Arendt argued that while the Greeks never worked out an explicit concept of freedom, in their political life they understood freedom in an exceptionally clear way. To grasp the essence of freedom it helps to go back and retrieve the original understanding of freedom that is implicit in the non-philosophical writings of the Greeks.

> Let us therefore go back once more to antiquity, i.e., to its political and *pre-philosophical* traditions, certainly not for the sake of erudition and not even because of the continuity of our tradition, but merely because a freedom experienced in the process of acting and nothing else – though, of course, mankind never lost this experience altogether – has never again been articulated with the same classical clarity.[102]

---

[100] BPF, 157–158.   [101] BPF, 145.   [102] BPF, 165 (italics added).

142 Classical Political Philosophy

This does not mean that to grasp what freedom is we only have to explicate the Greek understanding of freedom; it means that in our own attempts to think through the nature of freedom it would help to be guided initially by the testimony of the Greeks.

How then did the Greeks originally understand freedom?

The Greeks assumed we are not free if we are subject to the will of another, Arendt noted, and they delimited a private sphere within which each citizen was supposed to be sovereign. A male citizen was sovereign within his household in the sense that he had absolute power in his own domain. And a male citizen had sovereignty over his body in the sense that it was legally inviolable. In Athens after Solon, citizens could not be enslaved for debt or tortured in a court of law, and it was a crime to manhandle or even touch a citizen without his consent.[103] For the Greeks it was essential for a polis to ensure that each citizen was sovereign in the private sphere.

The Greeks also assumed we are not free if we are subject to the necessities of life. Arendt noted that, for Aristotle, freedom required liberation from the activities and relationships necessary for survival and prosperity: "This prerequisite of freedom ruled out all ways of life chiefly devoted to keeping one's self alive – not only labor, which was the way of life of the slave, but also the working life of the free craftsman and the acquisitive life of the merchant. In short, it excluded everybody who involuntarily or voluntarily, for his whole life or temporarily, had lost the free disposition of his movements and activities."[104] It was generally assumed that to master the necessities of life one had to master others, to rule over family and slaves as the head of a household. Liberation from necessity required sovereign rule in domestic life, it was thought, so the freedom of citizens in the polis required the domination of slaves in the household.

But the sovereignty of a master is not the political freedom of a citizen. Arendt pointed out that in the *Politics* Aristotle took for granted the difference between freedom and sovereignty: "the life of a free man is better than the life like that of a master of slaves."[105] The distinction between freedom and sovereignty applies not only to the difference between the citizen of the polis and the master of the house, but also to the difference between the citizen of the polis and the ruler of a kingdom.

---

[103] Arendt noted that at his execution Socrates was expected to drink hemlock by himself, since to force him to drink it would have violated his status as a citizen (OR, 12).

[104] HC, 12.   [105] Aristotle, *Politics*, 549 (1325a24).

Later Political Theory

On this point Arendt referred to the story of Otanes, the Persian who refused the chance to be king, who said he was "willing neither to rule nor to be ruled," and who was the only free man in the Persian Empire, according to Herodotus.[106] She concluded that, for the Greeks, sovereignty and freedom were not just different but incompatible: "To be free meant both not to be subject to the necessity of life or to the command of another and not to be in command oneself. It meant neither to rule nor to be ruled."[107] The sovereign ruler is not yet free as long as he remains in a realm dominated by the concern for survival and prosperity, whether that realm is a household or an empire.

Finally, freedom required overcoming the love of life and the fear of death. This is explicit in Seneca's maxim that "life is slavery without the virtue that knows how to die."[108] For Arendt this elevation of freedom over life was essential to the Greek elevation of the city over the household, citizenship over rulership, the polis over the *oikos*, politics over economics, the world over bare life: "To leave the household, originally in order to embark upon some adventure and glorious enterprise and later simply to devote one's life to the affairs of the city, demanded courage because only in the household was one primarily concerned with one's own life and survival. Whoever entered the political realm had first to be ready to risk his life, and too great love for life obstructed freedom, was a sure sign of slavishness."[109]

In short, freedom required liberation – not just from the necessities of life, but from the realm dominated by the care for life; not just from the rule of masters and tyrants, but from the realm of rulership itself.

But liberation is not yet freedom. There were clear differences in ancient Greece between the liberty of an emancipated slave and the freedom of an enfranchised citizen. So the Greeks, Arendt argued, took for granted a set of "truisms" that modern political theory has neglected: "that liberation and freedom are not the same; that liberation may be the condition of freedom but by no means leads automatically to it; that the notion of liberty implied in liberation can only be negative, and hence, that even the intention of liberating is not identical with the desire for freedom."[110]

Freedom was first of all a political matter, according to Arendt. A polis was free if its citizens had a certain equal status and equal rights: equality under the law (*isonomia*); the right to speak openly in public (*parrhesia*); and the right to address the assembly (*isegoria*). These rights were not

---

[106] Herodotus, *The History*, trans. David Grene (Chicago: University of Chicago Press, 1987), 250.
[107] HC, 32. [108] HC, 36. [109] HC, 36. [110] OR, 29.

Classical Political Philosophy

meant to circumscribe a private realm in which citizens were not subject to the power of the government; they were meant to ensure that all citizens had an equal share of power. To be free was to be able to participate in governing the city. This understanding of freedom was implicit in Greek literature. Its clearest expression is perhaps in *The Suppliant Women* by Euripides, where a foreigner asks who is king in Athens, and Theseus explains that there is no king:

> [Athens] is not ruled by one man, but is a free city. Here the people rule, and power is held yearly by turns. They do not give the most to the rich; the poor also have an equal share ... Freedom is this: "Who has good counsel to offer the polis?" He who does so wins fame; he who does not is silent. Where could greater equality be found?[111]

Freedom here is a matter not of private liberty but of public power. It is tied to equality among citizens and the right to engage in the deliberations of the assembly.[112] True freedom appears in the experience of action.

Arendt thought this understanding of freedom was obscured when philosophers transposed the question of freedom from the political realm to the psychic realm, where freedom is not a matter of action but of choice and will. This transposition is especially clear in the philosophy of the Stoics. Arendt focused on the Stoic philosopher Epictetus, who was not a citizen but a former slave, and who, understandably, was not concerned with politics but deeply concerned with questions of sovereignty and liberty. According to Epictetus, we are wrong to think that a good and happy life depends on our worldly situation. Worldly things are simply external impressions; what matters is not things themselves but our judgments about them. Our judgments are usually dominated by our passions; our desires make things seem desirable, and our fears make them seem fearful. But if we abandon our worldly cares and master our passions, we find that our power to judge and to choose is absolutely sovereign. If we give up trying to control what is beyond our control (the world), and focus only on controlling what can be controlled (the self), then nothing can make us unhappy and no one can force us to do what is wrong.

---

[111] This citation is of two passages: lines 405–408 and 437–441. The translation is partly my own, partly that of David Kovacs (ed. and trans.), Euripides, *Suppliant Women; Electra; Heracles* (Cambridge, MA: Harvard University Press, 1998), and partly that of David Grene and Richmond Lattimore in *Euripides: The Complete Greek Tragedies*, ed. David Grene and Richmond Lattimore (Chicago: University of Chicago Press, 1958).

[112] This passage is cited both by Finley and Foucault: M. I. Finley, *Politics in the Ancient World* (Cambridge: Cambridge University Press, 1983), 136; Michel Foucault, *Fearless Speech*, ed. Joseph Pearson (Los Angeles: Semiotext(e), 2001), 60–61.

Later Political Theory

Stoic philosophy teaches us how to live an invincibly serene and virtuous life. The task of philosophy is to turn our cares away from the world towards the mastery of the self. The man who has mastered himself liberates himself from all compulsion and achieves an unworldly but absolute liberty. Epictetus declares that in his inner life man is sovereign: "man ... has nothing more sovereign [κυριότερος] than his power to choose [προαίρεσις] ... all else is subject to this, and the power to choose itself is free from slavery and subjection."[113] In the world we may be enslaved by men and subject to fate, but in his inner life the philosopher is invincible: "I must die. I must be imprisoned. I must suffer exile. But must I die groaning? Must I whine as well? Can anyone prevent me from going into exile with a smile? ... Chain me? My leg you will chain–yes, but not my power to choose – no, not even Zeus can conquer that."[114]

Epictetus altered the question of freedom in three ways, according to Arendt. First, he displaced the notion of freedom from the political to the psychic realm; freedom was understood in light of the inner experience of choice rather than the worldly experience of action. Second, Epictetus conceived freedom in terms of the power to choose between alternatives (*liberum arbitrium*) rather than in terms of the power to do. Third, he interpreted this inner experience in terms of the experiences of mastery and slavery, sovereignty and liberation: "Epictetus transposed these worldly relationships into relationships within man's own self."[115] This transposition led Epictetus to conceive of the self in terms of the household. The independence of the psyche was understood in terms of sovereign power, and freedom was understood in terms of liberation from compulsion. So the ideal of freedom changed. The exemplar of freedom was no longer the citizen but the sovereign:

> Because of the philosophic shift from action to will-power, from freedom as a state of being manifest in action to the *liberum arbitrium*, the ideal of freedom ... became sovereignty, the ideal of a free will, independent from others and eventually prevailing against them.[116]

Freedom was conceived as sovereignty of the inner man.

This Stoic concept of freedom was altered by Christian thinkers, according to Arendt, and this alteration was based on the differences between Stoic and Christian views of virtue. As long as virtue consists of mastering our passions and choosing the best course of action, a good life is

---

[113] Epictetus, cited by Arendt, LMW, 78. [114] Epictetus, cited by Arendt, LMW, 79.
[115] BPF, 148. [116] BPF, 163.

Classical Political Philosophy

146

entirely within our power. But if virtue consists in not simply doing but being good – once anger is equated with murder and lust with adultery – then a good life is no longer entirely in our power. Our inner self is not sovereign. I can choose to control my lust, but I cannot choose not to lust. I can force myself to restrain my anger, but I cannot force myself to love my enemies. With Christianity, Arendt argued, "The chief task of the spirit is not just to rule over the appetites and to make the flesh obey but to bring about its mortification – to crucify it 'with its passions and desires' (Galatians 5:24), which in fact is beyond human power."[117] For Arendt it was St. Paul, in his Epistle to the Romans, who first described the weakness of the will and pointed to the gap between what I will and what I can do. Paul wrote:

> I do not understand my own actions. For I do not do what I want, but I do the very thing I hate ... I can will what is right, but I cannot do it. For I do not do the good I want, but the evil I do not want is what I do. Now if I do what I do not want, it is no longer I that do it, but sin that dwells within me [ἡ οἰκοῦσα ἐν ἐμοὶ ἁμαρτία].[118]

Paul transformed the Stoic image of the self as a house ruled by a sovereign. If lust, anger, and pride are sins, then sin dwells within me and dominates my life. I am no longer the master of my house. Sin rules, and I am its slave: "With my mind I am a servant to the law of God, but with my flesh I am a slave to the law of sin."[119] How to be free of sin? We cannot free ourselves, but can only be liberated by the grace of God. And this grace does not depend on human will or exertion, but comes to those who from the heart obey God as their sovereign Lord.

> Thanks be to God that you, having once been slaves of sin, have become obedient from the heart to the form of teaching to which you were entrusted, and that you, having been set free from sin, have become servants of righteousness.[120]

Paul refigured the nature of freedom. Like Epictetus, he understood freedom as liberation from slavery. But freedom was no longer the self-liberation of the inner man from subjection to the external world. Freedom was liberation from the powers of sin that dominate us, and this liberation

---

[117] LMW, 70.
[118] *New Greek–English Interlinear New Testament,* The New Revised Standard Version, ed. J. D. Douglas, trans. Robert K. Brown and Philip W. Comfort (Wheaton, IL: Tyndale House Publishers, 1990), 550. (Romans 7:15–20.)
[119] *New Greek–English Interlinear New Testament,* 550. (Romans 7:25.)
[120] *New Greek–English Interlinear New Testament,* 547. (Romans 6:17–18.)

Later Political Theory   147

comes through divine redemption and through absolute obedience to the will of the Lord. True freedom demands total submission.

In the Epistle to the Romans, Paul transposed this demand for inward obedience into the realm of worldly power. We should faithfully serve rulers who are themselves servants of God.

> Let every person be subject to the governing authorities [ἐξουσίαις], for there is no authority except from God, and those authorities that exist have been instituted by God. Therefore, whoever opposes the authority opposes the ordinance of God, and those who oppose will incur judgment. For the rulers are not fearsome to good conduct but to evil. Do you want not to fear the authority? Then do what is good, and you will receive its praise; for the authority is God's servant for your good.[121]

This transposition altered the concept of freedom by subordinating worldly freedom to spiritual freedom. Freedom of action, speech, and belief could be restricted by the worldly authorities in order to make possible the spiritual liberation of Christian life. It was this Christian liberty that the Puritans sought in America: in the words of the Puritan Jonathan Boucher, "true liberty" was not "a right to do everything that we please," but "a liberty to do every thing that is right, and being restrained from doing any thing that is wrong."[122] This Christian concept of freedom was perfectly compatible with the abolition of what for the Greeks were two essential conditions of freedom: the sovereignty of the citizens in their private life, and their right to engage in politics.

What mattered to Arendt was that both Stoic and Christian thinkers understood freedom in terms of liberation, sovereignty, and will, and that these terms were not based on specifically political experiences but were derived from the experience of slavery, mastery, and willpower.

When modern theorists ask about the nature of freedom, Arendt argued, they tend to understand political freedom in this inherited vocabulary. Proponents of positive freedom understand freedom as the collective sovereignty of the general will. Rousseau, she pointed out, explicitly conceived of "political power in the strict image of individual will-power," and derived his theory of popular sovereignty directly from his concept of the will.[123] Whenever we speak of the "sovereignty" of a nation, or the "will" of a people, we still think of political freedom in these terms. On the

---

[121] *New Greek–English Interlinear New Testament*, 567. (Romans 13:1–4.)

[122] Jonathan Boucher, cited in Eric Foner, *The Story of American Freedom* (New York: W. W. Norton, 1998), 5.

[123] BPF, 163.

148 Classical Political Philosophy

other hand, proponents of negative freedom understand freedom as individual sovereignty and personal autonomy. In the words of John Stuart Mill, "Over himself, over his own body and mind, the individual is sovereign."[124] Yet this negative concept of freedom seems narrow and hollow since it does not entail either the economic independence or the right to self-government that for the Greeks was essential to political freedom.

The interpretation of freedom as sovereignty obscures the essence of freedom, in Arendt's view. But the traditional questions of free will and popular sovereignty seem so basic and self-evident that we can scarcely conceive of a freedom that has nothing to do with sovereignty, will, or liberation.

> Within the conceptual framework of traditional philosophy, it is indeed very difficult to understand how freedom and non-sovereignty can exist together or, to put it another way, how freedom could have been given to men under the condition of non-sovereignty.[125]

To understand what freedom is, she thought, we have to detach the concept of freedom from notions of sovereignty and will.

> Freedom and sovereignty are so little identical that they cannot even exist simultaneously. Where men wish to be sovereign, as individuals or as organized groups, they must submit to the oppression of the will, be this the individual will with which I force myself, or the "general will" of an organized group. If men wish to be free, it is precisely sovereignty they must renounce.[126]

One task of her phenomenology was to bring to light and grasp in concepts an experience of freedom that cannot be understood in terms of willpower or sovereignty. We will follow how she did this in Chapter 6.

Authority

We tend to think of authority as essential to politics. It seems some form of authority is an irreducible part of any political system. Arendt began her reflections on the subject by contesting this basic point.

> Authority as the one, if not the decisive, factor in human communities did not always exist, though it can look back on a long history, and the

---

[124] John Stuart Mill, *On Liberty* (New York: Penguin, 1984), 69.   [125] BPF, 164.
[126] BPF, 164–165.

Later Political Theory 149

experiences on which this concept is based are not necessarily present in all bodies politic.[127]

This sounds strange. What would be a politics without authority?

This question is not just academic. In her view, the history of modern politics is the story of the ever-widening erosion of all traditional authorities: "In the modern world authority has disappeared almost to the vanishing point."[128] If authority is essential to political community, then the loss of authority in the modern world looks like a catastrophe.

Arendt argued that the modern crisis of authority began with the emergence of secular politics. In medieval political theory, the authority of worldly powers was unquestionably grounded in the authority of the Church. It was the separation of politics and religion in the modern age that raised questions about the source of political authority: "Secularization, the emancipation of the secular realm from the tutelage of the Church, inevitably posed the problem of how to found and constitute a new authority."[129] In her view, the task of thinking is not to find or recover a transcendent source of political authority (divine or natural), but to conceive of political authority independent of extra-political or extra-human sources.

Her thinking was guided by a few questions: What is authority? Where did our inherited concepts of authority come from? How was the notion of authority introduced into the political realm? What were the political experiences from which it was born? How has it been displaced and transformed over time? How does it belong or not belong to the sphere of politics?

Arendt thought the concept of authority was foreign to Greek politics: "Neither the Greek language nor the varied political experiences of Greek history shows any knowledge of authority and the kind of rule it implies."[130] She cited the historian Dio Cassius who, in his history of Rome, noted that there was no word for authority in Greek, and that the Latin word *auctoritas* "is altogether impossible to Hellenize."[131]

The lack of authority in Greek politics was tied to the centrality of persuasion. Persuasion was central to Greek thought because politics implies equality. To try to persuade other citizens is to speak to them as equals who have the right to make their own decisions. Authority by contrast implies a hierarchy. To acknowledge others as authorities is to

---

[127] BPF, 104.   [128] BPF, 103–104.   [129] OR, 160.   [130] BPF, 104.

[131] BPF, 289. Arendt quoted Dio Cassius without translating the Greek: ἑλληνίσαι αὐτο καθάπαξ ἀδύνατον ἐστι. The English is my translation.

recognize their superior status, character, or knowledge: "Authority ... is incompatible with persuasion, which presupposes equality and works through a process of argumentation. Where arguments are used, authority is left in abeyance. Against the egalitarian order of persuasion stands the authoritarian order, which is always hierarchical."[132] Since life in the polis was based on the principle that all citizens were equal, and that differences were resolved through debate and persuasion, there was little room in Greek politics for official authorities.

For Arendt, it was Plato who first tried to introduce something like authority into political life.[133] The execution of Socrates showed that neither truth nor justice were safe in a polis governed through persuasion. In his search for an alternative to persuasion, Plato was guided by a number of models drawn from outside the political realm: the relation between a ship's captain and his crew; between a general and his soldiers; between a doctor and his patients; between an architect and his workers. In each of these models there is a free obedience based on neither persuasion nor violence but on the recognition of superior expertise. Plato argued there should be a similar relationship between the philosophers and citizens of a polis. The polis should be ruled by kings who are also philosophers, since philosophers have left the cave of opinion and gone up to the realm of truth – they have seen what a city is, what man is, what justice is, and this knowledge makes them best able to organize and rule the city. The philosopher's authority would come from his expertise in statecraft and statesmanship: "Here the concept of the expert enters the realm of political action for the first time, and the statesman is understood to be competent to deal with human affairs in the same sense as the carpenter is competent to make furniture or the physician to heal the sick."[134] The philosopher's claim to rule is based on his superior wisdom. Just as a doctor should not have to threaten patients to enlist their obedience, so the philosopher-king should not have to force citizens to obey. The compelling force should come not from the power of the ruler but from the self-evident truth of the ideas: "Very early in his search [Plato] must have discovered that truth, namely, the truths we call self-evident, compels the mind, and that this coercion, though it needs not violence to be effective, is stronger than persuasion and argument."[135] The ideal polis is not governed through persuasion but ruled by reason.

Plato interpreted ideas as absolute standards of right, Arendt argued, so that knowledge of the ideas could serve as the source of authority for the

---

[132] BPF, 93.   [133] BPF, 67.   [134] BPF, 111.   [135] BPF, 107.

Later Political Theory 151

laws of the city. He assumed political power is legitimate only if guided and checked by laws based in a transcendent source of authority. Arendt thought this assumption is still with us:

> This aspect of Plato's doctrine of ideas had the greatest influence on the Western tradition ... The essential characteristic of specifically authoritarian forms of government – that the source of their authority, which legitimates the exercise of power, must be beyond the sphere of power and, like the law of nature or the commands of God, must not be man-made – goes back to this applicability of the ideas in Plato's political philosophy.[136]

The interpretation of essence as idea lent a certain plausibility to Plato's analogy between technical experts and political leaders. This analogy let Plato introduce into the political sphere the concept of rule, "the notion that men can lawfully and politically live together only when some are entitled to command and the others forced to obey."[137]

> For our purposes it is essential to remember that the element of rule, as reflected in our present concept of authority so tremendously influenced by Platonic thinking, can be traced to a conflict between philosophy and politics, but not to specifically political experiences, that is, experiences immediately derived from the realm of human affairs.[138]

Plato's attempt to introduce a transcendent source of authority into the polis was based on the assumption that politics is ultimately a matter of rule.

Aristotle also tried to introduce into the polis a kind of authority that would legitimate the division of citizens into rulers and ruled, Arendt argued, and this led him to think of politics in nonpolitical terms.

> There can be no question that Aristotle, like Plato before him, meant to introduce a kind of authority into the handling of public affairs and the life of the polis, and no doubt for very good political reasons. Yet he too had to resort to a kind of makeshift solution in order to make plausible the introduction into the political realm of a distinction between rulers and ruled, between those who command and those who obey. And he too could take his examples and models only from a pre-political sphere, from the private realm of the household and the experiences of a slave economy. This leads him into glaringly contradictory statements, insofar as he superimposes on the actions and life in the polis those standards which, as he explains elsewhere, are valid only for the behavior and life in the household community.[139]

---

[136] BPF, 111. [137] HC, 222. [138] BPF, 113. [139] BPF, 118.

Classical Political Philosophy

While Plato thought of political authority in terms of the hierarchy between expert and layman, Aristotle thought political authority should be based on the natural hierarchy of the young and the old. How should we distinguish between those who should rule and those who should be ruled? Aristotle wrote: "Nature has given the distinction by making those of the same race partly younger and partly older, for whom it is proper that the former are ruled and the latter rule."[140] For Arendt, the hierarchy between young and old belongs to the sphere of education, and this hierarchy is incompatible with the equality essential to political life:

> The relation between old and young is educational in essence . . . Then, as well as now, nothing is more questionable than the political relevance of examples drawn from the field of education. In the political realm we deal always with adults who are past the age of education, properly speaking, and politics or the right to participate in the management of public affairs begins precisely where education has come to an end.[141]

In her view, Aristotle's idea of a gerontocracy based on the natural hierarchy between the old and the young conflicts directly with his own definition of the polis as a community of equals united for the sake of the best life possible.[142]

When Plato and Aristotle tried to introduce a kind of authority into political life, Arendt concluded, they had to rely on nonpolitical models and examples precisely because the experience of authority was foreign to Greek politics.

> The grandiose attempts of Greek philosophy to find a concept of authority which would prevent deterioration of the polis and safeguard the life of the philosopher foundered on the fact that in the realm of Greek political life there was no awareness of authority based on immediate political experience. Hence all prototypes by which subsequent generations understood the content of authority were drawn from specifically unpolitical experiences.[143]

In Greek politics there were magistrates with official powers, but no apolitical source of political authority.

To recover the original sense of authority, Arendt returned to the Romans. In her view, the Roman understanding of authority rested on several basic assumptions: that Rome owed its glory to the founders who had fathered the city; that the founding fathers were owed the deference

---

[140] Aristotle, *Politics*, 603 (1332b35).   [141] BPF, 118–119.
[142] Aristotle, *Politics*, 571 (1328a35).   [143] BPF, 119.

Later Political Theory

153

and obedience of later generations; that their wisdom and deeds were examples of greatness that all citizens were bound to follow; and that the first duty of citizens was to venerate the ancestors and to preserve their patrimony. To found a city was to lay down the sacred principles that would govern a people's way of life: "At the heart of Roman politics ... stands the conviction of the sacredness of the foundation, in the sense that once something has been founded it remains binding for all future generations. To be engaged in politics meant first and foremost to preserve the founding of the city of Rome."[144] The preservation of the ancestors' patrimony was accomplished through tradition, the handing-down (*tradere*) of their words and deeds: "Tradition preserved the past by handing down from one generation to the next the testimony of the ancestors, who had first witnessed and created the sacred founding."[145] The veneration of the ancestors was essential to Roman religion since, Arendt noted, the Romans understood religion as being bound to the beginning: "Here religion literally meant *re-ligare*: to be tied back, obligated, to the enormous, almost superhuman and hence always legendary effort to lay the foundations, to build the cornerstone, to found for eternity. To be religious meant to be tied to the past."[146] Political authority in Rome was understood in terms of these interwoven notions of foundation, tradition, and religion.

Authority was also understood in terms of the etymology of the word *auctoritas*. This meant the specific status proper to an *auctor* – an author or founder. The *auctor* of a building was distinguished from its *artifices*, the men who actually built it: "The author in this case is not the builder but the one who inspired the whole enterprise and whose spirit, therefore, much more than the spirit of the actual builder, is represented in the building itself. In distinction to the *artifex*, who only made it, he is the actual 'author' of the building, namely its founder."[147] In this sense, Aeneas was thought to be the founder rather than the builder of Rome. In *The Aeneid*, the act of foundation consisted not simply in the victory of the Trojans over the Latins, but in the mutual promises exchanged by Aeneas and Latinus. Aeneas promised the Latins "I will not make the Italians underlings to Trojans. For myself I ask no kingdom. Let both nations, both unconquered, both subject to equal laws, commit themselves to an eternal union."[148] *The Aeneid* here laid out the principle that war should end not with conquest for the victors and slavery for the

---

[144] BPF, 120.   [145] BPF, 124.   [146] BPF, 121.   [147] BPF, 122.
[148] Virgil, *The Aeneid*, trans. Robert Fitzgerald (New York: Random House, 1981), 374.

Classical Political Philosophy

vanquished, but with a new alliance of old enemies, who would become allies under the auspices of Roman law. Arendt noted:

> Since Rome was founded on this treaty-law between two different and naturally hostile people, it could become Rome's mission eventually 'to lay all the world beneath laws – *totem sub leges mitteret orbem*. The genius of Roman politics – not only according to Virgil but, generally, according to Roman self-interpretation – lay in the very *principles* which attend the legendary foundation of the city.[149]

Aeneas was the *auctor* of the Roman people not just because he defeated the Latins but because he established the principle of alliance that would govern Roman politics. His status as *auctor* – his authority – not only made his promise binding for all future generations, but also made his act a precedent that was to govern all acts of war and peace. The founders of Rome were authorities, Arendt argued, in the sense that their words and deeds were taken as guiding precedents for their descendants.

> Thus precedents, the deeds of the ancestors and the usage that grew out of them, were always binding. Anything that happened was transformed into an example, and the *auctoritas maiorum* became identical with authoritative models for actual behavior, with the moral political standard as such.[150]

The authority of the founders was handed down through tradition, and it was by following tradition that Roman leaders acquired their authority: "As long as this tradition was uninterrupted, authority was inviolate; and to act without authority and tradition, without accepted, time-honored standards and models, without the help of the wisdom of the founding fathers, was inconceivable."[151] There was a strict intrication of the concepts of foundation, tradition, religion, and authority – Romans derived their authority from their religious fidelity to the founding traditions of the city.

Arendt emphasized that in Latin *auctoritas* is not *potestas* – authority is not power. Cicero clearly distinguished the two in his treatise on the laws: "*Cum potestas in populo auctoritas in senatu sit*" – "while power resides in the people, authority rests with the Senate."[152] The Senate did not have the power to make political decisions, but the right to give advice and to approve or disapprove of whatever decisions were made. Arendt used the example of building to clarify this distinction: while the builder has the right to command the obedience of his workers, he does not necessarily have the authority of the founder or his heirs; his rule is

---

[149] OR, 210 (italics added).   [150] BPF, 123.   [151] BPF, 124.   [152] BPF, 122.

authoritative only if he follows the founding precedents and principles. The difference with Plato is clear: while the philosopher king derives authority from knowledge of the ideas (just as the architect derives his authority from his knowledge of houses), the Roman senator derives authority from fidelity to tradition. To have authority is to speak and act with the weight of tradition.

While the concept of authority originated in the sphere of politics, Arendt argued, the Romans abstracted it from political life and transposed it into the life of the mind: "The Romans felt they needed founding fathers and authoritative examples in matters of thought and ideas as well, and accepted the great 'ancestors' in Greece as their authorities for theory, philosophy, and poetry. The great Greek authors became authorities in the hands of the Romans, not of the Greeks."[153] In this way the concept of authority was uprooted from the experience of Roman politics and used in a derivative sense: "The notion of a spiritual tradition and of authority in matters of thought and ideas is here derived from the political realm and therefore essentially derivative – just as Plato's conception of the role of reason and ideas in politics was derived from the philosophical realm and became derivative in the realm of human affairs."[154]

The concept of authority was further displaced, Arendt argued, when Christians came to understand their Church in Roman terms: "The Apostles could become the 'founding fathers' of the Church, from whom she would derive her own testimony by way of tradition from generation to generation. Only when this had happened, one is tempted to say, had the Christian faith become a 'religion'."[155] Two aspects of this displacement were decisive for the genealogy of authority.

First, Christian thinkers retained the Roman distinction between power and authority. When the Roman Empire declined and the Church became involved in politics, Arendt argued, the Church did not pursue power so much as authority.

> The Church, when she embarked upon her great political career in the fifth century, at once adopted the Roman distinction between authority and power, claiming for herself the old authority of the Senate and leaving the power ... to the princes of the world. Thus at the close of the fifth century, Pope Gelasius I could write to Emperor Anastaius I: "Two are the things by which the world is chiefly ruled: the sacred authority of the Popes and the royal power."[156]

---

[153] BPF, 124.   [154] BPF, 124.   [155] BPF, 126.   [156] BPF, 126–127.

156   Classical Political Philosophy

As Roman emperors needed approval from the Senate to give authority to
their rule, so medieval kings needed the authority conferred by the investi-
ture of the Pope. The preeminence of spiritual authority over worldly
power was demonstrated in 1077 when Emperor Henry IV unsuccessfully
challenged the authority of the Church, and had to stand barefoot in the
snow to beg the Pope's forgiveness. Royal power needed the authority of
divine sanction.

A second mutation in the genealogy of authority, for Arendt, came
when Christian thinkers tried to understand their experience of faith in
terms of Greek philosophy. Long after the Academy and Lyceum were
closed, Christian thinkers formulated Church doctrine in Neoplatonic and
Aristotelean terms. Plato's doctrine of ideas and Aristotle's notion of
natural law came to dominate political theory.

> It is only in the Christian era that Plato's invisible spiritual yardsticks, by
> which the visible, concrete affairs of men were to be measured and judged,
> have unfolded their full political effectiveness. Precisely those parts of
> Christian doctrine which would have had great difficulty in fitting in and
> being assimilated to the Roman political structure – namely, the revealed
> commandments and truths of a genuinely transcendent authority ... –
> could be integrated into the Roman foundation legend via Plato. God's
> revelation could now be interpreted politically as if the standards for human
> conduct and the principle of political communities, intuitively anticipated
> by Plato, had been finally revealed directly...[57]

One irony of history, for Arendt, is that Plato's political philosophy was
first taken seriously not by the Athenians but by Christians, who interpreted the revelations of the Bible in terms of the Roman concept of
authority and the Platonic doctrine of ideas.

Christian thinkers laid down an assumption that still underlies much
political philosophy: that political institutions are authoritative only if they
are sanctioned by a source of authority that transcends the political realm.
Arendt summarized her argument in a few dense sentences:

> To the extent that the Catholic Church incorporated Greek philosophy
> into the structure of its doctrines and dogmatic beliefs, it amalgamated the
> Roman political concept of authority, which inevitably was based on a
> beginning, a founding in the past, with the Greek [Platonic] notion of
> transcending measurements and rules. General and transcendent standards
> under which the particular and immanent could be subsumed were now

[57] BPF, 127.

Later Political Theory 157

required for any political order, moral rules for all interhuman behavior, and rational measurements for the guidance of all individual judgment.[158]

This amalgamation of notions underlies the assumption that political power, to have authority, must be restrained and guided by laws grounded in standards that transcend the realm of politics.

In light of this assumption, the modern crisis of authority looks like a catastrophe. In the absence of authoritative standards against which political power can be checked and measured, it seems, governments can only be based on the principle that might makes right. But Arendt raised another possibility – that authority is not essential to political life, and that political authority does not have to be derived from extra-political sources, whether natural or divine.

> To live in a political realm with neither authority nor the concomitant awareness that the source of authority transcends power and those who are in power, means to be confronted anew, without the religious trust in a sacred beginning and without the protection of traditional and therefore self-evident standards of behavior, by the elementary problems of human living-together.[159]

We now confront the basic questions of political life without the false security of traditional authorities. The task of thinking is not to ground political authority on apolitical standards of right, but to understand how authority can be established within the political sphere itself. We will see in Chapter 6 how Arendt took on this task.

Law

What is the genealogy of the concept of law? How did the Greeks and Romans understand the nature of law? How was that understanding inherited and transformed by Christian thinkers? How did this heritage guide or misguide the thinking of the American revolutionaries? What understanding of law is implicit in the founding documents of the United States?

The American revolutionaries inherited the assumption that laws must be grounded on an apolitical source of authority, according to Arendt. They could not conceive of laws that did not rest on such grounds. In her book *On Revolution* she noted that John Adams insisted that "it was the general opinion of ancient nations that the Divinity alone was adequate to

[158] BPF, 128. [159] BPF, 141.

158 Classical Political Philosophy

the important office of giving laws to men," and that human laws had to be based on "rights antecedent to all earthly government . . . derived from the great Legislator of the universe."[160]

Arendt thought Adams was simply wrong: "neither the Greek *nomos* nor the Roman *lex* was of divine origin, [and] neither the Greek nor the Roman concept of legislation needed divine inspiration."[161] The Greeks thought laws were essentially artificial, and this artificiality was implicit both in the conceptual opposition of law and nature (νόμος vs. φύσις), and in the etymology of the word itself (which derived from νέμω, to allot, to divide up pasture, to dwell):

> The very word νόμος, which, apart from its etymological significance, receives its full meaning as the opposite of φύσις or things that are natural, stresses the 'artificial', conventional, man-made nature of the laws . . . Obviously, no idea of a "higher law" could possibly make sense with respect to this νόμος, and even Plato's laws are not derived from a "higher law" which would not only determine their usefulness but constitute their very legality and validity.[162]

The Latin etymology of the word *lex* also implied that, unlike the customs given to a people by the gods, laws are human institutions that need no higher source of authority: "The original meaning of the word *lex* is 'intimate connection' or relationship, namely something which connects two things or two partners whom external circumstances have brought together. Therefore, the existence of a people in the sense of an ethnic, tribal, organic unity is quite independent of all laws."[163]

Other thinkers confirm that Greek and Roman legislators did not justify their laws by appealing to natural law or divine sanction. M. I. Finley wrote: "Neither Greek nor Roman religion had the substantive doctrines or the ecclesiastical machinery to sanction (or legitimate) a particular ruler, regime or system. Lawgivers, rhetoricians and ideologists all spoke in the name of justice, but I am unaware of a single claim to divine sanction for a particular measure, regime, reform or revolution."[164] This view of law is foreign to modern thinkers, who have been baffled by the absence in Greek and Roman thought of the problem of legitimacy – the question of how to ground and validate human laws. Finley candidly admitted he was baffled by "the absence of any need to grapple with the problem of legitimacy, which today 'figures at the very heart of our concern with

[160] OR, 186.   [161] OR, 186.   [162] OR, 186–187.   [163] OR, 187.
[164] Finley, *Politics in the Ancient World*, 132.

Later Political Theory 159

the nature and value of modern society' as 'a main dimension of political culture.'" For Finley this absence is inexplicable: "It is not at all obvious why a problem that came to the fore in the Middle Ages and has been important ever since should not have arisen in antiquity, and I have no explanation to offer."[165] Why was the question of legitimacy absent from classical political thought? How did that question come to seem fundamental to political theory?

Arendt hinted at an answer in her reading of Paul's Epistle to the Romans. Paul understood sin and freedom in terms of law: "With my mind I am a servant to the law of God, but with my flesh I am a slave to the law of sin."[166] And Paul understood law in terms of servitude and sovereignty, Arendt argued: "Law itself is understood as the voice of a master demanding obedience; the Thou shalt of the law demands and expects a voluntary act of submission, an I-will of agreement."[167] Paul understood law in these terms, Arendt thought, because the model of law was no longer the *nomoi* of the Greek lawgivers or the treaties of the Romans, but the commandments of the Hebrew Bible. In Christian thought, the Ten Commandments provided both a model for political laws and an apolitical standard against which they could be measured.

> The model in whose image Western Mankind had construed the quintessence of all laws, even of those whose Roman origin was beyond doubt, and even in juridical interpretation that used all the terms of Roman jurisdiction – this model was itself not Roman at all; it was Hebrew in origin and represented by the divine Commandments of the Decalogue.[168]

Secular law was understood as a kind of commandment, an imperative expressing the will of a sovereign, and the will of a sovereign was legitimate only if it was sanctioned by divine will. Human laws had to be grounded in divine law, and the contract between subjects and their ruler had to be grounded in the covenant between men and their Creator. This concept of law rests on several assumptions: that law is an imperative that expresses the will of a sovereign; that the validity of a law rests on the authority of the lawgiver; and that human law is authoritative only if it conforms to divine law.

This concept of law was inherited by modern political thinkers, according to Arendt, and it guided their thinking even when they replaced

---

[165] Finley, *Politics in the Ancient World*, 131.
[166] *New Greek–English Interlinear New Testament*, 550. (Romans 7:25.)   [167] LMW, 68.
[168] OR, 189.

160   Classical Political Philosophy

the sovereignty of the king with the sovereignty of the people, when they tried to ground human laws on natural laws, and when they sought to discover divine law through the light of reason rather than through the voice of conscience or the revelation of the scriptures:

> And the model itself did not change when in the seventeenth and eighteenth centuries natural law stepped into the place of divinity–into the place, that is, which once had been held by the Hebrew God who was a lawmaker because he was the Maker of the Universe, a place which then had been occupied by Christ, the visible representative and bodily incarnation of God on earth, from whom then the vicars of Christ, the Roman popes and bishops as well as the kings who followed them, had derived their authority ... The point of the matter has always been that natural law itself needed divine sanction to become binding for men.[169]

If laws are commands, Arendt noted, their validity depends on the authority of the lawgiver, and human lawgivers have authority only insofar as they do the will of God. The question of legitimacy – the quest for a source of authority outside the political sphere that could validate human laws – appeared only after laws were understood as imperatives.

> These historical reminiscences and reflections are to suggest that the whole problem of an absolute which would bestow validity upon positive, man-made laws was partly an inheritance of absolutism, which in turn had fallen heir to those long centuries when no secular realm existed in the Occident that was not ultimately rooted in the sanction given to it by the Church, and when therefore secular laws were understood as the mundane expression of a divinely ordained law. This, however, is only part of the story. It was of even greater importance and impact that the very word 'law' had assumed an altogether different meaning throughout these centuries. What mattered was that ... the laws themselves were understood to be commandments, that they were construed in accordance with the voice of God, who tells men: *Thou shalt not.* Such commandments obviously could not be binding without a higher, religious sanction.[170]

It was this concept of law as imperative that the American revolutionaries inherited, and that led them to believe that the basic principles of the United States had to be grounded on the laws of nature and nature's God. We will see in Chapter 6 how Arendt tried to critically dismantle this inherited concept of law.

[169] OR, 189–190.   [170] OR, 189.

Principle

What is a principle? Arendt argued that political authority, in the original sense of the word, was for the Romans derived from religious fidelity to the principles that had governed the foundation of Rome and had been handed down through tradition: "The genius of Roman politics – not only according to Virgil but, generally, according to Roman self-interpretation – lay in the very principles which attend the legendary foundation of the city."[171] But this reference to "principles" is ambiguous since the word has several senses. To understand these different senses we have to briefly trace the lineage of the concept of principle. What did the word "principle" originally mean? How has that original meaning changed over time? How have modern thinkers conceived of principles? How might modern concepts distort our understanding of principles?

The Latin *principium* translates the Greek verb *archein* (ἄρχειν): to begin, to come first, to lead. *Archein* is what the best warriors did in Homer – they did not command others but initiated action and led the way, as when Odysseus led other warriors to and from the camp of Achilles.[172] An *archon* (ἄρχων) in this sense was first among equals, the leader of peers rather than the ruler of subordinates.[173] Arendt argued it was only after Homer, in Herodotus and Pindar, that *archein* came to mean primarily to rule or dominate, and an *archon* became primarily not a leader but a ruler: "Thus the role of the beginner and leader, who was a *primus inter pares* (in the case of Homer, a king among kings), changed into that of a ruler."[174]

Aristotle in his metaphysics brought together these two senses of *archein* (to begin and to rule). The principle or *arche* of an action is both what begins the action and what governs its performance. In the *Nicomachean Ethics*, the word "*arche*" has several senses. In the most general sense, the *arche* of an action is the man who performs it; more precisely, it is our power to decide what to do and how to do it. But ultimately the *arche* of an action is the end towards which the act is directed and for whose sake it

---

[171] OR, 210.
[172] See Homer, *The Iliad*, trans. Richmond Lattimore (Chicago: University of Chicago Press, 1961), 89 (Book IX, Line 657). Homer, *Homeri Opera: Iliadis I–XII*, ed. David B. Monro and Thomas W. Allen (Oxford: Oxford University Press, 1989), 197.
[173] Here I am indebted to Reiner Schürmann, *Heidegger on Being and Acting: From Principles to Anarchy* (Bloomington: Indiana University Press, 1990). See especially chapter 6.
[174] HC, 189. See also "Ruling and Being Ruled" in TWB, 56–68.

162 Classical Political Philosophy

is done.[175] Aristotle gave several examples of this kind of principle: the principle that initiates and governs production is the product to be made; the principle of exercise is health; the principle of virtuous action is simply virtue, since virtue is an end in itself.[176] In each case, the principle of action is an end that arouses our desire (*orexis*) and that we perceive with our reason (*logos*).[177] This concept of action could be called teleocratic, in that action is always initiated and governed (*kratein*) by an already existing end (*telos*).

But in Aristotle the word *arche* is ambiguous. On the one hand, the *arche* of a being is its innermost core. Principles inhere in things themselves, apart from the mind that perceives them. On the other hand, in the *Metaphysics*, Aristotle also uses the word to name the axioms laid down by the mind itself – the basic propositions from which demonstrations begin and from which later conclusions are deduced.[178]

In modern thought, this second sense of "principle" became the primary sense of the term. This shift is explicit in Descartes, who rejected the Aristotelean concept of *telos* in his *Principles of Philosophy*. While natural things may have an inherent *telos*, Descartes wrote, we should not be so arrogant as to suppose that we can know them with certainty. The search for final causes should be banished from philosophy.

> When dealing with natural things we will, then, never derive any explanations from the purposes which God or nature may have had in view when creating them and we shall entirely banish from our philosophy the search for final causes.[179]

The word "principle" for Descartes does not mean "final cause" but rather "basic proposition". Instead of looking for the natural ends that initiate and govern the motion of things, we should look for truths that are absolutely indubitable, fundamental propositions on which all knowledge

---

[175] In general, each man is the principle of his action: ἄνθρωπος εἶναι ἀρχὴ τῶν πράξεων. (Aristotle, *Nicomachean Ethics*, 138–139) (1112b32). But, more precisely, every practical principle has two sides. The principle of action (in the sense of its source of motion or "efficient cause") is *prohairesis*, the faculty of choice: πράξεως μὲν οὖν ἀρχὴ προαίρεσις. (Aristotle, *Nichomachean Ethics*, 329) (1139a32). The principle of action (in the sense of its *telos* or "final cause") is the end towards which it is directed: αἱ μὲν γὰρ ἀρχαὶ τῶν πρακτῶν τὸ οὗ ἕνεκα τὰ πρακτά (Aristotle, *Nichomachean Ethics*, 338–339) (1140b18).

[176] Aristotle, *Nicomachean Ethics*, 337 (1040b6).

[177] Aristotle, *Nicomachean Ethics*, 329 (1039a34).

[178] Aristotle laid out his concept of *arche* at the start of Book Five. See Aristotle, *Metaphysics*, 209–211 (1012b34–1013a24).

[179] René Descartes, *Selected Philosophical Writings*, trans. John Cottingham, Robert Stoothoff, and Dugald Murdoch (Cambridge: Cambridge University Press, 1990), 169.

Later Political Theory 163

may be based. Principles for Descartes are not the essential grounds of things, but are self-evident truths.

This modern concept of principle was brought into political philosophy by Locke, who wanted political theorists to think like mathematicians. In Locke's view, the task of the political philosopher is to find the fundamental principles of government and to deduce from them the natural rights and duties of citizens.

> I doubt not but from self-evident propositions, by necessary consequences, as incontestable as those in mathematics, the measures of right and wrong might be made out, to any one that will apply himself with the same indifferency and attention to the one as he does to the other of these sciences.[180]

Locke gave several examples of such self-evident propositions:

> "Where there is no property there is not injustice," is a proposition as certain as any demonstration in Euclid: for the idea of property being a right to anything, and the idea to which the name "injustice" is given being the invasion or violation of that right, it is evident that these ideas, being thus established, and these names annexed to them, I can as certainly know this proposition to be true, as that a triangle has three angles equal to two right ones. Again: "No government allows absolute liberty." The idea of government being the establishment of society upon certain rules or laws which require conformity to them; and the idea of absolute liberty being for any one to do whatever he pleases; I am as capable of being certain of the truth of this proposition as of any in the mathematics.[181]

This approach to political philosophy was deeply indebted to Plato. In Arendt's view, Plato "discovered that truth, namely, the truths we call self-evident, compels the mind, and that this coercion, though it needs not violence to be effective, is stronger than persuasion and argument."[182] Locke renewed the Platonic attempt to limit or eliminate politics by finding absolute measures from which codes of conduct could be derived. And he conceived these measures as essentially the same as the axioms of mathematics. Principles for Locke are not the grounds of action; they are self-evident truths.

The original sense of the word "principle" did not wholly disappear. It was retained and refined most notably by Montesquieu in *The Spirit of the Laws*. Montesquieu asked two questions: What are the different forms of

---

[180] John Locke, *An Essay Concerning Human Understanding* (London: Oxford University Press, 1904), 208.
[181] Locke, *Human Understanding*, 208.   [182] BPF, 107.

164   Classical Political Philosophy

government? What makes governments act as they do? Montesquieu's answers to the first question are traditional: a republic is a lawful government ruled by the people; a monarchy is a lawful government ruled by a king; and a tyranny is a lawless government under the will of one man. But in Arendt's view, Montesquieu's second question is "entirely original," and his answer is original as well: in each form of government the actions of both rulers and ruled are inspired and guided by a basic principle, a "spirit of the laws," that gives sense and force to specific codes of conduct. The principle of action in a republic is virtue; the principle of action in a monarchy is honor; and the principle of action in a tyranny is fear.[183] Arendt stressed that these principles of government are not goals of action; they do not direct action as the idea of the final product directs the process of production. Nor are these principles the same as motives; it is the principles themselves that determine the typical motives of public action: the principle of virtue underlies the "love of equality" that motivates action in a republic, just as the principle of honor underlies the "passion for distinction" that motivates action in a monarchy.[184] These principles of government are the underlying grounds on which goals and motives are based, "the very criteria according to which all public life is led and judged."[185]

These various concepts of principle were inherited by the American revolutionaries. When Jefferson spoke of "principles" of government he was using a concept of principle derived primarily from Locke; the principles set down in the Declaration are supposed to be self-evident truths from which the right to revolution can be deduced. But this concept of principle grasps only part of the Declaration. In Chapter 6 we will see how Arendt tried to critically dismantle the concept of principle foregrounded in the Declaration of Independence, and to bring to light a deeper understanding of principle implicit in the Declaration as an act of revolution.

One task of political theory, for Arendt, is to trace the genealogy of basic concepts. Through her genealogies she tried to demonstrate the provenance of inherited concepts by bringing to light the basic experiences from

---

[183] EU, 329.
[184] EU, 336. The classic example of an aristocracy governed by the principle of honor, for Arendt, was the society of the Homeric heroes. Twice she cites the principle that governs the actions of all the warriors: αἰὲν ἀριστεύειν καὶ ὑπείροχον ἔμμεναι ἄλλων – "Always to be best, and to stand out above others". Homer, *The Iliad*, 158 and 255. Homer, *Iliadis*, 126 and 247. See HC, 41 and BPF, 152.
[185] EU, 332.

which they were derived. But this demonstration is only a first step – its point is to undermine trust in these concepts and to deprive them of their seeming self-evidence. The next step is to rethink them on the basis of the way political phenomena actually appear in experience – to mark the limits of inherited concepts, to sense what eludes their grasp, and to revise and refine them in order to grasp and illuminate what they have distorted or obscured.

How then did Arendt rethink these basic concepts of political theory?

CHAPTER 6

Rethinking the Classical Legacy

The Legacy of Classical Political Philosophy

Political theory today is still indebted to classical philosophy, Arendt argued: "The political philosophies of Plato and Aristotle have dominated all subsequent political thought."[1] Her argument was not that the theories of Plato and Aristotle have much influence today, but that the language of Plato and Aristotle set the terms of much later philosophy, and that assumptions implicit in these terms continue to guide or misguide the thinking of political theorists. It is commonly assumed that:

Politics is a universal and necessary sphere of human life. All human community is by nature political.

Politics is a means to higher ends. Political life aims at something beyond itself.

Politics is ultimately a matter of rule. In any political community some people must be entitled to command and others must be required to obey.

Rule is legitimate when it is governed by the right ideas or ends. The right to rule must be based on standards and aims that check and guide political power. Otherwise, rule is based simply on might and violence.

These ideas or ends must transcend politics. The ends and principles of government will never be secure if they can be altered or abolished by political means. They must not rest on the opinions of citizens but on absolute grounds, such as the nature of man, the idea of justice, the laws of nature and nature's God.

These ideas or ends can be discovered by philosophy. They cannot be reached through debate and persuasion; they have to be found and fixed by philosophical theory.

These assumptions underlie a number of traditional questions. The notion that politics is a matter of rule leads to the belief that the most

[1] BPF, 106.

166

The Legacy of Classical Political Philosophy

basic political question is: Who should rule whom? The notion that politics is a means to an end underlies the question: What is the proper end of government? The attempt to find extrapolitical ideas and ends leads to questions such as: What is the ideal political community? What is the *telos* of man? What basic rights can be deduced from human nature? How can laws be set above men? What transcendent principles can ground the authority of human laws? By what standards should we guide and judge action in the political realm? Arendt objected to these questions for two reasons: they create false problems; and they perpetuate the misleading assumptions they take for granted.

Arendt argued that these assumptions have led philosophers to systematically misconceive the nature of power, violence, authority, government, law, and freedom. These misconceptions have to be made explicit before we can begin to rethink them. For the sake of simplicity we can only touch on them here.

Politics has been seen as essentially a fight for power. In her essay *On Violence*, Arendt cited the dictum of C. Wright Mills: "all politics is a struggle for power."[2] But she could have cited many others. Emmanuel Lévinas wrote that "[Politics is] the art of foreseeing war and winning it by every means."[3] Carl Schmitt argued that "The specific political distinction to which political actions and motives can be reduced is that between friend and enemy."[4] Chantal Mouffe has argued that "Politics ... is not an exchange of opinions but a contest for power."[5] And Michel Foucault said that "the set of relations of force in a given society constitutes the domain of the political, and ... a politics is a more-or-less global strategy for coordinating and directing those relations."[6] Throughout the philosophical tradition – and across the political spectrum from left to right – politics has been commonly conceived as a struggle for power.

Political power in turn has been conceived as power over others. Arendt cited thinkers who conceived power in terms of rule. Voltaire wrote that, "Power consists in making others act as I choose." Bertrand de Jouvenel wrote, "To command and to be obeyed: without that, there is no Power – with it no other attribute is needed for it to be ... The thing without

---

[2] OV, 35.

[3] Emmanuel Lévinas, *Totality and Infinity*, trans. Alphonso Lingis (Pittsburgh: Duquesne University Press, 1969), 21.

[4] Carl Schmitt, *The Concept of the Political*, trans. George Schwab (Chicago: University of Chicago Press, 1996), 26.

[5] Chantal Mouffe, *On the Political* (New York: Routledge, 2005), 51.

[6] Michel Foucault, *Power/Knowledge*, ed. Colin Gordon (New York: Pantheon, 1980), 189.

168 Rethinking the Classical Legacy

which it cannot be: that essence is command."[7] But her critique also applies to theorists who no longer conceive power in terms of rule, but who still understand power as the ability to restrain and direct the actions of others. Foucault, for example, defined the exercise of power as "a way of acting upon an acting subject or acting subjects ... a set of actions upon other actions."[8]

Violence has often been conceived as power in its purest form: "If the essence of power is the effectiveness of command, then there is no greater power than that which grows out of the barrel of a gun."[9] Violence and power were equated not just by Mao Zedong, Arendt noted, but also by American theorists such as C. Wright Mills ("the ultimate kind of power is violence").[10] This view of power prevails across the political spectrum: "there exists a consensus among political theorists from Left to Right to the effect that violence is nothing more than the most flagrant manifestation of power."[11]

Authority has been conceived as a way to command obedience, in Arendt's view, and so has been conceived as simply a different form of power. In everyday language, "power" and "authority" are often used as synonyms. Since authority is able to inspire a relatively free and voluntary obedience, rule by authority seems to be the only alternative to rule based on the threat of violence.

Government has been conceived as an instrument of rule. This conception underlies the traditional interpretation of different kinds of government as different forms of rule: monarchy is rule by one; oligarchy is rule by a few; plutocracy is rule by the rich; theocracy is rule by God; and democracy is supposedly the rule of the people.

Law too has been conceived in terms of rule. Arendt cited the claim of Passerin d'Entrèves that the essence of law lies in "the simple relation of command and obedience."[12] She could have also cited Hobbes: "A Law is the Command of him, or them that have the Sovereign Power, given to them that be his or their subjects."[13] This conception takes law as essentially the imperative of a sovereign power.

---

[7] OV, 36–37.
[8] Michel Foucault, "The Subject and Power," in the Afterword of Hubert Dreyfus and Paul Rabinow, *Michel Foucault: Beyond Structuralism and Hermeneutics* (Chicago: University of Chicago Press, 1983), 221.
[9] OV, 37.   [10] OV, 35.   [11] OV, 35.   [12] OV, 39.
[13] Thomas Hobbes, *A Dialogue between a Philosopher and a Student of the Common Laws of England*, ed. Joseph Cropsey (Chicago: University of Chicago Press, 1997), 71. Hobbes says the same thing in *Leviathan*: "Law, properly is the word of him, that by right hath command over others." Hobbes, *Leviathan*, ed. Richard Tuck (Cambridge: Cambridge University Press, 1991), 111.

Rethinking the Classical Legacy

Finally, *freedom* has been conceived in terms of sovereignty, according to Arendt. To be sovereign is to rule, and to rule is to have power over one's domain and to be able to do as one wills. Sovereignty means both to rule oneself and not to be ruled by others, to master oneself through willpower rather than to be subject to one's passions, and not to be subject to the will of a higher power. To be sovereign in this sense is to be free. If law is a kind of commandment given by the ruler to the ruled, then we are free to the extent that we give the law to ourselves, by making our own laws or making the law our own. We are unfree to the extent that we are subject to the laws of others.

Rethinking the Classical Legacy

Arendt argued these concepts fail to fully grasp the basic realities of politics, and this failure is evident in the confused way we use these words. She saw the source of this confusion in the assumption that politics is ultimately a matter of rule, and that the fundamental problem of political philosophy is the question: Who rules whom?

> It is, I think, a rather sad reflection on the present state of political science that our terminology does not distinguish among such key words as power, strength, force, authority, and, finally, violence – all of which refer to distinct, different phenomena and would hardly exist unless they did ... To use them as synonyms not only indicates a certain deafness to linguistic meanings, which would be serious enough, but it has also resulted in a kind of blindness to the realities they correspond to. In such a situation it is always tempting to introduce new definitions, but–though I shall briefly yield to temptation–what is involved is not simply a matter of careless speech. Behind the apparent confusion is a firm conviction in whose light all distinctions would be, at best, of minor importance: the conviction that the most crucial political issue is, and always has been, the question of Who rules Whom? Power, strength, force, authority, violence – these are but words to indicate the means by which man rules over man; they are held to be synonyms because they have the same function. It is only after one ceases to reduce public affairs to the business of domination that the original data in the realm of human affairs will appear, or, rather, reappear, in their authentic diversity.[14]

Her project was to distill and clarify the sense of these key words. This distillation was not a matter of stipulating new definitions, but of explicating the authentic insights implicit in the original senses of words, drawing

---

[14] OV, 43–44.

170 Rethinking the Classical Legacy

finer distinctions between phenomena, and refining our nontheoretical understanding of political phenomena in order to construct pure theoretical concepts.[15]

To rethink inherited concepts we first have to ask about their limits: What political phenomena elude or resist these concepts? What do they fail to comprehend? What experiences or events exceed their grasp?

Power

Arendt thought the limits of the common concept of power are exposed most clearly by the phenomenon of revolution.

> It is particularly tempting to think of power in terms of command and obedience, and hence to equate power with violence, in a discussion of what actually is only one of power's special cases – namely, the power of government. Since in foreign relations as well as domestic affairs violence appears as a last resort to keep the power structure intact against individual challengers – the foreign enemy, the native criminal – it looks indeed as though violence were the prerequisite of power and power nothing but a façade, the velvet glove which either conceals the iron hand or will turn out to belong to a paper tiger. On closer inspection, though, this notion loses much of its plausibility. For our purposes, the gap between theory and reality is perhaps best illustrated by the phenomenon of revolution.[16]

We can look to the history of revolutions to refine our understanding of political power.

If power were the ability to command obedience, she argued, and if obedience were best ensured through force, then revolutions would be won by whoever had superior instruments of coercion and violence. We would expect poorly armed revolutionaries to fail, and well-armed regimes to hold power. But the history of violent revolutions since 1776 tells a different story. For more than 200 years, poorly armed revolutionaries have managed to overthrow regimes with vastly superior firepower. How was that possible?

Even stranger is the history of nonviolent revolutions. Arendt pointed to the Hungarian Revolution of 1956, when soldiers sent to disperse

---

[15] A pure concept grasps what something is in its pure form. We rarely find the basic realities of politics in a pure form; most power relations are a mix of coercion, persuasion, personal authority, and official authority. It is precisely because these phenomena usually appear together that they are so easily confused: "These distinctions, though by no means arbitrary, hardly ever correspond to watertight compartments in the real world, from which they are nevertheless drawn" (OV, 46).

[16] OV, 47.

Rethinking the Classical Legacy

anti-government demonstrators instead joined the demonstrations and helped to bring down the Communist regime. But her claims were most clearly confirmed by the nonviolent revolutions the took place after her death (Manila in 1986, Prague in 1989, Belgrade in 2000, etc.). When soldiers and police simply stopped obeying orders, some of the most ruthless dictatorships of the twentieth century collapsed in the face of massive nonviolent resistance. If power grows out of the barrel of a gun, nonviolent revolution would seem impossible. And yet the impossible has happened over and over again.

What then do revolutions show about the nature of power?

The example of violent revolution shows that power depends on something more basic than weapons or armies, according to Arendt: it depends on organization. It is possible for small but disciplined groups to dominate huge but disorganized masses: "A comparatively small but well-organized group of men can rule almost indefinitely over large and populous empires."[17] In the same way, it is possible for poorly armed but well-coordinated armies to defeat larger and stronger foes:

> Even the most despotic domination we know of, the rule of masters over slaves, did not rest on superior means of coercion as such, but on a superior organization of power – that is, on the organized solidarity of the masters. Single men without others to support them never have enough power to use violence successfully ... And as for actual warfare, we have seen in Vietnam how an enormous superiority in the means of violence can become helpless if confronted with an ill-equipped but well-organized opponent.[18]

If power depends on organization, and if the hierarchical command structure itself is only one possible form of organization, then there should also be nonhierarchical forms of power, power that cannot be understood in terms of command and obedience.

The example of nonviolent revolution shows that power depends on something more basic than organization, according to Arendt: it depends on support for the organization and for its leaders. A regime can maintain control as long as it has the support of its power base – not necessarily the support of the people, but the support of the army, police, and civilian collaborators.[19] Once a regime loses this base of support, it can be toppled by nonviolent means.

---

[17] HC, 200.   [18] OV, 50–51.

[19] Arendt sometimes said that power resides in the people, but she knew it was naïve to think regimes collapse automatically when they no longer have any popular support. Regimes can usually maintain control as long as they can rely on the police, the army, and civilian collaborators:

Rethinking the Classical Legacy

> In a contest of violence against violence the superiority of the government has always been absolute; but this superiority lasts only as long as the power structure of the government is intact – that is, as long as commands are obeyed and the army or police forces are prepared to use their weapons. When this is no longer the case, the situation changes abruptly. Not only is the rebellion not put down, but the arms themselves change hands–sometimes, as in the Hungarian revolution, within a few hours ... Where commands are not obeyed, the means of violence are of no use; and the question of this obedience is not decided by the command-obedience relation but by opinion, and, of course, by the number of those who share it.[20]

The power of leaders depends on the support of their followers; when that support dissolves their power collapses.

What then is the essence of power? How is it different from strength, force, authority, and violence? How can we detach these concepts from the concept of rule?

In the most basic sense, Arendt thought, power is simply the ability to do. While power is commonly conceived as the ability of a leader to command the obedience of followers, that power of command depends on the support of the followers, and it vanishes once the leader no longer has their support. The power of leader and followers together – the group's concerted power – depends on something even more basic: the ability of the group to act together. The essence of power for Arendt is not the ability to command obedience but its underlying condition of possibility: the capacity for concerted action.[21]

> Power corresponds to the human ability not just to act but to act in concert. Power is never the property of an individual; it belongs to a group and remains in existence only so long as the group keeps together. When we say of somebody that he is "in power" we actually refer to his being empowered by a certain number of people to act in their name. The moment the group,

---

"Generally speaking, we may say that no revolution is even possible where the authority of the body politic is truly intact, and this means, under modern conditions, where the armed forces can be trusted to obey the civil authorities" (OR, 116). Mass protests against a regime can make manifest its lack of popular support, but such protests are effective only when they can persuade those who are propping up a regime to abandon their support.

[20] OV, 48–49.

[21] Jürgen Habermas does not quite do justice to Arendt on this point. In "Hannah Arendt: On the Concept of Power," he wrote that Arendt "understands power as the capacity to agree in uncoerced communication on some community action." Uncoerced agreement is not essential to power for Arendt. The power of a group is measured simply by the range of what it can do together; what matters is that members of a group can act in concert, not whether they have agreed without coercion to work toward some common end. See Jürgen Habermas, *Philosophical-Political Profiles*, trans. Frederick G. Lawrence (Cambridge, MA: MIT Press, 1983).

Rethinking the Classical Legacy

from which the power originated to begin with (*potestas in populo*, without a people or group there is no power), disappears, "his power" also vanishes.[22]

A leader's power to command obedience ultimately depends on her followers' capacity to act. If their ability to act in concert is diminished (whether through internal divisions, a collapse of discipline, or an incapacity to communicate) the leader's power is diminished as well.

In other words, Arendt distinguished two levels of power: *power-over-others* and *power-to-do*. We commonly think of political power as *power-over-others*, since political power has been generally used for domination and warfare, so that political institutions seem to be essentially instruments of rule and conquest, and it seems reasonable to conclude that government is essentially "the rule of men over men based on the means of legitimate, that is allegedly legitimate, violence."[23] But Arendt argued that power-over-others always depends on a more basic power-to-do. The power of a small ruling class over a large but atomized population depends on the power of the rulers to do things together – to defend themselves, to maintain order, to enforce their decrees – just as the powerlessness of the atomized population is based on their inability to act in concert. But the political power-to-do generated by group solidarity does not necessarily have to be used for domination and warfare, i.e. power-over others. Power-over-others is just one possible application of a group's power-to-do.

Arendt's distinction between two kinds of power is clearest in the case of tyranny. Of all political leaders, tyrants can have the greatest power-over others, in the sense that there is no limit to what they can decree, and nothing to check and restrain their rule. But tyrannical power can most easily be held over people deprived of their *power-to-act* together – people divided by mistrust, dominated by fear, and confined by mechanisms of surveillance and control. Tyrants hold power by making their people powerless. Hence the peculiar nature of tyranny: the stronger the tyrant, the weaker the country. The greater a tyrant's power to command, the less a people are able to act in their own interest or even in their own self-defense: "Tyranny prevents the development of power, not only in a particular segment of the public realm but in its entirety; it generates, in other words, impotence as naturally as other bodies politic generate power."[24] A classic example is Athens, which was relatively weak under the tyranny of Peisistratos, and became the most powerful polis in Greece under the democratic reforms of Cleisthenes. Traditional concepts of

---

[22] OV, 44.   [23] OV, 35.   [24] HC, 202.

174 Rethinking the Classical Legacy

power would lead us to expect that countries are more powerful the greater the ruler's power of command. Arendt's distinction between two kinds of power (power-over-others and power-to-do) helps to clarify why countries with all-powerful rulers tend to be fragile and weak, while leaders with limited powers can preside over countries that are dynamic and even domineering.

The key point for Arendt is that power exists only among human beings in the plural. The individual as such is powerless. The traditional concept of power, which focuses on a leader's power to command while overlooking its roots in her followers' power to act, leads us to think of power as something that could be possessed by one person alone. The basic error is to think of power on the model of strength.

Strength

Arendt argued that strength, in contrast to power, is a property of individuals. A person's strengths are those abilities that are entirely her own.

> Strength unequivocally designates something in the singular, an individual entity; it is the property inherent in an object or person and belongs to its character, which may prove itself in relation to other things or persons, but is essentially independent of them.[25]

Strength belongs to each person in the singular, while power exists only among people in the plural. And individual strength is usually no match for the power of a group: "The strength of even the strongest individual can always be overpowered by the many, who often will combine for no other purpose than to ruin strength precisely because of its peculiar independence."[26] It is this dissymmetry between strength and power that makes possible the peculiar tyranny of the weak over the strong.

Force

Force, in contrast to both strength and power, is something impersonal, according to Arendt. In her view, "force" strictly speaking refers to the pressure of impersonal objects or the dynamism of impersonal movements.

> Force ... should be reserved, in terminological language, for the "forces of nature" or the "force of circumstances" (*la force des choses*), that is, to indicate the energy released by physical or social movements.[27]

[25] OV, 44. [26] OV, 44. [27] OV, 44–45.

Rethinking the Classical Legacy

This kernel of sense is implicit in our everyday language when we speak of the "force of gravity," the "force of impact," the "force of compulsion," "market forces," or the "forces of production."

Authority

Authority is "the most elusive" of political phenomena, for Arendt, and also the most often misunderstood.[28] It is not a matter of coercion, since coercion is unnecessary as long as authority is recognized; people in positions of power tend to fall back on coercion or violence only when their authority begins to collapse. And authority is not a matter of persuasion, since persuasion can occur between equals, while authority always implies a hierarchy between those with authority and those without.

> If authority is to be defined at all, then, it must be in contradistinction to both coercion by force and persuasion through arguments. (The authoritarian relation between the one who commands and the one who obeys rests neither on common reason nor on the power of the one who commands; what they have in common is the hierarchy itself, whose rightness and legitimacy both recognize and where both have their predetermined stable place).[29]

The distinctive character of authority is evident in the free obedience it inspires: "Its hallmark is unquestioning recognition by those who are asked to obey; neither coercion nor persuasion is required."[30] This free obedience is ultimately grounded in a respect for some kind of recognized superiority. Authority can be conferred by superior insight; we see others as "authorities" when we recognize they really know what they are talking about. It can also be conferred by superior character; we recognize the "moral authority" of people who have led exemplary lives. Arendt also noted this superiority can be either personal or official: "Authority . . . can be vested in persons – as, for instance, in the relation between parent and child, between teacher and pupil – or it can be vested in offices, as, for instance, in the Roman senate (*auctoritas in senatu*) or in the hierarchical offices of the church."[31] While official authorities may have the right to give orders, the phenomenon of personal authority shows that authority in itself does not necessarily confer the ability to command obedience; we can follow the advice of a doctor or scholarly authority without granting her the right to tell us what to do. Authority is not the ability to command

[28] OV, 45.   [29] BPF, 93.   [30] OV, 45.   [31] OV, 45.

176   Rethinking the Classical Legacy

obedience but the ability to inspire respect. Since it depends on respect, it lasts only as long as respect is intact; when this respect dissolves, authority collapses. The speech proper to authority is not command, threat, or persuasion, but a kind of advice whose weight and force cannot safely be ignored: "The authoritative character of the 'augmentation' of the [Roman] elders lies in its being a mere advice, needing neither the form of command nor external coercion to make itself heard."[32] Authority may confer a kind of power, such as the ability to sway public opinion, but this power is a matter of influence rather than rule.

Violence

Violence, for Arendt, is essentially a means to an end: "Violence is by nature instrumental; like all means, it always stands in need of guidance and justification through the end it pursues."[33] So violence is not essentially irrational: "Violence, being instrumental by nature, is rational to the extent that it is effective in reaching the end that must justify it."[34] But while violence may be justified as a means to just ends, violence is always illegitimate within the sphere of politics. "Violence can be justifiable, but it will never be legitimate."[35] Since violence is not simply a matter of compulsion but of injury or violation, it is by definition extrapolitical. "To be political, to live in a polis, meant that everything was decided through words and persuasion and not through force and violence."[36] The various forms of violence (war, domination, terrorism, etc.) are matters of political concern, but they are not themselves political phenomena. Political life begins to break down precisely when public life starts to be ruled by intimidation and violence. Totalitarianism is anti-political in part because it sanctions violence and intimidation in public life. Politics is defined by the exclusion of violence.

Power and violence are essentially different, according to Arendt. While violence is a means to an end, power precedes the distinction between ends and means.

> This, of course is not to deny that governments pursue policies and employ their power to achieve prescribed goals. But the power structure itself precedes and outlasts all aims, so that power, far from being the means to an end, is actually the very condition enabling a group of people to think and act in terms of the means-end category.[37]

[32] BPF, 123.   [33] OV, 51.   [34] OV, 79.   [35] OV, 52.   [36] HC, 26.   [37] OV, 51.

Rethinking the Classical Legacy

While groups use power to achieve goals, the power of a group is independent of any specific goal for which power is used. It is true that most political groups crystallize around a specific aim, and they tend to dissolve when that aim is achieved, so it seems that the aim is primary and the power of a group depends on a common aim. But in principle it is always possible for a group to outlast the aim for which it formed and to pursue other aims, and this shows that the power of a group does not depend on any common aim. Power in this sense is the condition of possibility of effective action. The ability of a group to act in concert first makes it possible for the group to set goals and work towards them. Political power is not a means to an end; it is "an end in itself."[38]

Government

For Arendt the essence of government is simply power: "Power is indeed the essence of all government, but violence is not."[39] Governments are essentially organizations through which groups generate, regulate, and direct their power-to-act. It is futile to try to define government in terms of a purpose or end, for Arendt. If the essence of government is power, and if power precedes the distinction between means and ends, then it makes no sense to ask about the proper end of government.

> Since government is essentially organized and institutionalized power, the current question What is the end of government? does not make much sense either. The question will be either question-begging–to enable men to live together – or dangerously utopian – to promote happiness or to realize a classless society or some other nonpolitical ideal, which if tried out in earnest cannot but end in some kind of tyranny.[40]

It is a mistake to define government as essentially an instrument, whether as a means to rule and conquest, or as a means to security and self-preservation. Such definitions confuse the usual ends of government with its essence. Governments have no proper function or natural end, and it is precisely this lack of function or end that makes political institutions possible. Since government is a power structure that precedes the schema of means and ends, the absence of a naturally given end makes possible a form of community open to endless debate over questions of ends: How best to live together?

---

[38] OV, 51.   [39] OV, 51.   [40] OV, 51–52.

178 Rethinking the Classical Legacy

Contracts

If power is the essence of government, for Arendt, contracts are a means by which power is generated and sustained.

> In distinction to strength, which is the gift and possession of every man in his isolation against all other men, power comes into being only if and when men join themselves together for the purpose of action, and it will disappear when, for whatever reason, they disperse and desert one another. Hence, binding and promising, combining and covenanting are the means by which power is kept in existence; where and when men succeed in keeping intact the power which sprang up between them during the course of any particular act or deed, they are already in the process of foundation, of constituting a stable worldly structure to house, as it were, their combined power of action.[41]

Power is generated when people unite for the sake of action, and it exists only as long as the group stays united. The power of a group depends on the solidarity of its members, and this solidarity may be secured through oaths of allegiance or mutual promises.

Arendt distinguished two kinds of contract. A contract may be horizontal in the sense that it presupposes equality among those who enter into it. A group may come into being when a number of people pledge their commitment to one another. Such a group may choose a leader, but the allegiance of each member to the leader is secondary to the members' allegiance to each other. The act of coming together generates a collective power-to-do, and each member has a share of this power insofar as he or she has a part in its government.

> The mutual contract by which people bind themselves together in order to form a community is based on reciprocity and presupposes equality; its actual content is a promise, and its result is indeed a "society" or "cosociation" in the old Roman sense of *societas*, which means alliance. Such an alliance gathers together the isolated strength of the allied partners and binds them into a new power structure by virtue of 'free and sincere promises.'[42]

The crucial point, for Arendt, is that this form of government is especially conducive to the debate and deliberation essential to politics.

On the other hand, a contract may be vertical in the sense that it creates a hierarchy among those who enter into it. A group may come into being

---

[41] OR, 175. [42] OR, 170.

when a number of individuals each pledge their obedience to a single leader. The group is constituted by the allegiance of each member to the leader, and such groups can be extremely powerful as long as their leaders command the obedience of their followers. This kind of vertical contract is the basis of governments in which subjects consent to be ruled by a sovereign in exchange for the sovereign's protection.

> In the so-called social contract between a given society and its ruler, on the other hand, we deal with a fictitious, aboriginal act on the side of each member, by virtue of which he gives up his isolated strength and power to constitute a government; far from gaining new power, and possibly more than he had before, he resigns his power such as it is, and far from binding himself through promises, he merely expresses his "consent" to be ruled by the government, whose power consists of the sum total of forces which all individualized persons have channeled into it and which are monopolized by the government for the alleged benefit of all subjects.[43]

The crucial point, for Arendt, is that this form of government can dispense with politics altogether. All decisions can be made by a single leader, and the government can dispense with public debate or common deliberation.

The difference between these two kinds of contract is clear in the case of oligarchy. A few people may bind themselves together through a horizontal contract that prohibits relations of violence or hierarchy among members, and this contract can guarantee each member a say in deliberations over how their concerted power should be used. These few may then enter into a vertical contract with an atomized population, who consent to be ruled by the few in exchange for the protection of their safety and happiness. This vertical contract would institute an oligarchy – the rule of a few over many. But the horizontal contract among the oligarchs would allow the few to govern themselves without any form of hierarchy or rule.

Arendt argued these two kinds of contract, and the forms of government based on them, are essentially different.

> The [horizontal] mutual contract where power is constituted by means of promise contains *in nuce* both the republican principle, according to which power resides in the people ... and the federal principle ... according to which constituted political bodies can combine and enter into lasting alliances without losing their identity. It is equally obvious that

---

[43] OR, 170.

180   Rethinking the Classical Legacy

> the [vertical] social contract which demands the resignation of power to
> the government and the consent to its rule contains *in nuce* both
> the principle of absolute rulership ... and the national principle according
> to which there must be one representative of the nation as a whole, and
> where the government is understood to incorporate the will of all
> nationals.[44]

The horizontal contract among equals makes possible a form of government without rulership. The vertical contract among sovereign and subjects implicitly equates government with rule.

The equation of government with rule led modern political theorists to confuse these two kinds of contract, according to Arendt. Thinkers from Hobbes to Rousseau clearly recognized the difference between the two: the horizontal contract among individuals was supposed to constitute society, and the vertical contract between a society and its ruler was supposed to constitute the government. But the notion of rule led them to see these two kinds of contract as simply two sides of a single contract necessary for any political community.

> The decisive differences between these two kinds [of contract] (which
> hardly have more in common than a commonly shared and misleading
> name) were early neglected because the theorists themselves were primarily
> interested in finding a universal theory covering all forms of public rela-
> tionships, social as well as political, and all kinds of obligations; hence, the
> two possible alternatives of "social contract", which, as we shall see, actually
> are mutually exclusive, were seen, with more or less conceptual clarity, as
> aspects of a single twofold contract.[45]

The American revolutionaries inherited this confusion from British political theory.

The confusion of these two kinds of contract has obscured the nature of law, according to Arendt. Law has been traditionally conceived in terms of the vertical relation between ruler and subjects. In this view, a law is essentially the command of a sovereign. But – Arendt pointed out – this vertical relation is only one kind of power structure. Power may also be generated by a horizontal contract among equals, and this horizontal structure makes possible forms of government that exclude relations of rule among citizens. If the essence of government is not rule but power, not power-over others but the power-to-do, what then is the essence of law?

---

[44] OR, 171.   [45] OR, 169–170.

Rethinking the Classical Legacy 181

Law

Arendt argued that laws are in essence not imperatives but "directives" – not commandments but rules. The laws of a polity regulate how we live together, just as the rules of a game regulate how we play. We follow the laws of a community because we wish to live in it, just as we follow the rules of a game because we wish to play.

> The point of these rules is not that I submit to them voluntarily or recognize theoretically their validity, but that in practice I cannot enter the game unless I conform; my motive for acceptance is my wish to play, and since men exist only in the plural, my wish to play is identical with my wish to live. Every man is born into a community with preexisting laws which he "obeys" first of all because there is no other way for him to enter the great game of the world. I may wish to change the rules of the game, as the revolutionary does, or to make an exception for myself, as the criminal does; but to deny them on principle means no mere "disobedience," but the refusal to enter the human community . . . All laws are "'directives' rather than 'imperatives.'" They direct human intercourse as rules direct a game.[46]

One might object that this argument is absurd. Some laws may best be seen as directives, but others are obviously imperatives rather than directives. Think of monarchies where a sovereign's word is law. Such laws seem to be essentially a kind of command.

Arendt's argument aimed at a deeper level of law. Laws that take the form of commands presuppose a hierarchical power structure, and this hierarchy itself rests on the basic rules that govern the vertical relation between sovereign and subject. Sovereignty is made possible by rules that are not themselves laid down by the sovereign; commands always depend on rules that are not themselves commands. Sometimes these rules are explicit; an army may have rules that govern when soldiers should obey or disobey commands. Sometimes these rules are implicit; a culture may have a code of honor that governs who must obey whom. These basic rules do not command specific actions, but direct the interactions between those who command and those who obey. They are directives rather than imperatives. Law as imperative is made possible by law as directive.

How then are laws like the rules of a game?

For Arendt, humans can live together only by consenting to follow the basic laws of a community. Community is possible on the ground of this basic consent, just as games are possible on the basis of a shared consent to

---

[46] OV, 97.

182 Rethinking the Classical Legacy

the rules of the game. We follow basic laws because we want to live, just as we follow rules because we want to play.

The analogy between communities and games breaks down at one point: we choose the games we play, but for the most part we don't choose the communities in which we live. Initially we are simply born into communities we have not chosen, and we willingly or unwillingly consent to their laws. The fact that we must abide by laws in general does not mean that we have to accept the particular laws of our community. We can always try "to change the rules of the game, as the revolutionary does."[47]

The concept of directive clarifies the nature of law. It brackets certain traits that are implicit in the imperative conception of law, but that are inessential to law as such. It detaches the concept of law from notions of rule, will, and sovereignty. It frees questions of legitimacy from the quest for absolute, transcendent standards of right. And it dissolves the pseudo-problems inherent in common concepts of law. In particular, Arendt argued, the concept of law as directive dissolves the problem of the absolute:

> The common dilemma – either the law is absolutely valid and therefore needs for its legitimacy an immortal, divine legislator, or the law is simply a command with nothing behind it but the state's monopoly of violence – is a delusion.[48]

The problem of the absolute arises only if we conceive of law as a kind of commandment, according to Arendt: "Only to the extent that we understand by law a commandment to which men owe obedience regardless of their consent and mutual agreements, does the law require a transcendent source of authority for its validity, that is, an origin which must be beyond human power."[49] The concept of law as an imperative lends itself to philosophies that are anti-political, in that they aim to replace the deliberations of citizens with the commands of rulers who derive their authority either from the rational truth of philosophy or from the revealed truth of religion. By contrast, the concept of law as directive lets us grasp the nature of laws in polities that are not structured by vertical power relations between those who rule and those who are ruled.

Freedom

Arendt was highly critical of inherited concepts of freedom. Freedom cannot be conceived as liberation from subjection, she argued, because

---

[47] OV, 97.   [48] OV, 97.   [49] OR, 189.

Rethinking the Classical Legacy 183

while freedom requires liberation, liberation in itself is not freedom. Nor can freedom be conceived simply as freedom of choice or freedom from sin, since these concepts reduce freedom to a purely inner and unworldly condition. Nor can freedom be conceived as the negative liberty of individuals free of the constraints of government, or the positive liberty of people who rule themselves. Nor can freedom be conceived as the autonomy of a rational being who gives laws to herself. In each case freedom is conceived in terms of sovereignty and will, whether it is the inner sovereignty of the will (Epictetus), deliverance from sin through submission to the will of the Lord (Paul), the personal sovereignty of the individual who can do as she wills (Mill), the popular sovereignty of a group that is ruled by the general will (Rousseau), or the rational will of the autonomous individual (Kant).

These concepts of freedom contain two basic errors, for Arendt. The first is to conceive of freedom in terms of an individual will. This error has led philosophers to think of freedom starting from "Man" in the singular rather than humans in the plural. The second error is to conceive of freedom in terms of sovereignty: "their basic error seems to lie in that identification of sovereignty with freedom which has always been taken for granted by political as well as philosophic thought."[50] The identification of freedom with sovereignty is an error, for Arendt, because the ideal of absolute sovereignty is an illusion. To aspire to absolute sovereignty is to deny the plurality constitutive of human existence – the fact that being human means being with others.

> If it were true that sovereignty and freedom are the same, then indeed no man could be free, because sovereignty, the ideal of uncompromising self-sufficiency and mastership, is contradictory to the very condition of plurality. No man can be sovereign because not one man, but men, inhabit the earth.[51]

The illusion of sovereignty can be sustained in two ways: either through domination of one's self and of others; or through a retreat from the world into a realm of pure inwardness. In either case, Arendt thought, we are not really free.

The question is whether nonsovereign freedom is possible. Is there a way to be free that exceeds traditional concepts of freedom? Is true freedom possible under the human condition of plurality?

---

[50] HC, 234.   [51] HC, 234.

> The question which then arises is whether our notion that freedom and non-sovereignty are mutually exclusive is not defeated by reality, or to put it another way, whether the capacity for action does not harbor within itself certain potentialities which enable it to survive the disabilities of non-sovereignty.[52]

If absolute sovereignty is an illusion, what then is freedom?

Freedom in Arendt's view is primarily not a matter of thought or will but of action. We experience freedom not in choosing or willing but in doing. This experience is implicit in the classical interpretation of the Greek word for freedom.

> According to Greek etymology, that is, according to Greek self-interpretation, the root of the word for freedom, *eleutheria*, is *eleuthein hopos ero*, to go as I wish, and there is no doubt that the basic freedom was understood as freedom of movement. A person was free who could move as he wished; the I-can, not the I-will, was the criterion.[53]

The experience of freedom in worldly action is primary, Arendt claimed, while the experience of inner freedom is derivative: "The experiences of inner freedom are derivative in that they always presuppose a retreat from the world, where freedom was denied, into an inwardness to which no other has access."[54] The unworldly experience of inner freedom is possible only on the basis of our worldly existence. To be free of the world is still a way of being in the world.[55]

Essential to genuine freedom is the power to do. "For the ancients it was obvious that an agent could no longer be called free when he lacked the capacity to do – whereby it is irrelevant whether this failure is caused by exterior or by interior circumstances."[56] Negative liberty, autonomy, and freedom of choice are meaningless unless we have the power to do as we choose. Actual freedom is measured not by the absence of constraints, or by the capacity for self-rule, or by the ability to choose among alternatives. The measure of freedom is the range of what we can actually do.

The greater our power, the broader the range of what we can do. To increase our power-to-do is to increase our freedom. Hence, the most important instruments of freedom are the forms of mutual promises through which power is generated and sustained. Since the power generated by promises is possible only among human beings in the plural, the freedom opened up by such power is a nonsovereign freedom that accords with the human condition of plurality.

---

[52] HC, 235–236. [53] LMW, 19. [54] BPF, 146. [55] HC, 76. [56] BPF, 161.

Rethinking the Classical Legacy 185

> The faculty of promising is . . . the only alternative to a mastery which relies on domination of one's self and rule over others; it corresponds exactly to the existence of a freedom which was given under the condition of non-sovereignty.[57]

The freedom of people bound together by mutual promises is superior to the freedom of individual sovereignty for two reasons. First, any person or nation that isolates itself from others in order to preserve its sovereignty thereby reduces its power-to-do and so diminishes its real freedom; it is only through association with others that people increase their power-to-do and so expand the space of possibilities open to them. Second, any person or nation that avoids long-term commitments in order to preserve its future autonomy thereby reduces the temporal scope in which its power is effective and so again diminishes its real freedom. (It was this concern to preserve the will's autonomy that led Rousseau to conclude that "it is absurd for the will to bind itself for the future."[58]) By entering into long-term commitments, humans gain a measure of control over the future, and this control enormously increases their power-to-do and so increases their freedom. Arendt argued that it is only by renouncing the ideal of self-sufficiency and mastery, and by entering into contracts with others, that people together achieve real freedom. This freedom alone gives us a certain limited sovereignty.

> Sovereignty, which is always spurious if claimed by an isolated single entity, be it the individual entity of the person or the collective entity of a nation, assumes, in the case of many men mutually bound by promises, a certain limited reality. The sovereignty resides in the resulting, limited independence from the incalculability of the future, and its limits are the same as those inherent in the faculty itself of making and keeping promises. The sovereignty of a body of people bound and kept together, not by an identical will which somehow magically inspires them all, but by an agreed purpose for which alone the promises are valid and binding, shows itself quite clearly in its unquestioned superiority over those who are completely free, unbound by any promises and unkept by any purpose. This superiority derives from the capacity to dispose of the future as though it were the present, that is, the enormous and truly miraculous enlargement of the very dimension in which power can be effective.[59]

True freedom depends on power, and power is generated when people come together and act in concert. Freedom belongs not to sovereign monads but to humans in the plural. This insight throws new light on

[57] HC, 244.   [58] BPF, 164.   [59] HC, 245.

the relation between freedom and the mutual promises that constitute political communities. Such contracts are not just restrictions on individual liberty; they are the means by which freedom is increased and sustained.

True freedom is paradoxical, Arendt argued. Actions are free only if they are not determined by what came before: "An act can only be called free if it is not affected or caused by anything preceding it."[60] Freedom interrupts the chain of causes and effects and disrupts the quasi-automatic process of ruled-governed behavior. Free action does not simply follow from preexisting motives and move toward preestablished aims; it breaks with things as they are and brings something new into the world.

> Freedom as related to politics is ... the freedom to call something into being which did not exist before, which was not given, not even as an object of cognition or imagination, and which therefore, strictly speaking, could not be known. Action, to be free, must be free from motive on one side, and from its intended goal as a predictable effect on the other. This is not to say that motives and aims are not important factors in every single act, but they are its determining factors, and action is free to the extent that it can transcend them.[61]

This sounds strange because freedom eludes our usual ways of thinking. The idea of free action as an absolute beginning seems unthinkable. But it does not just *seem* unthinkable, Arendt argued, it *is* unthinkable in terms of traditional concepts of causality and continuity. The metaphysics we have inherited from Aristotle not only "denies the future as an authentic tense," but also obscures "the abyss of nothingness that opens up before any deed that cannot be accounted for by a reliable chain of cause and effect and is inexplicable in Aristotelean categories of potentiality and actuality."[62] Yet the unthinkable happens. Every free action "looks like a miracle."[63] People who take action confront "the abyss of freedom."[64] "This sounds stranger than it actually is. It is in the very nature of every new beginning that it breaks into the world as an 'infinite improbability,' and yet it is precisely this infinitely improbable which actually constitutes the very texture of everything we call real."[65]

Freedom in this sense is grounded in the human condition of *natality* – in the fact that each human being is born into the world as someone singular and new, with the capacity to bring something new into the world through free action. "Action has the closest connection with the human

[60] LMW, 210.   [61] BPF, 151.   [62] LMW, 15 and 207.   [63] HC, 246.
[64] LMW, 195–217.   [65] BPF, 169.

Rethinking the Classical Legacy 187

condition of natality; the new beginning inherent in birth can make itself felt in the world only because the newcomer possesses the capacity of beginning something new, that is, of acting."[66] Since free action is the *raison d'être* of political life, the basic trait of humans as political animals is not mortality but natality.

If free action is not determined by motives and goals, it would seem to be arbitrary. But arbitrariness is not freedom. To be free, actions must have something that guides them without simply determining them. How can action not be arbitrary, and at the same time not determined by some anterior ground?

Arendt answered this question by rethinking the concept of *principle*. To act freely, in her view, is to act on principle. Principles do not *determine* actions in the way that goals and motives do – they are too broad to set specific aims or to dictate particular courses of action. But principles "inspire" actions, in the sense that they are the animating spirit in which actions are performed.

> Action insofar as it is free is neither under the guidance of intellect nor under the dictate of the will – although it needs both for the execution of any particular goal – but springs from something altogether different which (following Montesquieu's famous analysis of forms of government) I shall call a principle. Principles do not operate from within the self as motives do ... but inspire, as it were, from without; and they are much too general to prescribe particular goals, although every particular aim can be judged in the light of its principle once the act has been started.[67]

How does this view of principle differ from traditional concepts of *arche* or *principium*? A principle in this sense is not a self-evident proposition. Like Aristotle, Arendt conceived of each practical principle as an origin of action that governs the action throughout its performance. Unlike Aristotle, she did not understand the governing power of a principle in terms of movement towards a *telos* (neither a *telos* outside the activity, as in the case of production, nor a *telos* achieved in the action itself). Arendt was closer to Montesquieu's concept of principle as that which "sets in motion and guides actions" in the public sphere.[68] But her concept of principle is more specific and precise than Montesquieu's. To see this, we have to look at her use of the word "principle" in her discussion of the act of foundation.

---

[66] HC, 9.   [67] BPF, 152.   [68] EU, 331.

188   Rethinking the Classical Legacy

Think of the founding of Rome. Arendt noted that, in *The Aeneid*, Rome was founded not just through military victory but through the mutual promises that made allies of the Latins and Trojans, and this act of foundation established the principle of alliance that governed Roman politics. "The genius of Roman politics – not only according to Virgil but, generally, according to Roman self-interpretation – lay in the very *principles* which attend the legendary foundation of the city."[69] These principles were not as general as the virtue (the love of equality) that Montesquieu identified as the principle of the Roman Republic, but not as specific as the particular motives and aims of the action. They were specific enough to govern the act of foundation, but general enough that they could continue to inspire and guide the actions of later generations.

This link between freedom and principled action was key to her interpretation of the American Revolution, the Declaration of Independence, and the founding of the United States, as we will see in Chapter 7.

In short, Arendt distinguished several senses of freedom. In the most basic sense, freedom is grounded in the human condition of being with others in a common world; we are free insofar as we share with others a horizon of possibilities within which we can act. On a less basic level, freedom is the expanded space of possibilities open to people who form groups through mutual promises that generate the power to act in concert. On a more derivative level, political freedom is the ability of citizens in a polity to have a share in its power and a voice in decisions about what to do and how to live together; it consists of "the citizen's right of access to the public realm, in his share in public power – to be 'a participator in the government of affairs' in Jefferson's telling phrase."[70] In this sense, people are not politically free when their concerted power to act is controlled from above by a despot, or an oligarchy, or a faceless bureaucracy; a polity is free to the extent that citizens have the right and ability to govern themselves. And on the most derivative level, "political freedoms" mean simply the rights and liberties that make politics possible: freedom of assembly; freedom of speech; the right to dissent; and the right to vote.

For the sake of clarity, I have divided Arendt's work into two parts: her rethinking of the legacy of classical political philosophy (this chapter); and her history of the American Revolution (Chapter 7). But her thought was

---

[69] OR, 210 (italics added).   [70] OR, 127.

Rethinking the Classical Legacy 189

not so neatly divided. She did not interpret the Revolution by simply imposing her concepts on historical events – her conceptual work depended as much on her interpretation of history as her interpretation of history was informed by her theoretical concepts. The task of the thinker and the task of the historian are complementary: the study of actual events can help attune thinkers to what eludes traditional concepts; and the attempt to question and refine traditional concepts can help historians see the past in a new light.

How then did Arendt interpret the American Revolution?

CHAPTER 7

On Politics and Revolution

A Forgotten Legacy

In her essay *On Violence* Arendt made a striking claim: Americans have forgotten the legacy of the American Revolutionaries. "The heritage of the American Revolution is forgotten."[1] What was the heritage of the Revolution? How has it been forgotten?

For Arendt this forgetting was not a matter of knowledge but of understanding. What has been lost is not the factual history but the meaning of events. The factual record is a text that we have to interpret to understand the meaning of the story, the nature of revolution, the experience of the revolutionaries, the principles that guided them, and the spirit that inspired their acts. We know a great deal about the Revolution, but we fail to fully understand it, and this failure of understanding is at the heart of our failure to remember.

Arendt explained this loss in two ways.

First, she claimed the revolutionaries themselves failed to fully grasp the meaning of the Revolution. This failure was not a lapse they could have avoided, but the inevitable result of their limited perspective. The actors in a historical drama can never fully understand the meaning of events as they live through them, since events always exceed the intentions and expectations of those who participate in them. People do not "make" history in the same way they make products or stories: "In contradistinction to fabrication, where the light by which to judge the finished product is provided by the image or model perceived beforehand by the craftsman's eye, the light that illuminates processes of action, and therefore all historical processes, appears only at their end, frequently when all the participants are dead."[2] Events are never wholly determined by the goals and motives of the actors, but are always the result of developments no one

[1] OV, 6. [2] HC, 192.

190

A Forgotten Legacy

could foresee or control. The meaning of events can only become clear in retrospect.

But this limited perspective does not fully explain the loss of understanding. After the War of Independence and the framing of the Constitution, the revolutionaries had the rest of their lives to reflect on what had happened. How could they have failed to fully grasp the meaning of the Revolution?

Arendt made a second argument: the colonists in America had been led by force of circumstances to develop relatively democratic practices of self-government. The town meetings and colonial assemblies had opened up a limited public realm and made possible the reemergence of a somewhat inclusive political sphere. The rebirth of a democratic political life in the colonies was a radical innovation that marked "a new beginning in the very midst of the history of Western mankind."[3] These practical innovations and political experiences allowed the colonists to understand the realities of political life better than the British and European theorists from whom they inherited their conceptual language. But despite their innovations in political practice, in their political theories the colonists remained bound to the conceptual framework of the European tradition: "The novelty of the New World's political development was nowhere matched by an adequate development of new thought."[4] Instead of rethinking inherited concepts in light of their own experiences, the colonists interpreted their experiences in terms of inherited concepts. There was a gap between the colonists' theoretical language and their nontheoretical understanding of politics. When the Revolution forced the colonists to justify their actions in theoretical terms, they fell back on formulas that had the authority of tradition but that failed to do justice to their real insights. So their practical understanding of politics remained theoretically inarticulate: "whenever they thought in general or in theoretical terms, that is, not in terms of action and the foundation of political institutions, their thought would remain shallow and the depth of their experience would remain inarticulate."[5] When the Revolution was over, and the revolutionaries tried in retrospect to articulate the truth of their experiences, their thinking was guided or misguided by the limits of traditional political philosophy.

> As far as Jefferson and the men of the American Revolution are concerned –
> again with the possible exception of John Adams – the truth of their

---

[3] OR, 194.   [4] OR, 195.
[5] Hannah Arendt, "Action and the 'Pursuit of Happiness,'" in *Politische Ordnung und Menschliche Existenz* (Munich: Verlag C. H. Beck, 1962), 10.

On Politics and Revolution

192

experience rarely came out when they spoke in generalities. Some of them, it is true, would get indignant about "the nonsense of Plato", but this did not prevent their thought from being predetermined by Plato's "foggy mind" rather than by their own experiences whenever they tried to express themselves in conceptual language.[6]

The revolutionaries failed to fully articulate the meaning of the Revolution because they interpreted it in traditional terms rather than revising and refining traditional terms in light of their actual experience.

This failure of thought led to a failure of public memory. Since the revolutionaries did not conceive of their experiences in terms that could fully grasp the meaning of events, they died without leaving behind a conceptual language that articulated and preserved their deepest insights. The truth of their experience remained largely unspoken.

> The American failure to remember can be traced back to this fateful failure of post-revolutionary thought. For if it is true that all thought begins with remembrance, it is also true that no remembrance remains secure unless it is condensed and distilled into a framework of conceptual notions within which it can further exercise itself. Experiences and even the stories which grow out of what men do and endure, of happenings and events, sink back into the futility inherent in the living word and living deed unless they are talked about over and over again. What saves the affairs of mortal men from their inherent futility is nothing but this incessant talk about them, which in its turn remains futile unless certain concepts, certain guideposts for future remembrance, and even for sheer reference, arise out of it.[7]

The colonists had broken with traditional practices of government, so the meaning of the Revolution could not be grasped in the terms of traditional political theory. But the revolutionaries failed to translate their experiences into a lasting conceptual framework, so that what was unprecedented in the revolution was obscured by the false clarity of received ideas. "The American failure to remember" is not a lack of knowledge but a lack of understanding. This lack of understanding has generated superficial interpretations of the past, which distort and conceal the meaning of the Revolution even as they claim to preserve and explain it.

Interpretations of the Revolution

Arendt specifically criticized three interpretations of the American Revolution.

---

[6] OR, 129.   [7] OR, 220.

Interpretations of the Revolution 193

1. *Classic liberal interpretations of the Revolution.* The American revolutionaries inherited from British political theory the language of liberalism. Classic liberals assume that each human being is endowed with natural rights; that the purpose of government is to protect those rights; that laws are instituted to establish a sphere of private life in which individuals can freely pursue their own ends as long as they do not violate the rights and liberties of others. Civil laws are just insofar as they rest on natural laws, and they are legitimate insofar as they have the consent of the governed. The consent of the governed is best achieved through representative government, in which the rights and interests of the governed are safeguarded by their representatives.

For the most part, the Revolutionaries interpreted their history in these terms. Most historians have followed their lead – the American Revolution has largely been interpreted as a triumph of classic liberalism: the colonists rebelled against an unrepresentative government that trampled their rights, and they successfully established a limited government based on human rights, legal equality, rule of law, and the consent of the governed.

The problem with this interpretation, Arendt argued, is that it does not quite explain why the revolutionaries founded a republic rather than a monarchy. One can have a liberal government under an enlightened monarch, and there is no reason why a constitutional monarchy cannot be a limited government based on human rights, legal equality, rule of law, and the consent of the governed. In some cases, a constitutional monarchy is actually more likely to protect civil rights and civil liberties than a republic, which is always liable to degenerate into a tyranny of the majority. The revolutionaries eventually decided a republic would most likely secure the ends of liberal government, but it seems implausible that liberal ideals were the only factor in that decision. Arendt argued that more was at stake in the American Revolution than liberal ideals.

> The guarantee of civil liberties and the pursuit of private happiness had long been regarded as essential in all non-tyrannical governments where the rulers governed within the limits of the law. If nothing more was at stake, then the revolutionary changes of government, the abolition of monarchy and the establishment of republics must be regarded as accidents, provoked by no more than the wrong-headedness of the old regimes. Had this been the case, reforms and not revolution, the exchange of a bad ruler for a better one rather than a change of government, should have been the answer.[8]

[8] OR, 134.

194   On Politics and Revolution

Liberal interpretations cannot fully explain several aspects of the Revolution: why events led the revolutionaries from the rejection of a particular monarch to a rejection of monarchy in general; why (in Jefferson's words) "the contests of that day were contests of principle, between the advocates of republican, and those of kingly government;"[9] why many Americans came to regard monarchy as a form of government fit for slaves;[10] and why most of the revolutionaries came to believe (in Jefferson's words) that freedom depended on a citizen's right to be "a participator in the government of affairs."[11]

2. *Christian interpretations of the Revolution.* In the traditional language of Christian political theories, human authority is valid insofar as it derives from divine authority; civil rights are legitimate insofar as they protect God-given rights; civil laws are just only to the extent that they conform to divine law. Governments are just and legitimate only as long as they represent the will of God.

The language of Christian political theory was sometimes explicit in the discourse of the revolutionaries. The Articles of Confederation of 1776 invoked "the Great Governor of the World." The Declaration of Independence declared that the principles of American government are based on "the Laws of Nature and of Nature's God," and the rights enumerated in the Declaration are said to be those with which all men have been "endowed by their Creator." Christian interpretations of American history tend to focus on this strand of revolutionary discourse, and sometimes even see the Revolution as an attempt to found a Christian nation.

Such interpretations rely on a selective reading of history. The belief that the revolutionaries meant to found a Christian nation is not supported by the facts. Arendt noted that the Constitution of 1787 never refers to God, and prohibits the use of religious tests to disqualify candidates for public office. The original opponents of the Constitution denounced it as an irreligious and Godless document, and yet it was ratified by a majority of state conventions. A treaty ratified by the Senate in 1797 made this explicit: "The government of the United States of America is not, in any

---

[9] OR, 33.
[10] The people of Malden, Massachusetts, urged the revolutionaries to declare independence from Britain, and to renounce "with disdain our connection with a kingdom of slaves" (OR, 310.).
[11] OR, 127.

sense, founded on the Christian religion."[12] Christian interpretations of American history focus on only one strand of colonial thought, and overlook the secular dimension of the Revolution.

3. *Social interpretations of the Revolution.* Arendt argued that, after 1776, freedom and revolution came to be understood less in political than in social terms. During the French Revolution it appeared that political liberties were meaningless in certain social conditions. Citizens with political rights were not free in a meaningful sense if they were utterly destitute, exploited, and oppressed. Real freedom required radical social change, and social change seemed less likely to be effected through political means than through government by decree or force. So the political questions that obsessed the American Revolutionaries were displaced by what French Revolutionaries called "the social question":

> From the later stages of the French Revolution up to the revolutions of our own time it appeared to revolutionary men more important to change the fabric of society, as it had been changed in America prior to its Revolution, than to change the structure of the political realm.[13]

The shift from political to social aims was explicitly recognized by Robespierre: "Republic? Monarchy? I know only the social question."[14] In the nineteenth century, Arendt argued, revolution came to be understood as essentially a social phenomenon – not the founding of a new political order but a radical transformation of society. Historians who approach the Revolution with the tools of social science have shifted attention from the actions of the revolutionaries to the underlying social and economic conditions that determined the course of events.

From this point of view, the American Revolution hardly seems like a revolution at all. The superficial shift from monarchy to a republic seems to hide an underlying continuity in social and economic structures. In Arendt's time the most famous proponent of this view was Charles Beard, whose history of the Revolution concluded that "The Constitution was essentially an economic document" designed to protect the class interests of the ruling elite.[15] In this account, the Constitutional Convention of

---

[12] *Treaties and Other International Acts of the United States of America*, vol. 2, ed. Hunter Miller (Washington: United States Government Printing Office, 1931), 349–385.
[13] OR, 25.   [14] OR, 56.
[15] Charles Beard, *An Economic Interpretation of the Constitution* (New York: Macmillan, 1936), 324.

1787 was not the culmination of the Revolution, but a betrayal of the possibilities of social change opened up by the upheaval of 1776.[16]

For Arendt, social interpretations of history are problematic in several ways. They tend to underemphasize the political dimension of the Revolution. They tend to approach the ideas of the revolutionaries not as a possible source of insight but as ideologies to be critiqued from the ostensibly superior perspective of social science or critical theory. And they tend to interpret the revolution in America in light of later revolutions and in terms of concepts grounded in experiences foreign to the experience of the American revolutionaries. Her deepest objection to these interpretations of American history is that they understand the Revolution in terms of inadequate concepts of politics and freedom.

These three failures of interpretation are not arbitrary mistakes, according to Arendt. They are grounded in the failures of post-revolutionary thought: "The result of the 'American' aversion from conceptual thought has been that the interpretation of American history, ever since Tocqueville, succumbed to theories whose roots of experience lay elsewhere."[17] Liberal, Christian, and social interpretations of Revolutionary history are inadequate because they conceal and forget the meaning of the Revolution under the guise of remembering it.

But the heritage of the Revolution has not vanished without a trace. The insights of the revolutionaries are preserved not in their theories, Arendt argued, but in their practical political documents and their nontheoretical writings.

> Still, there are more than a few instances when their profoundly revolutionary acting and thinking broke the shell of an inheritance which had degenerated into platitudes and when their words matched the greatness and novelty of their deeds. Among these instances is the Declaration of Independence.[18]

While the revolutionaries failed to articulate their practical understanding of politics in theoretical terms, their testimonies contain implicit insights that are far more incisive and illuminating than their explicit theories. A gap between explicit theory and implicit insight runs through all of their writings, including the Declaration of Independence. Arendt aimed to reinterpret the American Revolution in light of the authentic political insights implicit in the revolutionaries' nontheoretical writings.

---

[16] I am indebted here to Bruce Ackerman's discussion of Beard and Arendt in his book *We The People: Foundations* (Cambridge, MA: Harvard University Press, 1991), 200–229.

[17] OR, 220. [18] OR, 129.

How then did Arendt interpret the American Revolution? How did she read the writings of the revolutionaries?

Tasks of Interpretation

Arendt's approach to the Declaration was complex. She distinguished between theory and nontheoretical understanding, and between theoretical discourse (which uses precise and definite concepts) and ordinary language (which articulates our nontheoretical understanding). In her view, the task of theory is to refine our nontheoretical understanding of beings, and so theoretical language should explicate and clarify the nontheoretical insights implicit in the ordinary senses of words. But Arendt recognized that thinkers may work out theoretical concepts by abstracting words from everyday language while ignoring the insights implicit in their ordinary sense. And she recognized that writers may also borrow theoretical terms to try to articulate nontheoretical insights for which they have no other words. In both cases, a word may have at least two senses: a theoretical sense and a nontheoretical sense; and these two senses may actually conflict with one another. So there may be a tension in any text between explicit theory and implicit understanding, between the theoretical sense of words (the concepts they designate) and their nontheoretical sense (the insights they express). Such a tension is bound to produce ambiguities or inconsistencies in a text.

The possibility of this tension complicates the task of the historian. Arendt did not reject the tasks that commonly govern the interpretation of historical documents. It is necessary to learn the original language of a text, to read it in context, and to try to discern the intentions of the writer. But in her reading of the Declaration she tried to refine and supplement these principles. Her aim was not just to reconstruct the revolutionaries' self-interpretation, but also to show the tensions and blind spots in this self-interpretation in order to bring to light and make explicit the deeper understanding of politics implicit in their actions and words.

So Arendt's reading of revolutionary documents was guided by several tasks: (1) to understand the practical context in which the revolutionaries acted; (2) to learn the theoretical languages in which they thought and spoke; (3) to understand the testimonies of the revolutionaries in their own terms; (4) to look for tensions, ambiguities, or inconsistencies in their writings; (5) to read these tensions as symptoms of a gap between the theoretical concepts and the nontheoretical insights of the revolutionaries; (6) to show the limitations of their theoretical concepts by pointing out what they fail to grasp in the revolutionaries' testimony and in the unfolding of events; (7) to make explicit the nontheoretical political insights implicit in the words and actions of the revolutionaries; (8) to theoretically articulate these insights by rethinking inherited concepts; and (9) to clarify the meaning of the Revolution by reinterpreting events in light of this critical rethinking of traditional political theory.

These tasks of reading are part of the larger task of thought and remembrance. If the heritage of the American Revolution is forgotten, if this forgetting occurred because the revolutionary generation failed to rethink inherited concepts on the basis of their own experiences, if they did not do justice to their own experiences and insights when they interpreted them in terms of traditional theories, then we perpetuate this forgetting if we simply reconstruct the political theories of the founders. To recover the heritage of the Revolution, to understand the meaning of our history, we have to critically reread the testimony of the revolutionaries and critically rethink the concepts in which they thought. This is not to impose contemporary concepts on history, but to bring to light what has remained invisible and unthought in the American political tradition. The task of remembrance is a task of thinking.

Colonial Experiences

Arendt's interpretation of the Revolution started with a few simple arguments. The demands of emigration pushed the colonists to organize themselves into self-governing bodies through charters, covenants, and compacts. Through the practice of self-government the colonists developed a practical understanding of politics that diverged from traditional theories. This nontheoretical understanding of politics was handed down to the American revolutionaries and the writers of the Declaration of Independence. So the political principles implicit in the Declaration of Independence are not primarily derived from inherited theories, but were rooted in the practical experiences of the colonists.

The early colonists had little theoretical interest in politics in general or democracy in particular. If anything, they were proudly anti-political and anti-democratic. John Cotton, a leader of the Massachusetts Bay Colony, conceived of "Theocracy ... as the best form of government," and dismissed democracy with the question "if the people be governors, who shall be governed?"[19] Despite their aversion to democracy in theory, in practice

[19] OR, 171 and 308.

Colonial Experiences 199

the early settlers quickly developed relatively democratic forms of self-government. Their indifference to politics vanished in the face of dire circumstances – their mutual dependence, their need for effective group action, and the absence of any outside authorities. Arendt argued that the force of circumstances led the colonists to set up institutions of self-government, and that the experience of self-government led them to a few basic insights into the nature of political action.

> No theory, theological or political or philosophical, but their own decision to leave the Old World behind and to venture forth into an enterprise entirely of their own led into a sequence of acts and occurrences in which they would have perished, had they not turned their minds to the matter long and intensely enough to discover, almost by inadvertence, the elementary grammar of political action . . . What they discovered, to be sure, was no theory of social contract in either of its two forms, but rather the few elementary truths on which this theory rests.[20]

The theories of the colonists were less important to Arendt than the nontheoretical understanding of political matters implicit in their actions and words. Her task as an interpreter of the revolution was not to reconstruct the colonists' political theories but to retrieve their nontheoretical insights:

> For our purpose in general, and our attempt to determine with some measure of certainty the essential character of the revolutionary spirit in particular, it may be worthwhile to pause here long enough to *translate*, however tentatively, the gist of these pre-revolutionary and even pre-colonial experiences into the less direct but more articulate language of political thought.[21]

She aimed to translate the colonists' practical insights into theoretical terms.

Arendt focused in particular on the contracts by which the colonists organized themselves into self-governing communities. These contracts were economic and religious as well as political. They included the charters with which investors formed joint stock companies to finance the new settlements, the covenants with which the Puritans established new churches, and the compacts with which the settlers founded new towns. To follow her argument, it helps to look closely at three such contracts.

1. The Charter of the Massachusetts Bay Company made the company a self-governing body. It gave the stockholders the right to elect their

---

[20] OR, 173–174.   [21] OR, 174 (italics added).

200 On Politics and Revolution

leaders, and gave these leaders the "full Power and authoritie" to appoint officers, to hold assemblies, and to make and enforce laws within the company. It promised that "all such Orders, Lawes, Statuts and ordinances, Instructions and Directions ... shalbe carefullie and dulie observed." And it proclaimed that all members of the colony and their descendants would enjoy "all liberties and Immunities of free and natural subjects ... as if they and everie of them were borne within the Realme of England."[22]

2. The covenant of the first church of Boston actually preceded the incorporation of Boston itself. In the covenant, the settlers formed a congregation by promising to each other to live a Christian life:

> Wee whose names are hereunder written, being by His most wise, & good Providence brought together into this part of America in the Bay of Massachusetts, & desirous to unite our selves into one Congregation, or Church, under the Lord Jesus Christ our Head, in such sort as becometh all those whom he hath Redeemed, & Sanctifyed to Himselfe, do hereby solemnly, and religiously (as in His most Holy Proesence) Promisse, & bind o'selves, to walke in all our wayes according to the Rule of the Gospell, & in all sincere Conformity to His holy Ordinance, & in mutuall love, & respect each to other, so neere as God shall give us grace.[23]

In the churches established by such covenants, it was customary for congregations to decide the criteria for membership, and to appoint their ministers by vote. The first written ballot in America was actually used by the Salem congregation to elect a new minister.[24]

3. The Mayflower Compact, which the Pilgrims wrote at sea and signed the day they arrived in America, created a "civill Body Politick" on the basis of mutual promises.

> We, whose names are underwritten, the Loyal Subjects of our dread Sovereigne Lord, King James ... Having undertaken for the Glory of God, and Advancement of the Christian Faith, and the Honour of our King and Country, a Voyage to plant the first colony in the Northerne Parts of Virginia; doe, by these Presents, solemnly and mutually in the Presence of God and one of another, covenant and combine ourselves together into a civill Body Politick, for our better Ordering and Preservation, and Furtherance of the ends aforesaid; And by Virtue hereof do enact, constitute, and

---

[22] *The Charter of the Massachusetts Bay Colony: A Primary Source Investigation*, ed. Barbara A. Moe (New York: Rosen Publishing Group, 2002), 96.

[23] http://www.firstchurchbostonhistory.org/covenant.html.

[24] See Douglas Campbell, *The Puritan in Holland, England, and America*, vol. 2 (New York: Harper & Brothers, 1892), 437.

Colonial Experiences

frame such just and equall Laws, Ordinances, Acts, Constitutions, and Offices, from time to time, as shall be thought most meete and convenient for the Generall Good of the Colonie; unto which we promise all due Submission and Obedience.[25]

It is worth noting that the Pilgrims landed several hundred miles north of their land grant in Virginia, and were not authorized by the king to settle in Plymouth. Nevertheless, they authorized themselves to settle there, and gave themselves the right to elect their own governor.

These three contracts share certain features. All gave full members an equal say in electing leaders. All were based on the unanimous consent of the founding members, and all were guaranteed by mutual promises of support.

Arendt noted that these charters, covenants, and compacts became precedents for the founding of new communities. "This deed quickly became a precedent, and when, less than twenty years later [1639], colonists from Massachusetts emigrated to Connecticut, they framed their own 'Fundamental Orders' and 'plantation covenant' in a still uncharted wilderness, so that when the royal charter finally arrived to unite the new settlements into the colony of Connecticut it sanctioned and confirmed an already existing system of government."[26] Arendt also noted that these civil bodies quickly became more democratic. This was especially the case in the Massachusetts Bay Colony. Less than a year after the colonists arrived in America they turned the company charter into a kind of constitution. In 1631 the company gave almost 120 settlers the rights of the original stockholders. By 1641 all men in the colony were free to attend meetings in their towns, and by 1647 all men had the right to vote in town meetings. Despite their distrust of democracy in theory, in practice they quickly moved towards relatively inclusive and egalitarian forms of self-government.

Arendt claimed the colonists' use of contracts to form self-governing bodies was rooted not in theory but in a practical understanding of the nature of action and power. "Nothing but the simple and obvious insight into the elementary structure of joint enterprise as such ... caused these men to become obsessed with the notion of compact and prompted them

---

[25] David A. Weir, *Early New England: A Covenanted Society* (Grand Rapids, MI: Eerdmans Publishing Company, 2005), 85.
[26] OR, 167–168.

202 On Politics and Revolution

again and again 'to promise and bind' themselves to one another."[27] This claim requires some qualification.

It is true that the colonists worked out their forms of government in response to the practical demands of their situation. Once they found themselves cut off from established political powers and authorities, it quickly became clear that people were not going to follow leaders or obey laws they did not support. In the absence of traditional means of coercion and enforcement, there was no way to make people obey laws or leaders imposed on them from above. The most effective way to ensure that people supported the authorities was to give every full member of the community a say in the deliberations by which leaders were chosen and laws were made, in exchange for a promise to abide by whatever decisions the community reached. Town governments had to be inclusive in order to be effective. In practice this meant that all men who were independent enough to flout the authorities with impunity had to be included in the deliberations by which leaders were chosen and laws were established, since it was only when men had the opportunity to participate in the group's deliberations that they felt obliged to respect its decisions. Conversely, the colonists felt free to exclude from their meetings all those who were physically weak enough, or dependent enough on others, that they could be forced or coerced into obedience in other ways. It was also for practical reasons that town meetings were typically governed by the principle of consensus rather than of majority decision. In practice, a bare majority was rarely sufficient to make decisions authoritative; people in the minority could simply disregard majority decisions they disagreed with. Town meetings aimed at consensus because decisions were usually respected only when they had the support of all free men. (This view of colonial history is not confined to Arendt. Others have also argued that it was not theories but practical considerations that drove the first settlers to proto-democratic forms of self-government: "Not the principled notions of the New Englanders but the stern necessities of enforcement sustained town-meeting democracy in Massachusetts.")[28]

Arendt's claim is slightly misleading. It implies that the colonists' contracts were simply a natural solution to a practical problem. But there is no reason the contracts had to be horizontal (between equals) rather than

---

[27] OR, 173.

[28] Michael Zuckerman, "The Social Context of Democracy in Massachusetts," *The William and Mary Quarterly* 25:4 (October 1968): 523–544. Here I am gratefully indebted to Zuckerman.

Colonial Experiences

203

vertical (between each member of a group and a single leader). If the king had financed the colonists and had appointed representatives to rule them— to be responsible for their safety and welfare in exchange for their absolute obedience, then the contracts uniting the settlers would have been radically different. The colonists' decisions to organize themselves by means of horizontal contracts drew on a number of customs: as members of joint stock companies they were accustomed to an equal say in company business; as members of Puritan congregations they were accustomed to appointing their own ministers; and as Britons they were accustomed to the "liberties and Immunities of free and naturall Subjects." It was only in the context of these customs that it might have seemed "natural" to found communities on the principles of equality, common deliberation, and mutual promises.

What did the experience of self-government teach the colonists about the realities of politics? What were the insights they derived from their experiences?

Arendt argued that the colonists learned from experience two insights into the nature of action. First, that action requires plurality – individuals can initiate projects, but they need others to help carry them out. And second, that to act effectively a group does not have to be united by a common ancestry, similar motives, or shared beliefs; they only have to be united by a common interest:

> We then may say that the specifically American experience had taught the men of the Revolution that action, though it may be started in isolation and decided upon by single individuals for very different motives, can be accomplished only by some joint effort in which the motivations of single individuals – for instance, whether or not they are an "undesirable lot" – no longer counts, so that homogeneity of past and origin, the decisive principle of the nation-state, is not required.[29]

What united the colonists from the start was not a shared ancestry, language, religion, or nationality, but a practical commitment to the common good made necessary by the solidarity and mutual reliance required for concerted action.

The experience of concerted action led the colonists to a practical insight into the nature of power – that political power is generated and sustained by mutual promises. Arendt wrote that the demands of action taught the colonists:

---

[29] OR, 174.

> Power comes into being only if and when men join themselves together for the purpose of action, and it will disappear when, for whatever reason, they disperse and desert one another. Hence, binding and promising, combining and covenanting are the means by which power is kept in existence; where and when men succeed in keeping intact the power which sprang up between them during the course of any particular act or deed, they are already in the process of foundation, of constituting a stable worldly structure to house, as it were, their combined power of action.[30]

This practical understanding of power was essential to what happened in America:

> In other words, what had happened in colonial America prior to the Revolution (and what had happened in no other part of the world, neither in the old countries nor in the new colonies) was, theoretically speaking, that action had led to the formation of power and that power was kept in existence by the then newly discovered means of promise and covenant.[31]

Arendt's formulation here is not quite precise: what the colonists discovered was not that the power to act was sustained by mutual promises, but that these promises could constitute a purely horizontal contract among equals, rather than a vertical contract of allegiance between ruler and subjects.

Most importantly, Arendt argued, the effectiveness of these horizontal contracts led to an insight into the nature of politics. The colonists learned it is possible to form political communities that exclude any form of rule.

> The unique and all-decisive distinction between the settlements of North America and all other colonial enterprises was that only the British emigrants had insisted, from the very beginning, that they constitute themselves into "civil bodies politic." These bodies, moreover, were not conceived as governments, strictly speaking; they did not imply *rule* and the division of people into *rulers* and *ruled*.[32]

This does not mean that rule was absent in colonial America. There were obviously relations of domination between men and women, parents and children, masters and slaves, Europeans and Indians. What mattered to Arendt was that the colonists effectively founded polities based on the principle of equality among qualified "citizens," and that within these polities there were elected leaders but no constitutive hierarchy between rulers entitled to command and subjects obliged to obey.

---

[30] OR, 175.   [31] OR, 175–176.   [32] OR, 168 (italics added).

Colonial Experiences

The compacts also showed the difference between power, violence, and authority, according to Arendt. The proliferation of new settlements showed that polities could be founded without recourse to violence and without the authority of a higher power:

> The really astounding fact in the whole story is that their obvious fear of one another was accompanied by the no less obvious confidence they had in their own power, granted and confirmed by no one and as yet unsupported by any means of violence, to combine themselves into a "civil Body Politick" which, held together solely by the strength of mutual promise "in the Presence of God and one another", supposedly was powerful enough to "enact, constitute, and frame" all necessary laws and instruments of government.[33]

In the Massachusetts Bay Charter, for example, the "full Power and authoritie" of the elected leaders comes from the support and respect of those who elected them rather than from any claim to represent a higher authority. Arendt noted that when some of the colonists left Massachusetts to found Connecticut, they were able to establish a government by mutual agreement and to govern themselves for twenty three years before a royal charter retrospectively sanctioned their colony. In light of these events, it became clear that the local and colonial governments derived their effective authority not from the king but from the support and respect of the colonists themselves. This insight was not lost on the revolutionaries. John Adams stressed that the first colonial governments did not derive their authority from the British monarchy:

> The first planters of Plymouth were "our ancestors" in the strictest sense. They had no charter or patent for the land they took possession of; and derived no authority from the English parliament or crown to set up their government. They purchased land of the Indians, and set up a government of their own, on the simple principle of nature; ... and [they] continued to exercise all the powers of government, legislative, executive, and judicial, upon the plain ground of an *original contract among independent individuals*.[34]

The experience of self-government taught the colonists that political authority did not have to depend on the authority of a sovereign ruler.

The compacts also made it clear that political authority does not have to depend on religious authority. While in theory the Puritans believed that the laws of men had to rest on the commandments of God, Arendt noted,

---

[33] OR, 167.   [34] OR, 310 (Arendt's italics).

On Politics and Revolution

in practice they had discovered a way to make laws whose authority did not depend on any kind of higher law: "the act of mutual promise is by definition enacted 'in the presence of one another'; it is in principle independent of religious sanction."[35]

The experience of self-government also led to a new view of law and consent, according to Arendt. In drafting their compacts, the colonists assumed that the legitimacy of the laws rested on the consent of the community. But the consent implied in a horizontal contract among equals is essentially different from the consent implied in a vertical contract between ruler and subjects. In a vertical contract, subjects promise to obey the laws of a ruler, and in return the ruler promises to protect their basic rights and liberties. As long as these rights and liberties are secure, the subjects owe the ruler their unconditional obedience. "Consent" in this case means acquiescence to the will of a ruler. In a horizontal contract among equals, on the other hand, members of a community make laws through common deliberation and mutual promises, and the laws derive their legitimacy from the support of the community. Members are obliged to follow the laws because they had a chance to participate in making them, and because they have the chance to dissent and to try to persuade their peers that the laws should be changed. "Consent" in this case means an active support of communal agreements. The laws created by a horizontal contract are not imperatives but directives, and they rest not on a passive acquiescence to the will of a ruler but on an active fidelity to the mutual promises on which the laws are based. The spirit of American politics, for Arendt, was born of this new understanding of law:

> If Montesquieu was right – and I believe he was – that there is such a thing as "the spirit of the laws," which varies from country to country and is different in the various forms of government, then we may say that *consent*, not in the very old sense of mere acquiescence, with its distinction between rule over willing subjects and rule over unwilling ones, but in the sense of active support and continuing participation in all matters of public interest, is the spirit of American law.[36]

The spirit of American laws is this principle of consent: that laws are agreements; that they are legitimate to the extent that they have the active support of the people; that people are bound to follow the laws because they have the right to participate in the political process by which

---

[35] OR, 171.   [36] CR, 85 (italics added).

Colonial Experiences 207

they are made or rescinded, and also the right to dissent and to alter or abolish the laws.

Arendt thought the notion of consent in politics is often a fiction. It is a fiction to say, for example, that people consent to be ruled by a government in exchange for its protection. "Theoretically, this consent has been construed to be the result of a social contract, which in its more common form – the contract between and people and its government – is indeed easy to denounce as mere fiction."[37] It is also a mistake to think that a consent to the basic constitution of a society implies a consent to all its laws: "It is often argued that the consent to the constitution, the *consensus universalis*, implies consent to statutory laws as well, because in representative government the people have helped to make them. This consent, I think, is indeed entirely fictitious; under the present circumstances, at any rate, it has lost all plausibility."[38] It is also a fiction to attribute a kind of voluntary assent to laws by people who are excluded from the political community (e.g. disenfranchised women, children, slaves). Those who are excluded from politics are involuntarily subjected to the laws imposed on them.

But Arendt argued the notion of consent captures something essential to political institutions. We are all born into institutions we have not made or chosen; we have been thrown into them rather than joining them voluntarily. They depend for their existence on our willing or unwilling support. We are responsible for them to the extent that we have some room to act and to the degree that, however unwillingly, we tacitly support them. In this sense, tacit consent is not a matter of voluntary agreement to contracts we may choose to enter; it is a matter of responsibility for the institutions we are born into, institutions we have neither chosen nor made. In her view, this responsibility is a basic trait of human existence:

> Every man is born a member of a particular community and can survive only if he is welcomed and made at home within it. A kind of consent is implied in every newborn's factual situation; namely, a kind of conformity to the rules under which the great game of the world is played in the particular group to which he belongs by birth. We all live and survive by a kind of tacit consent, which, however, it would be difficult to call voluntary ... Seen from this perspective, tacit consent is not a fiction; it is inherent in the human condition.[39]

[37] CR, 85. [38] CR, 89. [39] CR, 88.

On Politics and Revolution

Her point is that we are responsible not only for what we have voluntarily chosen or done. We all find ourselves in institutions we have not chosen, but which depend for their existence on our (voluntary or involuntary) support.

Arendt thought the experience of self-government made this kind of consent glaringly obvious to the colonists: "the point is that [consent] was no mere fiction in the American pre-Revolutionary experience."[40] The New England town meetings aimed at consensus precisely because the colonists knew from experience that the effective authority of the laws depended on the consent of the townsmen. The practical need for consensus led to a clear understanding of consent.

> Consent as it is implied in the right to dissent – the spirit of American law and the quintessence of American government – spells out and articulates the tacit consent given in exchange for the community's tacit welcome of new arrivals, of the inner immigration through which it constantly renews itself.[41]

In other words, the experience of self-government taught the colonists that the power of political institutions ultimately depends on the willing or unwilling support of those who belong to them. The political principles of consent and dissent help to maintain that support by giving citizens a way to actively take responsibility for inherited institutions, whether that responsibility takes the form of preserving, altering, or abolishing them.

Experience in self-government also showed the basic role of opinion in politics. Precisely because the power of a community depends on the citizens' consent to its institutions, Arendt argued, these institutions ultimately rest on the citizens' opinions:

> It is the people's support that lends power to the institutions of a country, and this support is but the continuation of the consent that brought the laws into existence to begin with ... All political institutions are manifestations and materializations of power; they petrify and decay as soon as the living power of the people ceases to uphold them. This is what Madison meant when he said "all governments rest on opinion," a word no less true for the various forms of monarchy than for democracies.[42]

The power of political bodies, for Arendt, rests on the opinions of their members.

The experience of self-government also changed the colonists' understanding of freedom, in her view. In the British liberal tradition, liberty

---

[40] CR, 85.   [41] CR, 88.   [42] OV, 41.

Colonial Experiences

was conceived as liberation from subjection and independence from the arbitrary will of others. The purpose of government was to protect the right to liberty through laws that secured civil rights and civil liberties. Governments were instituted to establish a sphere of private life in which individuals could freely pursue their own ends as long as they respected the rights and liberties of others. Liberty was supposed to exist outside the political realm, in the sphere of private life. Arendt argued that in town meetings and colonial assemblies the colonists experienced a freedom that exceeded this inherited concept of liberty: not freedom from the power of a ruler, but the freedom that comes from having a share in the power of a self-governing body. Once the colonists had tasted this freedom, they were tempted to retrospectively reinterpret their history by positing this freedom as the end for the sake of which their ancestors had come to America. Arendt laid out this argument in a few sentences worth quoting in full.

> Thus Jefferson himself – in a paper for the Virginia Convention of 1774 which in many respects anticipated the Declaration of Independence – had declared that "our ancestors" when they left the "British dominions in Europe" exercised "a right which nature has given all men, . . . of establishing new societies, under such laws and regulations as to them shall seem most likely to promote public happiness." If Jefferson was right and it was in quest of "public happiness" that the "free inhabitants of the British dominions" had emigrated to America, then the New World must have been the breeding grounds of revolutionaries from the beginning. And, by the same token, they must have been prompted even then by some sort of dissatisfaction with the rights and liberties of Englishmen, prompted by a desire for some kind of freedom which the "free inhabitants" of the mother country did not enjoy. This freedom they called later, when they had come to taste it, "public happiness", and it consisted in the citizen's right of access to the public realm, in his share in public power – to be "a participator in the government of affairs" in Jefferson's telling phrase – as distinct from the generally recognized rights of subjects to be protected by the government in the pursuit of private happiness even against public power.[43]

In America the colonists discovered a kind of freedom that British subjects did not have – not just the liberty of individuals who are free from the power of government in their private lives, but also the freedom of citizens who have the power to enter public life and to govern themselves. The colonists rediscovered political freedom in the Greek sense of the term: they were free in the sense that they were able to participate in self-government as equals who were willing neither to rule nor to be ruled.

[43] OR, 127.

On Politics and Revolution

This new experience of freedom led the colonists to a new sense of the dignity and happiness of political life. They were heirs to a philosophical tradition that assumed the active life was lower than the contemplative life, and that the highest happiness lay in philosophy rather than politics. Politics was supposed to be only a means to a higher end, and public life was merely a burden one assumed for the sake of a secure and prosperous private life. Arendt thought the experience of self-government led the colonists to a different estimation of politics. In the town meetings and colonial assemblies they learned that public life liberated them from the isolation and weightlessness of private matters, and that the gravity of political action and the solidarity of political life afforded them a distinct kind of happiness, what they called "public happiness."

> They knew very well, and John Adams was bold enough to formulate this knowledge time and again, that the people went to the town assemblies, as their representatives later were to go to the famous Conventions, neither exclusively because of duty nor, and even less, to serve their own interests but most of all because they enjoyed the discussions, the deliberations, and the making of decisions.[44]

The experience of public life led the colonists to value self-government over any form of rule, and led them to believe it is better to live as a citizen among equals than to live as the subject of even the most enlightened ruler.

Finally, Arendt suggested, these "civil bodies politick" led the colonists to a deep understanding of the ethos of democratic self-government. The town meetings and colonial assemblies were governed by the principles of common deliberation and mutual promises, and so the colonists developed a respect for the virtues of deliberative discourse: civility, judgment, impartiality, mutual respect. They also developed a sense of the sanctity of mutual promises; the obligation to support common agreements was for them a matter of sacred honor. And they developed a sense of public spirit: a concern for the common good; a commitment to public service; and a willingness to subordinate certain private interests to the interests of the community as a whole. The colonists developed a political ethos – a set of principles, virtues, and concerns essential to the success of self-government. In Arendt's view, politics has an ethical basis in the sense that political life demands of citizens a specific ethos: "Every organization of men, be it social or political, ultimately relies on man's capacity for making promises and keeping them. The only strictly moral duty of the

---

[44] OR, 119.

The Revolution

citizen is this twofold willingness to give and keep reliable assurance as to his future conduct, which forms the pre-political condition of all other, specifically political virtues."[45] The demands of self-government pushed them to develop an ethos that supported their political institutions.

In sum: Arendt argued that the practical demands of emigration and settlement led the colonists to develop a distinctive political culture. Pushed by the need for collective order and effective group action, they learned to use covenants and compacts to organize themselves into relatively democratic communities. It quickly became clear that in the absence of official authorities the most practical form of government was self-government. The best way to get people to support town governments was to hold town meetings and to include in the political process all those who could not simply be forced to obey. Democracy was necessary where force did not work. The experience of self-government gave the colonists real insight into the basic realities of political life: action, power, authority, law, consent, and freedom. It also led them to appreciate the happiness of political action and the dignity of political life. The emergence of town meetings and colonial assemblies marked a new birth of politics in the modern age. But despite their innovations in political practice, the colonists remained bound to the conceptual framework of European political theory and their practical insights remained theoretically inarticulate.

Arendt's interpretation of colonial history framed her view of the Revolution. How then did she interpret the American Revolution?

The Revolution

Arendt distinguished revolutions from similar phenomena, such as rebellions, restorations, civil wars, and *coups d'état*. "Revolutions are more than successful insurrections and ... we are not justified in calling every *coup d'état* a revolution or even in detecting one in each civil war."[46] In a rebellion, people rise up against an oppressive government. In a restoration, an illegitimate ruler is deposed and replaced with a legitimate heir to power. In a civil war, different factions of a nation engage in open combat. In a *coup d'état*, a small group seizes power by force. Even in the common sense of the word, "revolution" refers to something distinct – a fundamental change in the form of government and the birth of a new political order.

---

[45] CR, 92.   [46] OR, 34.

This concept of revolution is relatively recent: "The modern concept of revolution, inextricably bound up with the notion that the course of history suddenly begins anew, that an entirely new story, a story never known or told before, is about to unfold, was unknown prior to the two great revolutions at the end of the eighteenth century."[47] Before the American War of Independence, the word "revolution" had been used to name restorations of monarchical power, such as the return of the Stuart monarchy in 1660, and the overthrow of James II and the coronation of William and Mary in 1688. When "revolution" was first applied to political events, the word still had the sense of cyclical motion. It meant not a new beginning but a return to the old order of things.[48] While the word "revolution" existed in the eighteenth century, eighteenth-century political discourse had no concept for what happened in America between 1776 and 1787. "Although there were enough words in pre-modern political language to describe the uprising of subjects against a ruler, there was none which would describe a change so radical that the subjects became rulers themselves."[49]

Arendt argued that premodern political language lacked a concept of revolution because revolution itself is a distinctly modern phenomenon: "revolutions, properly speaking, did not exist prior to the modern age."[50] There were of course rebellions before 1776, but these rebellions were not revolutions in the modern sense of the word: "The aim of such rebellions was not a challenge of authority or the established order of things as such; it was always a matter of exchanging the person who happened to be in authority, be it the exchange of a usurper for the legitimate king or the exchange of a tyrant who had abused his power for a lawful ruler."[51] While there had often been revolts in which subjects exchanged a bad ruler for a better one, Arendt thought, there had rarely been popular uprisings that aimed to change the form of government itself.

To grasp what a revolution is we have to understand the events that engendered the modern sense of the word.

> If we want to learn what a revolution is – its general implications for man as a political being, its political significance for the world we live in, its role in modern history – we must turn to those historical moments when revolution made its full appearance, assumed a kind of definite shape, and began to cast its spell over the minds of men, quite independent of the abuses and cruelties and deprivations of liberty which might have caused them to rebel.

---

[47] OR, 28.   [48] OR, 42.   [49] OR, 41.   [50] OR, 12.   [51] OR, 40.

The Revolution

> We must turn, in other words, to the French and the American Revolutions...[52]

What happened in America between 1776 and 1787? What was the nature of the event? What does it mean to call the event a revolution? What is revolution?

Arendt stressed that the American Revolution began as a restoration – an attempt by the colonists to correct abuses of power by the British authorities, and to restore their civil rights and civil liberties as British subjects. The colonists claimed their actions were firmly based on precedent. In particular, they appropriated the language of the Glorious Revolution of 1688 in order to claim as a precedent the events that had deposed James II and established William and Mary on the British throne. They called the Continental Congress a "convention" after the illegal meeting of Parliament that presided over the events of 1688. They called their statement of principles a "Bill of Rights," and modeled it on the Bill of Rights adopted by Parliament in 1689. Above all, by calling themselves "revolutionaries" they claimed to be more faithful to the legacy of the Glorious Revolution than the British authorities.[53] The colonists at first aimed only to restore the old order of things: "They pleaded in all sincerity that they wanted to revolve back to old times when things had been as they ought to be."[54] Ben Franklin wrote that, at the start of the Revolution, no one wanted independence from Britain: "I never had heard in any Conversation from any Person drunk or sober, the least Expression of a wish for a Separation, or Hint that such a Thing would be advantageous to America."[55] The initial aim of the revolutionaries was to restore the old order.

But the aim of the Revolution changed. The goal of reconciliation with Britain gave way to the goal of independence, and the aim of the revolutionaries shifted from the restoration of a constitutional monarchy to the foundation of a republic.

It was not inevitable that the United States would become a republic. Arendt noted that some colonists envisioned a new American monarchy: "even in 1776 a correspondent to Samuel Adams could still write: 'We now have a fair opportunity of choosing what form of government

---

[52] OR, 43–44.

[53] Thomas Paine wrote: "It is somewhat extraordinary, that the offence for which James II was expelled, that of setting up power by assumption, should be reenacted, under another shape and form, by the parliament that expelled him. It shows, that the rights of man were but imperfectly understood at the Revolution." Thomas Paine, *The Rights of Man* (New York: Penguin, 1985), 43.

[54] OR, 44.   [55] OR, 44.

214 On Politics and Revolution

we think proper, and contract with any nation we please for a king to reign over us'."[56] A new monarchy would have been consistent with the original aims of the revolutionaries: since the revolutionaries first aimed only to restore their civil rights and civil liberties, these rights and liberties could well have been protected under a constitutional monarchy.

> Constitutional government was even then, as it is still today, limited government, in the sense in which the eighteenth century spoke of a "limited monarchy", namely, a monarchy limited in its power by virtue of laws. Civil liberties as well as private welfare lie within the range of limited government, and their safeguard does not depend on the form of government.[57]

If the aim of the Revolution were only to restore a limited constitutional government, it is not clear why the revolutionaries moved from the condemnation of a particular monarch to a condemnation of monarchy in general, or why they eventually decided that the only form of government worthy of a free people was a republic. Why did the Revolution end in the foundation of a republic?

Arendt answered these questions with a simple thesis: in the course of events the aim of the revolutionaries shifted from liberation to freedom.

Liberation in her view means emancipation from subjection. To be liberated means to be free from any higher power. Liberation aims at negative freedom: to be at liberty means to be free from any form of constraint or compulsion. The civil liberties guaranteed by liberal government are negative freedoms in this sense – freedom of speech means freedom from restraints on speech; freedom of movement means freedom from constraints on movement. The aim of classic political liberalism is to limit the power of government and so to protect these essentially negative liberties.

Freedom, on the other hand, is for Arendt the space of possibilities that are actually open to us. To be free means not simply to be free of constraints, but to have the power to act. The measure of freedom is the range of what we can actually do. Freedom in this sense depends on power. Power is generated when people form communities that can act in concert. The power-to-act generated by political communities increases the range of what citizens can do. Political power in this sense opens a space of freedom.

---

[56] OR, 297. [57] OR, 143.

The Revolution 215

Civil liberties and political freedom are thus distinct, according to Arendt. Liberty means limits on the power of government; freedom means a share in the power of government. Emancipation from oppression is a matter of liberation; enfranchisement as a citizen is a matter of freedom.

But civil liberties and political freedom are intrinsically related, Arendt argued, since liberty is a condition of political freedom. No political community is possible without the right to free speech, the right to assemble, without the security guaranteed by the right to life, etc. The liberties protected by liberal government are the conditions but not the essence of political freedom: "All these liberties, to which we might add our own claims to be free from want and fear, are of course essentially negative; they are the results of liberation but they are by no means the actual content of freedom, which, as we shall see later, is participation in public affairs, or admission to the public realm."[58]

What happened during the Revolution was that the struggle for liberation became a fight for political freedom. Before 1776 the practice of self-government had allowed the colonists to experience a certain degree political freedom: "What was a passion and a 'taste' in France clearly was an experience in America."[59] But the Revolution forced them to engage in public life with unprecedented commitment and intensity; from 1765 to 1775, in response to a series of acts by Parliament that interfered with their customary self-government, the colonists learned to organize meetings, demonstrations, boycotts, civic associations, committees of correspondence, committees of public safety, militias, illegal assemblies, and finally Continental Congresses. It was in the course of events that the revolutionaries fully realized the power of concerted action and the happiness of public life.

> It was in the very nature of their enterprise that they discovered their own capacity and desire for the "charms of liberty", as John Jay once called them, only in the very act of liberation. For the acts and deeds which liberation demanded of them threw them into public business, where, intentionally or more often unexpectedly, they began to constitute that space of appearances where freedom can unfold its charms and become a visible, tangible reality.[60]

The struggle for liberation led the revolutionaries to embrace political life. It forced them into "the speechmaking and decision-taking, the oratory and the business, the thinking and the persuading, and the actual doing"

---

[58] OR, 32.   [59] OR, 119.   [60] OR, 33.

216   On Politics and Revolution

that is the gist of politics.[61] The life-or-death stakes of their enterprise minimized the factionalism and the power struggles that we today tend to identify with politics. And against the weight of their whole tradition – for which public life was supposed to be a burden, and politics a necessary evil – they discovered that political action gave them an unexpected sense of happiness: "It was through these experiences that those who, in the words of John Adams, had been 'called without expectation and compelled without previous inclination' discovered that 'it is action, not rest, that constitutes our pleasure'."[62] The experience of political action pushed the revolutionaries to shift their aims from a defense of their civil rights and liberties to a fight for political freedom.[63]

This fight for political freedom is essential to revolution. While the end of rebellion is liberation, Arendt wrote, the end of revolution is freedom: "the aim of revolution was, and always has been, freedom."[64]

The revolutionaries ended up rejecting monarchy and founding a republic, she argued, precisely because the aim of the revolution shifted from liberation to freedom. While a constitutional monarchy could have protected their civil rights and civil liberties, only a republic could provide an institutional space for the practice of politics and the freedom of self-government.

> The difficulty here is that revolution as we know it in the modern age has always been concerned with both liberation and freedom. And since liberation, whose fruits are absence of restraint and possession of 'the power of locomotion', is indeed a condition of freedom ... it is frequently very difficult to say where the mere desire for liberation, to be free from oppression, ends, and the desire for freedom as the political way of life begins. The point of the matter is that while the former, the desire to be free from oppression, could have been fulfilled under monarchical – though not under tyrannical, let alone despotic – rulership, the latter necessitated the formation of a new, or rather rediscovered form of government; it demanded the constitution of a republic.[65]

Unlike the British in 1660 and 1688, the American revolutionaries were not content to exchange a bad ruler for a better one while retaining the

---

[61] OR, 34.   [62] OR, 34.

[63] This was also a thesis of Pauline Maier in *American Scripture*: "The experience of self-government under the ad-hoc institutions of the revolution itself provided a powerful argument for republicanism." Pauline Maier, *American Scripture: Making the Declaration of Independence* (New York: Knopf, 1997), 92.

[64] OR, 11.   [65] OR, 33.

The Revolution 217

same form of government. They aimed to found a new form of government.

Founding a new form of government is essential to revolution, for Arendt:

> Only where change occurs in the sense of a new beginning, where violence is used to constitute an altogether different form of government, to bring about the formation of a new body politic, where the liberation from oppression aims at least at the constitution of freedom, can we speak of revolution.[66]

A successful revolution ends in the constitution of a new form of government, a government that abolishes the division between ruler and subjects and that allows citizens to govern themselves.

Arendt thought this experience of political innovation was itself new: "This relatively new experience, new at any rate to those who made it, was at the same time the experience of man's faculty to begin something new."[67] And this new experience of political innovation was at the root of the revolutionaries' "pathos of novelty" – the sense that they were inaugurating a new order of the ages. Thomas Paine articulated this pathos when he wrote that "We have every opportunity and every encouragement before us, to form the noblest, purest constitution on the face of the earth. We have it in our power to begin the world over again ... The birthday of a new world is at hand."[68] This pathos of novelty distinguished the American Revolution from the restorations of 1660 and 1688. For Arendt, it is an essential trait of revolution: "Only where this pathos of novelty is present and where novelty is connected with the idea of freedom are we entitled to speak of revolution."[69]

Arendt suggested that one more trait may be essential to revolution. Both the American and the French Revolutions ended up founding secular states, and establishing a clear distinction between politics and religion. Political authority no longer needed the sanction of religious authority. Positive laws no longer had to be grounded on divine law. The realm of politics was no longer included within and subordinated to the realm of religion.

> Secularization, the separation of religion from politics and the rise of a secular realm with a dignity of its own, is certainly a crucial factor in the phenomenon of revolution. Indeed, it may ultimately turn out that what

---

[66] OR, 35.   [67] OR, 34.   [68] Thomas Paine, *Common Sense* (New York: Penguin, 1986), 120.
[69] OR, 34.

218 On Politics and Revolution

we call revolution is precisely that transitory phase which brings about the birth of a new, secular, realm.[70]

The secularization of politics may perhaps also be an essential trait of revolution. The American Revolution, in this way, marked the rebirth of politics as a distinct sphere of existence with a meaning and a dignity of its own.

What then is the meaning of revolution? What distinguishes revolution from other forms of political upheaval?

Arendt singled out four traits of the American Revolution. It aimed not just at liberation from oppression but at political freedom. It ended with the founding of a new form of government. It was marked by a pathos of novelty rooted in an intense experience of the human capacity for innovative action. And it separated politics from religion, and so marked the rebirth of politics as a distinct sphere of existence. The War for Independence gave the word "revolution" a new sense – revolution as a popular insurrection that aims to establish a sphere of political freedom by founding a new form of government. Arendt did not think this was the *only* proper sense of the word; but she thought it was a distinct sense, born of a distinct phenomenon of modern politics.

How did the revolutionaries themselves understand revolution?

On a practical level they understood the meaning of revolution, Arendt argued, but in their theorizing they failed to fully grasp and articulate what they were doing. It was clear to them that the aim of the Revolution was freedom: "once the revolutions had begun to run their course ... the novelty of the story and the innermost meaning of its plot became manifest to actors and spectators alike. As to the plot, it was unmistakably the emergence of freedom."[71] But they did not clearly distinguish between liberation and freedom, civil rights and political rights, freedom from tyranny and the freedom of self-government: "those who tried their hand at both liberation and the foundation of freedom more often than not did not distinguish between these matters very clearly either."[72] The revolutionaries acted on the practical understanding of politics that had developed from the first compacts among the colonists through decades of town meetings and colonial assemblies, and their actions revealed a new understanding of some of the basic realities of politics. But in their theories the revolutionaries remained indebted to the conceptual framework of

---

[70] OR, 26. [71] OR, 29. [72] OR, 33.

The Revolution 219

British political discourse, and the nontheoretical insights of the revolutionaries were interpreted or misinterpreted in terms of traditional political theory.

Political freedom, for example, was described in terms of civil liberties.

> Since their original intention had not been the foundation of freedom but the recovery of the rights and liberties of limited government, it was only natural that the men of the revolution, when finally confronted by the ultimate task of revolutionary government, the foundation of a republic, should be tempted to speak of the new freedom, born in the course of the revolution, in terms of ancient liberties.[73]

The revolutionaries justified their actions with appeals to the traditional rights to property and to representation for the purposes of taxation. They rejected the British claim that they were "virtually" represented in Parliament, and they argued that only the elected colonial assemblies had the authority to set taxes. In doing so, their defense of traditional rights merged with their claim to a right to self-government. And this claim was entirely new: "Among the rights, the old privileges and liberties of the people, the right to a share in government was conspicuously absent. And such a right to self-government is not even fully present in the famous right of representation for the purposes of taxation."[74] By conceiving their fight for political freedom as a defense of civil liberties, the revolutionaries obscured the real meaning of what they were doing.

In the same way, for Arendt, the revolutionaries' practical understanding of power was obscured by inherited concepts of sovereignty and rule. The colonists had learned to generate political power with horizontal contracts of mutual promises, and the Revolution showed how deeply this practice had taken root: "What the American Revolution actually did was to bring the new American experience and the new American concept of power out into the open."[75] The Revolution unleashed at the state and national level the colonial practice of covenant and compact: "Since the colonial governments had originally been made without any reference to king or prince, it was as though the Revolution liberated the power of covenant and constitution-making as it had showed itself in the earliest days of colonization."[76]

> The astounding fact that the Declaration of Independence was preceded, accompanied, and followed by constitution-making in all thirteen colonies

---

[73] OR, 155.   [74] OR, 41.   [75] OR, 166.   [76] OR, 168.

On Politics and Revolution

revealed all of a sudden to what extent and entirely new concept of power and authority, an entirely novel idea of what was of prime importance in the political realm had already developed in the New World, even though the inhabitants of this world spoke and thought in the terms of the Old World and referred to the same sources for inspiration and confirmation of their theories.[77]

The collapse of royal power in the colonies showed that the power of rulers is always derivative, in the sense that it derives from the support of a group and collapses when that group withdraws its support. The power of citizens acting in concert was shown when the colonists essentially forced the British to repeal unpopular policies (the Stamp Act and the Townsend duties). The Revolution itself showed the difference between power-over-others and the power-to-do, between the power to command generated by a vertical contract between ruler and subjects, and the concerted power generated by horizontal compacts among equals. Despite these experiences, Arendt argued, the revolutionaries continued to think of political power in terms of sovereignty and rule.

> Just as the old concept of liberty, because of the attempted restoration, came to exert a strong influence on the interpretation of the new experience of freedom, so the old understanding of power and authority, even if their former representatives were most violently denounced, almost automatically led the new experience of power to be channeled into concepts which had just been vacated.[78]

The revolutionaries abolished institutions of sovereign rule and established institutions of self-government. But by conceiving of self-government in terms of "self-rule" and "popular sovereignty," they obscured the nature of republican government and distorted their own practical understanding of political power.

So there was a gap between the revolutionaries' political theories and their nontheoretical understanding of politics. This gap ran through all revolutionary discourse, including the Declaration of Independence. To understand the Declaration, Arendt suggested, it is not enough to trace its language back to British political theories. We have to focus on tensions and ambiguities within the text of the Declaration, and to read them as symptoms of a tension between implicit insight and explicit theory. How then did Arendt read the Declaration of Independence?

---

[77] OR, 166.   [78] OR, 155.

The Declaration of Independence

In 1776 the revolutionaries confronted a fundamental problem: after the British dissolved the colonial assemblies, the revolutionaries had no lawful claim to power. Their lawmaking was illegal and their attempt to constitute a new government was unconstitutional. When they sought to declare independence and to establish a new political order, they could not legitimate their actions within the established order. They had no official authority.

This problem is inherent in all revolutionary action, according to Arendt. Revolutionary action is always caught in a vicious circle: it is legitimate within the order it seeks to found, and illegitimate within the order it seeks to replace.

> Those who get together to constitute a new government are themselves unconstitutional, that is, they have no authority to do what they have set out to achieve. The vicious circle in legislating is present not in ordinary lawmaking, but in laying down the fundamental law, the law of the land or the constitution which, from then on, is supposed to incarnate the 'higher law' from which all laws ultimately derive their authority.[79]

Ordinary lawmaking may be authorized by the basic laws of a constitution. But revolution – the act of laying down basic laws – cannot be authorized by any prior law.

> What the royal charters and the loyal attachment of the colonies to king and Parliament in England had done for the people in America was to provide their power with the additional weight of authority; so that the chief problem of the American Revolution, once this source of authority had been severed from the colonial body politic in the New World, turned out to be the establishment and foundation not of power but of authority.[80]

The fundamental problem was a problem of foundations: What is the source and ground of political authority?

Political authority became a problem only with the emergence of secular politics, according to Arendt. As long as politics was subordinated to religion, the authority of worldly power was unquestionably grounded in the authority of the church. It was the separation of politics and religion that raised questions about the source of political authority: "Secularization, the emancipation of the secular realm from the tutelage

---

[79] OR, 184.   [80] OR, 178.

On Politics and Revolution

of the Church, inevitably posed the problem of how to found and constitute a new authority."[81] The act of foundation made authority a problem.

The problem of authority is different from the problem of power. The colonists had learned to generate power through compacts of mutual promises, but power alone is not enough to found a stable and lasting government.

> While power, rooted in a people that had bound itself by mutual promises and lived in bodies constituted by compact, was enough "to go through a revolution" (without unleashing the boundless violence of the multitudes), it was by no means enough to establish a "perpetual union", that is, to found a new authority. Neither compact nor promise upon which compacts rest are sufficient to assure perpetuity, that is, to bestow upon the affairs of men that measure of stability without which they would be unable to build a world for their posterity, destined and designed to outlast their own mortal lives.[82]

To be stable, governments need not just power but authority. They have to inspire enough respect that citizens will support the laws and follow them freely. To found a government on a constitution that has nothing behind it but the will of a sovereign (whether that sovereign is a king, a class, or a majority) is to build a government on a foundation of sand. A constitution without authority may be changed at will or replaced whenever a new sovereign comes to power. The revolutionaries knew that the act of foundation would be futile if the constitution did not inspire (in the words of James Madison) "that veneration which time bestows on every thing, and without which the wisest and freest government would not possess the requisite stability."[83] They sought not just to constitute a new power structure but to found a new authority.

The Revolution raised basic questions: What legitimates fundamental laws? What gives authority to a constitution? What is the ultimate ground of political authority?

"The Laws of Nature and of Nature's God"

In her genealogy of authority, Arendt argued that Christian thinkers had adopted the Roman distinction between power and authority, conceding worldly power to kings but claiming authority for the Church. For centuries royal power had needed the sanction of the Church in order to

---

[81] OR, 160.   [82] OR, 182.   [83] OR, 203.

have authority. Christian thinkers had also adopted the Aristotelean notion of natural law and the Platonic assumption that the authority to rule is conferred by knowledge of transcendent and absolute standards of right, and they identified these absolute standards with the laws of God revealed in the scriptures and the laws of nature discoverable by reason. Worldly rulers had authority only if they obeyed the laws of nature and of God.

The American revolutionaries inherited this tradition, Arendt argued, and took for granted three basic assumptions: (1) political authority must be based on standards of right that are absolute, in the sense that they do not depend on us and are obligatory regardless of our consent; (2) political authority must be based on standards that are transcendent in the sense that they transcend human power and so transcend the realm of politics; (3) political authority ultimately has to be sanctioned by *religious* authority – "authority as such had become unthinkable without some sort of religious sanction."[84]

These assumptions underlie a traditional dilemma in political theory. It seems that political authorities are either sanctioned by a higher authority, or else they rule simply because they have power. Either laws are derived from a transcendent source of authority, and so are obligatory in and of themselves, or else laws are simply the dictates of those in power, commands that ultimately rest on nothing more than the threat of force. The revolutionaries seemed to be caught in this dilemma. They were acutely aware that they had no official authority, and that they were vulnerable to the accusation that the revolution was simply a war for power.

The revolutionaries responded to the problem of authority by falling back on traditional theories of natural right, Arendt argued, and by invoking a higher law of nature beyond the laws of human beings. They began the Declaration by appealing to "the Laws of Nature."

> For the men of the Revolution, who prided themselves on founding republics, that is, governments "of law and not of men", the problem of authority arose in the guise of the so-called "higher law" which would give sanction to positive, posited laws. No doubt, the laws owed their factual existence to the power of the people and their representatives in the legislatures; but these men could not at the same time represent the higher source from which these laws had to be derived in order to be authoritative and valid for all, the majorities and the minorities, the present and the future generations.[85]

---

[84] OR, 160.   [85] OR, 182.

224 On Politics and Revolution

The appeal to natural law responded to the demand for an absolute and transcendent source of political authority, since laws of nature are by definition independent of human thought and beyond human power.

But the appeal to natural law was not enough. Early modern political theorists assumed that natural laws in themselves had no authority unless they had been authored by a divine legislator. This assumption led Locke to conclude that the fundamental law of civil society could only be founded on an "appeal to God in Heaven." It led Rousseau to conclude that in order to establish human laws on higher laws "one would need gods." It led Robespierre to attempt to found a cult of the Supreme Being.[86] The revolutionaries inherited this assumption, which was implicit in traditional concepts of authority, and were unable to conceive of political authority without religious sanction. This is why they added to their appeal to natural law an appeal to "Nature's God."

> In order to be a source of authority and bestow validity upon man-made laws, one had to add to "the law of nature", as Jefferson did, "and nature's God", whereby it is of no great relevance if, in the mood of the time, this god addressed his creatures through the voice of conscience or enlightened them through the light of reason rather than through the revelation of the Bible. The point of the matter is that natural law itself needed divine sanction to become binding for men.[87]

To be authoritative, human law had to be founded on natural law, and natural law itself had to be authored by a divine legislator.

The same logic underlies the appeal to natural rights. Just as positive law had to be based on divine law, so positive rights had to be based on God-given rights. So the Declaration says not just that all men have certain unalienable rights, but that they are endowed with such rights by their Creator. The idea that positive rights must be derived from God-given rights followed from the assumption that political authority needed religious sanction. This assumption underlies the claim that American political institutions ultimately rest on a religious foundation – that (in the words of Justice William O. Douglas) "We are a religious people whose institutions presuppose a Supreme Being."[88]

This assumption is complicated by a stubborn fact: there is no mention of God in the Constitution of the United States. The founders who wrote it did not appeal to a Supreme Being. This absence of God in the Constitution did not go unnoticed in 1787. During and after the debates

---

[86] OR, 185 and 184.   [87] OR, 190.   [88] OR, 312.

The Declaration of Independence 225

over ratification, the Constitution was denounced as a godless document. Timothy Dwight lamented that "We formed our Constitution without any acknowledgment of God; without any recognition of His mercies to us, as a people, of His government, or even of His existence. The convention, by which it was formed, never asked even once, His direction, or his blessings, upon their labors. Thus we commenced our national existence under the present system, without God."[89] Yet after the process of debate and ratification, the Constitution was accepted as authoritative, and it continues to inspire a respect bordering on veneration.

How to explain this tension? The appeal to God seems essential to the authority of the Declaration. How could it fail to appear in the Constitution? To understand this tension we have to see the gap between the revolutionaries' theoretical concepts and their practical understanding of political authority.

In their *practical understanding* of political authority, the revolutionaries' thinking was rooted in the colonial experience of self-government. The first settlers had learned to use compacts to form political bodies that elected their own leaders and made their own laws, and the practice of self-government then expanded into town meetings and colonial assemblies. In these political bodies, it became clear that the authority of leaders and laws rested on the respect of the governed rather than on any claim to represent a higher authority. And this respect rested in turn on the fact that they had been chosen through a political process governed by principles of common deliberation and mutual promises. Members were obliged to respect the outcome of the process precisely because they had a chance to participate in deliberations and had an equal say in the final decision. Without quite understanding what they were doing, Arendt argued, the colonists learned to constitute political bodies whose authority did not depend on religious sanction: "the act of mutual promise ... is in principle independent of religious sanction."[90] In the practice of self-government they came to understand laws not as the commands of a ruler but as promises among equals. And so they came to understand that political authority does not necessarily depend on the sanction of a higher authority, but rests on the respect for laws inspired by the political process itself.

But in their *theorizing*, the revolutionaries still felt compelled to appeal to a higher authority, since they continued to think of politics in terms of

---

[89] Timothy Dwight, quoted in Isaac Kramnick and R. Laurence Moore, *The Godless Constitution* (New York: Norton, 1997), 105–106.
[90] OR, 171.

On Politics and Revolution

inherited concepts. Arendt traced the lineage of this inheritance in her genealogy of the concept of law. The traditional concept of law was in part the legacy of theories of absolute monarchy, for which worldly power needed the sanction of religious authority.

> The whole problem of an absolute which would bestow validity upon positive, man-made laws was partly an inheritance from absolutism, which in turn had fallen heir to those long centuries when no secular realm existed in the Occident that was not ultimately rooted in the sanction given to it by the Church, and when therefore secular laws were understood as the mundane expression of a divinely ordained law.[91]

More importantly, for Arendt, the traditional concept of law was the legacy of Christian theories of government, which conceived authority on the model of a divine ruler and conceived law on the model of divine commandments.

> It was of even greater importance and impact that the very word 'law' had assumed an altogether different meaning throughout these centuries. What mattered was that – the enormous influence of Roman jurisprudence and legislation upon the development of medieval as well as modern legal systems and interpretations notwithstanding – the laws themselves were understood to be commandments, that they were construed in accordance with the voice of God, who tells men: *Thou shalt not.* Such commandments obviously could not be binding without a higher, religious sanction.[92]

Law was understood on the model of divine commandment: "the model in whose image Western Mankind had construed the quintessence of all laws, even of those whose Roman origin was beyond doubt ... was itself not Roman at all; it was Hebrew in origin and represented by the divine Commandments of the Decalogue."[93] This model of law led the revolutionaries to assume that political laws were analogous to the laws of God, and that, in order to have authority, secular law had to be the mundane expression of divinely ordained law. Arendt argued that the revolutionaries felt compelled to appeal to an absolute and transcendent source of authority because in theory they continued to conceive of laws as commands.

> There was no avoiding the problem of the absolute ... because it proved to be inherent in the traditional concept of law. If the essence of secular law was a command, then a divinity, not nature but nature's God, not reason but a divinely informed reason, was needed to bestow validity on it.[94]

[91] OR, 189. [92] OR, 189. [93] OR, 189. [94] OR, 195.

The Declaration of Independence

The Declaration's appeal to God was required by the traditional concept of law and traditional theories of political authority.

This demand for a transcendent source of authority was based on a misconception of law, Arendt argued. Laws seem to require a transcendent source of authority only when they are conceived as commands that are obligatory in and of themselves.

> Only to the extent that we understand by law a commandment to which men owe obedience regardless of their consent and mutual agreements, does the law require a transcendent source of authority for its validity, that is, an origin which must be beyond human power.[95]

To conceive of laws as commandments is to think of them as imperatives. But laws are essentially directives. Laws do not need a transcendent source of authority in order to be authoritative.

> The common dilemma – either the law is absolutely valid and therefore needs for its legitimacy an immortal, divine legislator, or the law is simply a command with nothing behind it but the state's monopoly on violence – is a delusion. All laws are "'directives' rather than 'imperatives.'" They direct human intercourse as the rules direct the game.[96]

As a matter of theory, the appeals to the laws of nature and of nature's God were the solution to a false problem.

The Constitution of the United States is godless because it embodies the Founders' nontheoretical understanding of law. The Founders understood that political authority does not have to be based on religious authority, and that the fundamental laws of a people do not have to be based on natural or divine laws. They established a secular government, and a political sphere distinct from the sphere of religion.

The Declaration embodies the tension between this practical understanding of law and the concept of law the revolutionaries inherited from the tradition. The traditional concept of law led them to believe that laws needed religious sanction, even when experience had taught them in practice to create authoritative laws without any appeal to religious authority.[97]

A similar tension appears in the Declaration's Bill of Rights.

---

[95] OR, 189.   [96] OV, 97.
[97] Here I am indebted to Frederick M. Dolan, *Allegories of America: Narratives, Metaphysics, Politics* (Ithaca: Cornell University Press, 1994), 191.

228   On Politics and Revolution

"We Hold These Truths to be Self-Evident"

The Declaration has two sides. On the one hand, it is an act of revolution – an attempt to unite the colonists, to win over allies, to renounce allegiance to the British crown, and to found a new nation. On the other hand, it is a brief statement of political theory – an attempt to justify a break with Britain and to state the basic principles of a new government. In a sense the Declaration is two documents in one: a practical political document aimed at getting things done, and a theoretical document grounded on an appeal to self-evident truths.

The appeal to self-evident truth has a long history. Arendt argued that it goes back to Plato, who aimed to replace the self-government of citizens through persuasion with the rule of philosopher-kings through true knowledge.

> It was after Socrates' death that Plato began to discount persuasion as insufficient for the guidance of men and to seek for something liable to compel them without using external means of violence. Very early in his search he must have discovered that truth, namely, the truths we call *self-evident*, compels the mind, and that this coercion, though it needs not violence to be effective, is stronger than persuasion and argument.[98]

The task of the political philosopher, for Plato, is to know the true measures of right, to make these truths evident to reason, and to design an ideal polity on the basis of these self-evident truths. This task was taken up by John Locke, who aimed to discover principles of right that were as self-evident as the axioms of mathematics: "I doubt not but from self-evident propositions, by necessary consequences, as incontestable as those in mathematics, the measure of right and wrong might be made out."[99] This task passed from Locke to the American Revolutionaries, who justified their actions through an appeal to "self-evident" "truths." Jefferson later wrote that his intent in the Declaration was "to place before mankind the common sense of the subject in terms so plain and firm as to command their assent."[100] His model of self-evident truth was mathematical demonstration, the rigorous deduction of theorems from a few self-evident principles. In the Bill of Rights he imitated the form of mathematical

---

[98] BPF, 107–108 (italics added).
[99] John Locke, *An Essay Concerning Human Understanding* (London: Oxford University Press, 1904), 208.
[100] Jefferson, quoted in Garry Wills, *Inventing America: Jefferson's Declaration of Independence* (New York: Random House, 1978), 191.

The Declaration of Independence 229

reasoning, laying out a few principles of political theory and then deducing from them a right to revolution.

But the Declaration has another side. Arendt noted that it was also modeled on the colonial compacts that the first settlers used to found "civil bodies politic." Like those compacts, it contains a statement of basic principles, a pledge of mutual support, and the signatures of the founders. As a practical document – as an act of revolution rather than a statement of theory – the Declaration was part of a long tradition of colonial charters, covenants, and compacts.

So the Declaration is modeled on two different kinds of discourse, and these two forms of discourse have different kinds of validity. The principles of mathematics are absolutely valid, in that their validity does not depend on our consent. They are valid whether or not we agree with them, and they are beyond our power to change. As a theoretical document, the Declaration claims that its principles are valid in this absolute sense. By contrast, the principles in the founding charter of a political body derive their validity only from the agreement of the body; they are valid only as long as they are held by the body, and they can be altered or abolished whenever they lose the body's support. As a practical document the Declaration sought to establish its validity by claiming and winning over the support of the colonists. There is a tension in the Declaration between two kinds of discourse, and these two different claims to validity.

This tension produces a remarkable ambiguity. The Declaration's Bill of Rights begins with the words: "We hold these truths to be self-evident." These words are so familiar we tend not to notice that they are profoundly strange. Their strangeness comes from a tension between the affirmation "We hold" and the appeal to "self-evident" "truths."

The appeal to "self-evident" "truths" belongs to the discourse of theory. It implies the principles of the Declaration are absolutely valid, that they articulate absolute standards against which the relative legitimacy of governments can be measured, that their validity does not depend on their effectiveness or on the support of the people, that they are beyond human power, and that they transcend the realm of politics.

The affirmation "We hold" belongs to the discourse of practical politics, the language of compacts and reciprocal promises. It shows that the Declaration is in part an act of agreement. "We hold" implies that the Bill of Rights is part of an act of mutual commitment to a shared set of principles, that the validity of the principles depends on this commitment rather than on any claim to absolute truth. The value of these principles is not a matter of truth but of effectiveness – whether the principles seem

230 On Politics and Revolution

most likely to "effect" the safety and happiness of the people. And the meaning of these principles is not self-evident; they are open to interpretation.

It would make sense to say, "We hold these principles to be most likely to effect our safety and happiness." It would make sense to say, "These truths are self-evident." But to say "We hold these truths to be self-evident" is to say something profoundly strange. If the text is simply a statement of truth, the "We hold" is inexplicable. Why bother to affirm that "we hold" principles to be self-evident if those principles really are self-evidently true? If the text is a declaration of agreement, the claim to self-evidence is superfluous. Why bother to declare that principles are "self-evident," when what is at stake is whether they seem most likely to effect our safety and happiness?

Arendt argued that the words "We hold these truths to be self-evident" conflate in one sentence two essentially different kinds of discourse.

> Jefferson's famous words, "We hold these truths to be self-evident", combine in a historically unique manner the basis of agreement between those who have embarked upon revolution, an agreement necessarily relative because related to those who enter it, with an absolute, namely with a truth that needs no agreement since, because of its self-evidence, it compels without argumentative demonstration or political persuasion.[101]

In the affirmation of self-evidence there is a tension between two essentially different claims to validity.

There is an obvious historical explanation for this tension: in the first draft of the Declaration Jefferson wrote, "We hold these truths to be sacred and undeniable." The affirmation "We hold" makes sense in the context of this profession of faith. But Jefferson (perhaps influenced by Ben Franklin) later changed "sacred and undeniable" into "self-evident."[102] It may have been that, under the pressure of events, he did not realize it makes no sense to profess faith in something self-evident.

But Arendt suggested a more illuminating explanation: this tension was produced by the gap between the revolutionaries' political theories and their practical understanding of politics. The revolutionaries inherited from the philosophical tradition the theoretical project of founding a government on absolute and transcendent standards of right, political

---

[101] OR, 192.
[102] Carl Becker thought this change might have been made by Ben Franklin: Carl Becker, *The Declaration of Independence: A Study in the History of Political Ideas* (New York: Random House, 1922), 142. Garry Wills noted there is no evidence for this view (Wills, *Inventing America*, 238).

The Declaration of Independence

231

principles as clear and certain as the principles of mathematics. But they had also inherited from the earliest colonists the practice of constituting political bodies through compacts of mutual promises, and they knew that political principles did not depend for their authority on claims to absolute truth but that their authority rested on opinions about the way of life they made possible.

Arendt made three points about the claim to self-evidence.

First, she argued that the principles are not self-evident. Their meaning is not transparent, and a single meaning cannot be made obvious to any rational person. They have been interpreted differently by reasonable people for almost 250 years. The principles of the Declaration are not self-evidently true in the same sense as the axioms of mathematics. The claim to self-evidence should be understood rather as an affirmation of consensus among the revolutionaries, according to Arendt. To say they are self-evident is to affirm that we consider them beyond dispute.

> Thus in the Declaration of Independence, Jefferson declared certain "truths to be self-evident," because he wished to put the basic consent among the men of the revolution beyond dispute and argument; like mathematical axioms, they should express "beliefs of men" that "depend not on their own will, but follow involuntarily the evidence proposed to their minds." Yet by saying "We hold these truths to be self-evident," he conceded, albeit without becoming aware of it, that the statement "All men are created equal" is not self-evident but stands in need of agreement and consent – that equality, if it is to be politically relevant, is a matter of opinion, and not "the truth."[103]

To be clear: Arendt was not criticizing the principles of the Declaration. To deny the self-evidence of the principles is not to deny the principles themselves. She believed the rights set down by Jefferson are essential to political freedom. She did not believe they are self-evident.

Second, the attempt to base political authority on self-evident truth is misguided, according to Arendt. The search for absolute standards of right led the revolutionaries to misconceive the principles of government on the model of the principles of mathematics, and to misconceive political laws on the model of mathematical laws.

> The fallacy of this position was not only to equate this compelling evidence with right reason – the *dictamen rationis* or a veritable dictate of reason – but to believe that these mathematical 'laws' were of the same nature as the laws of a community, or that the former could somehow inspire the latter.[104]

[103] BPF, 246.   [104] OR, 193.

On Politics and Revolution

In her view, the "We hold" is an implicit concession by Jefferson that the principles of the Declaration did not have the same kind of validity as mathematical truths.

> Jefferson must have been dimly aware of this, for otherwise he would not have indulged in the somewhat incongruous phrase, "We hold these truths to be self-evident", but would have said: These truths are self-evident, namely, they possess a power to compel which is as irresistible as despotic power, they are not held by us but we are held by them; they stand in no need of agreement.[105]

It is simply fallacious to think that political principles are essentially the same as mathematical principles, and that the laws of a community are essentially the same as the laws of mathematics.

Third, Arendt argued it is anti-political to base arguments on claims to self-evident truth, since what is self-evident is not subject to debate, and debate is essential to politics.

> "All governments rest on opinion," James Madison said, and not even the most autocratic ruler or tyrant could ever rise to power, let alone keep it, without the support of those who are like-minded. By the same token, every claim in the sphere of human affairs to an absolute truth, whose validity needs no support from the side of opinion, strikes at the very roots of all politics and all governments.[106]

To claim that political principles are self-evidently true is to claim that they belong outside the political realm and are not open to debate.

The appeal to self-evident truths is ambiguous. It conflates two different kinds of discourse in a single sentence: a theoretical discourse that claims to be absolutely valid; and a practical discourse whose validity depends on consent. Arendt argued that this ambiguity results from a tension between the revolutionaries' political theories and their practical understanding of politics. The legacy of political philosophy led them to assume authority had to be grounded on a knowledge of absolute and transcendent standards of right. But the experience of self-government showed that political authority ultimately rested on the opinions of citizens. Arendt saw this sentence not as a claim to absolute truth but as the affirmation of a basic consensus of the American people. The affirmation would mean that all Americans support these principles at this level of generality, but that when it comes to specifying what they mean there is room for dissent and reasoned debate.

[105] OR, 193.   [106] BPF, 233.

The Declaration of Independence

"All Men are Created Equal"

The Declaration says that all men are by nature equal. The implication is that political inequality is unnatural. If humans are born equal, they become unequal through institutions that divide them into the rulers and the ruled.

Arendt stressed that this view differs from older concepts of political equality. For the classical Athenians, the value of equality under the law (isonomy) was not that it preserved the natural equality of men, but that it instituted a community of citizens in which men could meet as equals despite their natural inequality: "Isonomy guaranteed ἰσότης, equality, but not because all men were born or created equal, but, on the contrary, because men were by nature (φύσει) not equal, and needed an artificial institution, the polis, which by virtue of its νόμος [law] would make them equal."[107] Equality for the Greeks was strictly political rather than natural, social, or moral: "Equality existed only in this specifically political realm, where men met one another as citizens and not as private persons." So equality was essentially political – an artificial status rather than a natural condition: "The equality of the Greek polis, its isonomy, was an attribute of the polis and not of men, who received their equality by virtue of citizenship, not by virtue of birth."[108]

Arendt shared this view of political equality: "We are not born equal; we become equal as members of a group on the strength of our decision to guarantee ourselves mutually equal rights."[109] In her view, the principle of equality is based not on the nature of man but on the nature of politics. Politics is not possible except among citizens who are equal by law. This equality is an essential condition of a free polity. We hold the principle of equality not because it expresses a self-evident truth about human beings, but because it makes possible political freedom.

> That all men are created equal is not self-evident nor can it be proved. We hold this opinion because freedom is possible only among equals, and we believe that the joys and gratifications of free company are to be preferred to the doubtful pleasures of holding dominion ... These are matters of opinion and not of truth – as Jefferson, much against his will, admitted. Their validity depends upon free agreement and consent; they are arrived at by discursive, representative thinking; and they are communicated by means of persuasion and dissuasion.[110]

---

[107] OR, 30–31. [108] OR, 31. [109] OT, 301. [110] BPF, 247.

234 On Politics and Revolution

The validity of the principle of equality does not rest on self-evident truth but on the opinion that life in a free polity is better than life under any form of rule.

"Endowed by Their Creator with Certain Unalienable Rights"

The Declaration claims that all men by nature have rights. Arendt noted this claim implies a certain understanding of human nature. Rights are understood as properties that belong to the nature of each individual, just as natural substances have intrinsic and objective properties that exist in and of themselves. The idea is that positive laws can be based on natural laws, which can be derived from natural rights, which can be deduced from human nature.

> The very language of the Declaration of Independence as well as of the *Déclaration des Droits de l'Homme* – "inalienable," "given with birth," "self-evident truths" – implies the belief in a kind of human "nature" ... from which rights and laws could be deduced.[111]

Rights in the Declaration are understood in terms of human nature, and are conceived as inherent properties of "Man" in the singular.

Arendt had several arguments against this concept of rights.

First, she was critical of claims about human nature. Not that she denied that humans share certain basic and universal traits, but she denied we can grasp what makes us human using concepts of nature or essence derived from nonhuman beings: "It is highly unlikely that we, who can know, determine, and define the natural essences of all things surrounding us, which we are not, should ever be able to do the same for ourselves ... nothing entitles us to assume that man has a nature or essence in the same sense as other things."[112] Arguments that base political rights on human nature tend to uncritically take for granted traditional concepts of essence. We cannot simply assume that concepts of essence proper to nonhuman beings can also be used to grasp what makes us human.

She also argued that attempts to derive human rights from human nature are ultimately arbitrary. In *The Origins of Totalitarianism*, she noted that "the many recent attempts to frame a new bill of human rights ... have demonstrated that no one seems to be able to define with any assurance what these general human rights, as distinguished from the rights of citizens, really are."[113] In her view, the specific rights of citizens

---

[111] OT, 298. [112] HC, 10. [113] OT, 293.

The Declaration of Independence

can be derived from the nature of politics, but it seems impossible to derive any certain set of rights from the nature of Man in the singular.

Her third argument was based on her own experience as a stateless refugee. Traditional theories of human rights ascribe rights to "Man" in the singular. Individuals have rights, in this view, before or apart from any political community. But it was precisely when people were stripped of their citizenship and expelled from their political communities, she argued, that they were treated as if they had no rights at all.

> If a human being loses his political status, he should, according to the implications of [the doctrine of] the inborn and inalienable rights of man, come under exactly the situation for which the declarations of such general rights provided. Actually the opposite is the case. It seems that a man who is nothing but a man has lost the very qualities which make it possible for other people to treat him as a fellow-man.[114]

It was precisely those who mostly closely resembled the philosophical figure of Man in the singular, abstracted from any polity, who were treated as if they were not human. "The Rights of Man, supposedly inalienable, proved to be unenforceable – even in countries whose constitutions were based upon them – whenever people appeared who were no longer citizens of any sovereign state."[115] Human rights were not recognized and respected in people who did not belong to polities that guaranteed such rights. The disaster suffered by stateless refugees was not that they lost specific rights, but that they lost their place in a community that could guarantee any rights at all.

> Not the loss of specific rights, then, but the loss of a community willing and able to guarantee any rights whatsoever, has been the calamity which has befallen ever-increasing numbers of people. Man, it turns out, can lose all so-called rights of Man without losing his essential quality as man, his human dignity. Only the loss of a polity itself expels him from humanity.[116]

The situation of the stateless could not be understood or even described in terms of traditional theories of human rights, according to Arendt. Since traditional theories conceived human rights as the property of each individual prior to any polity, they were unable to grasp the significance of the loss of a polity, and were unable to conceive of a right that would secure people against this loss – the right to belong to a community that can guarantee one's rights are recognized and protected:

[114] OT, 300.   [115] OT, 293.   [116] OT, 297.

> The right that corresponds to this loss and that was never even mentioned among the human rights cannot be expressed in the categories of the eighteenth century because they presume that rights springs immediately from the "nature" of man.[117]

The experience of refugees suggests it is misleading to think of rights as essential traits of human nature, according to Arendt: "No matter how they have once been defined ... the real situation of those whom the twentieth century has driven outside the pale of the law shows that these are rights of citizens."[118] Rights actually exist only where they have been instituted, recognized, and guaranteed by a polity.

This concept of rights informed Arendt's view of American history. The "original crime" of the founders was not just the legalization of slavery, she argued, but the exclusion of even free blacks and Indians from belonging to "the American people." The *consensus universalis* articulated in the Constitution was that blacks and Indians were not part of "We the people" and could never become citizens of the United States. "Negroes and Indians ... had never been included in the original *consensus universalis* of the American republic. There was nothing in the Constitution or in the intent of the framers that could be so construed as to include the slave people in the original compact."[119] This denial of citizenship was effectively a denial of rights. "Negroes" and "Indians" were treated as if they had no rights precisely because they were not considered part of a national community willing to recognize them as citizens. This is explicit in *Dred Scott* v. *Sandford*. Chief Justice Roger Taney argued that "Persons of color" "are not included and were not intended to be included, under the word 'citizens' in the Constitution," and that "they had no rights which the white man was bound to respect."[120] America was founded on the principle that all men "are endowed by their Creator with certain unalienable rights," and yet the founders treated noncitizens as if they had no rights whatsoever. The fight of Black and Native Americans for political and civil rights has been at the same time a fight to become full citizens of the United States and to be fully included in the "we" of "We the People." This is why Arendt defined citizenship as "the right to have rights."[121] The link between rights and citizenship is obscured by the notion that humans have rights simply by virtue of being human. Humans have no rights, for

---

[117] OT, 297.   [118] OT, 295.   [119] CR, 90.
[120] *Dred Scott v. Sandford*, ed. Paul Finkelman (Boston: Bedford Books, 1997), 68, 58, and 61.
[121] OT, 296–297.

all practical purposes, except within communities willing to grant, recognize, and protect their rights.

Her arguments imply a threefold critique of the concept of rights implicit in the Declaration of Independence.

First, it is an error to try to think of rights starting from Man in the singular, or to try to derive rights from human nature. Rights belong to human beings in the plural. They are not essential properties of Man; they are the conditions of specific kinds of communities. They do not exist before or outside the communities that institute and recognize them. Arguments over rights should not focus on the question of human nature; they should focus on the question of how best to live together.

Second, political rights are derived from the nature of politics. Politics requires free assembly, free speech, the chance to have a voice in common deliberations. So among the essential conditions of a polity are the rights we call political: the right to assemble, the right to free speech, the right to vote. We should affirm these rights not because we believe they belong to the essence of Man, but because we believe that life in a polity is better than life under even the most enlightened ruler. Support for political rights ultimately rests on belief in the dignity of political life.

Last, the rights enumerated in the Declaration are not fundamental. More basic than the rights to life, liberty, and the pursuit of happiness is the right to belong to a community that will recognize and guarantee these rights, that is, the right to have rights at all: "We became aware of the existence of a right to have rights (and that means to live in a framework where one is judged by one's actions and opinions) and a right to belong to some kind of organized community, only when millions of people emerged who had lost and could not regain these rights because of the new global political situation."[122] The rights listed in the Declaration depend on this fundamental right to have rights, which was obscured by the assumption that rights are part of human nature, and which was revealed by the loss of all rights experienced by millions of stateless refugees including Arendt herself.[123] The right to have rights is at bottom the right to citizenship.

These thoughts guided Arendt's interpretation of the three basic rights mentioned in the Declaration.

---

[122] OT, 296–297.

[123] For a more detailed discussion of Arendt's theory of rights, see Jacques Derrida, *Cosmopolitanism and Forgiveness*, trans. Mark Dooley and Michael Hughes (New York: Routledge, 2001), 6–9, and Peg Birmingham, *Hannah Arendt and Human Rights: The Predicament of Common Responsibility* (Indianapolis: Indiana University Press, 2006).

238 On Politics and Revolution

"Life, Liberty, and the Pursuit of Happiness"

There has been much debate over the source of these words. The historian Carl Becker thought that Jefferson got them from the political theory of John Locke: "the Declaration, in its form, in its phraseology, follows closely certain sentences in Locke's second treatise on government."[124] In the *Second Treatise*, Locke derived a list of basic rights from a theory about the origin of society. Man in the state of nature is a sovereign individual – "absolute lord of his own person and possessions ... and subject to nobody" – and he has a natural right to his life, his liberty, and the fruits of his labor.[125] But since the enjoyment of these rights is not secure in a state of nature, man sacrifices his sovereign liberty and enters society: "he seeks out and is willing to join in society with others who are already united, or have a mind to unite, for the mutual preservation of their lives, liberties, and estates."[126] Governments exist to protect man's natural rights to life, liberty, and property. Becker did not claim that Jefferson simply copied Locke's treatise (Jefferson explicitly denied it), but he argued Locke's theory was so commonplace in colonial America that Jefferson drew on it indirectly when he sought to put into words "the common sense of the subject."[127]

Garry Wills has argued – against Becker – that Jefferson was primarily indebted not to Locke but to the Scottish philosopher Francis Hutcheson, who derived the basic rights of man from a different theory of society. Man cannot live in isolation, in his view; in order to survive and prosper we need the division of labor and exchange of goods. So man in the state of nature is not a sovereign individual but a member of society, which exists so that men can live safely and freely pursue happiness. As social beings, all men therefore have a natural right to life, to liberty, and to the pursuit of happiness. Governments exist in order to protect these rights, and the end of government is the safety and happiness of society as a whole. People may rightly abolish any government that fails to achieve these ends. Hutcheson wrote:

> But as the end of all civil power is ... the safety and happiness of the whole body, any power not naturally conducive to this end is unjust; which the

---

[124] Becker, *The Declaration of Independence*, 27.

[125] John Locke, *The Second Treatise of Government*, ed. Thomas Pearson (Indianapolis: Bobbs-Merrill Publishing, 1980), 70.

[126] Locke, *The Second Treatise*, 70–71.   [127] Becker, *The Declaration of Independence*, 25.

The Declaration of Independence 239

people ... may justly abolish again when they find it necessary to their safety to do so.[128]

Wills noted that the language of the Declaration is remarkably similar: "Whenever any form of government becomes destructive of these ends, it is the right of the people to alter or to abolish it, and to institute new government, laying its foundations on such principles, and organizing its powers in such form, as to them shall seem most likely to effect their safety and happiness." Wills did not claim Jefferson simply copied Hutcheson: "I do not argue for direct borrowing, since the Hutchesonian language was shared so widely by Scottish thinkers." But he did claim the Declaration was written in the theoretical language of Hutcheson and other Scottish thinkers: "Jefferson drew his ideas and words from these men, who stood at a conscious and deliberate distance from Locke's political principles."[129]

Despite their differences, both Locke and Hutcheson shared a few assumptions. Both assumed government is a means to an end. Both assumed the first end of government is the security and prosperity of human life. Both conceived of liberty negatively, as the absence of external constraint. Both assumed the ultimate end of government is the happiness of the individual citizen and of the people as a whole. And both assumed happiness lies outside politics, in the private sphere.

Arendt thought the experience of self-government gave the American colonists a deeper understanding of government and politics. In her view, the first colonists formed companies and "civil bodies politick" not for the sake of security but for the sake of action. Their initial goal was simply to cross the Atlantic and to settle in America. The experience of emigration and settlement showed that political bodies are not essentially means to an end; they are organizations that give people the power to act in concert, and this power structure precedes and makes possible concerted action towards any particular end. Political bodies of course use their power to achieve definite ends – not least of which is the security of life, liberty, and property – but what is essential to a political body is not any particular end but the concerted power-to-act that precedes both means and ends.

The experience of concerted action showed the colonists that by combining into "civil bodies politic" they could do together what none of them could do on their own. When they organized themselves into communities, they forfeited a degree of liberty and accepted certain constraints on their behavior; but at the same time they acquired a share of the

---

[128] Hutcheson, quoted in Wills, *Inventing America*, 238.   [129] Wills, *Inventing America*, 239.

240   On Politics and Revolution

community's power-to-do, and as members of a community they were able to do what no one of them could have done in isolation. By constituting themselves as a body they increased their power-to-act, and by increasing their power-to-act they vastly expanded the space of possibilities open to them – the space of real freedom. The experience of action gave the colonists a practical understanding of freedom deeper than inherited concepts of liberty. Since the concerted power of the polity expanded the real freedom of its members, political freedom meant not just protection from the power of government but also a share in the power of government. To be free came to mean more than to have rights that guaranteed limited government and rule of law; such rights are the condition but not the content of political freedom. To be free meant to be able to participate in self-government.

So in the Declaration the word "liberty" has two senses.

On the one hand, in claiming a right to liberty, the revolutionaries sought to reclaim the traditional liberties of English subjects. They could not claim these liberties as Englishmen because they were renouncing their allegiance to England, and because America was increasingly multiethnic. Arendt argued that the claim that all men have a right to liberty effectively meant (in the words of an anonymous revolutionary), "'Whether you be English, Irish, Germans, or Swedes, . . . you are entitled to all the liberties of Englishmen and the freedom of this constitution'." Arendt commented:

> What they were saying and proclaiming was in fact that those rights which up to now had been enjoyed only by Englishmen should be enjoyed in the future by all men – in other words, all men should live under constitutional, "limited" government.[130]

These liberties were essentially negative – they guaranteed subjects freedom from lawless or unjustified compulsion. In this sense, the word "liberty" signifies the traditional concept of freedom as individual sovereignty and absence of constraint.

On the other hand, the word "liberty" also had a nontheoretical sense. The revolutionaries were fighting a king who had taken the power to tax from the colonists' elected representatives, who had sought to limit town meetings, and who had finally dissolved the colonial assemblies. They were fighting not just for civil rights but for the right to govern themselves. The word "liberty" came to mean not just the right to limited and constitutional government, but also the right to self-government.

---

[130] OR, 148–149.

The Declaration of Independence   241

> The men of the revolutions ... could not possibly have had in mind merely those liberties which today we associate with constitutional government and which are properly called civil rights ... All these liberties, to which we might add our own claims to be free from want and fear, are of course essentially negative; they are the results of liberation but they are by no means the actual content of freedom, which, as we shall see later, is participation in public affairs, or admission to the public realm.[131]

If the revolutionaries had aimed only to recover their civil liberties, they could have kept a monarchical government and merely exchanged a bad ruler for a better one. The fact that they founded a republic shows that under the name of "liberty" they sought not simply civil liberties but political freedom in the original sense of the word.

The experience of political freedom was closely connected to what the revolutionaries called "public happiness." This phrase also had at least two senses. Arendt argued that public happiness meant the well-being of a polity in which citizens are free to participate in public life:

> This freedom they called ... "public happiness", and it consisted of the citizen's right of access to the public realm, in his share in public power – to be "a participator in the government of affairs" in Jefferson's telling phrase – as distinct from the generally recognized rights of subjects to be protected by the government in the pursuit of private happiness even against public power...[132]

But she also suggested the phrase "public happiness" drew some of its sense from the Americans' discovery that they actually enjoyed public life. "The Americans knew that public freedom consisted in having a share in public business, and that the activities connected with this business by no means constituted a burden but gave those who discharged them in public a feeling of happiness they could acquire nowhere else."[133] In the experience of self-government, the colonists acquired a taste for what Arendt called "the wine of action," "the charms of liberty," and "the joys and gratifications of free company."

This notion of public happiness contradicted a common assumption of traditional political theory. Since Aristotle, happiness had been understood as the end of government, and politics had been understood as a means to that end. Public life was supposed to be a burden, and happiness was supposed to lie in private life. Hence the corresponding notion that the political life is not an end in itself, and that a love of politics could only be explained in terms of a desire for power over others.

---

[131] OR, 32.   [132] OR, 127.   [133] OR, 119.

242   On Politics and Revolution

> The "participators in the government of affairs" were not supposed to be happy but to labor under a burden, happiness was not located in the public realm which the eighteenth century identified with the realm of government, but government was understood as a means to promote the happiness of society, the "only legitimate object of good government", so that any experience of happiness in the "participators" themselves could only be ascribed to an "inordinate passion for power", and the wish for participation on the side of the governed could only be justified by the need to check and control these "unjustifiable" tendencies of human nature.[134]

Arendt thought that the weight of this tradition kept the revolutionaries "from owning up to the rather obvious fact that they were enjoying what they were doing far beyond the call of duty."[135] The revolutionaries tended to speak of political life in clichés that covered the truth of their experience. Jefferson was speaking in platitudes when claimed that his real happiness lay in his private life, "In the lap and love of my family, in the society of my neighbors and my books, in the wholesome occupations of my farms and my affairs."[136]

But she also thought there are moments of candor in the testimony of the revolutionaries when a different understanding of happiness surfaces. Near the end of his life, Jefferson indirectly confessed that his years as a revolutionary had been among the best and happiest in his life:

> Jefferson's true notion of happiness comes out very clearly (without any of the distortions through the traditional, conventional framework of concepts which, it turned out, was harder to break than the structure of the traditional form of government) when he lets himself go in a mood of playful and sovereign irony and concludes one of his letters to Adams as follows: "May we meet there again, in Congress, with our antient colleagues, and receive with them the seal of approbation 'Well done, good and faithful servants.'" Here, behind the irony, we have the candid admission that life in Congress, the joys of discourse, of legislation, of transacting business, of persuading and being persuaded, were to Jefferson no less conclusively a foretaste of an eternal bliss to come than the delights of contemplation had been for medieval piety.[137]

Adams also located the highest happiness in the life of action: "it is action, not rest, that constitutes our pleasure."[138]

The word "happiness" in revolutionary discourse had several senses. It meant private happiness – both the happiness of the individual in private

---

[134] OR, 128.   [135] OR, 33.   [136] Jefferson, quoted in OR, 128–129.   [137] OR, 131.
[138] John Adams, quoted in OR, 34.

The Declaration of Independence 243

life, and the general welfare of society as a whole. But it also meant public happiness – both the well-being of the polity as a whole, and the specific happiness of participating in public life. Much is at stake in the distinction between public and private happiness. If the goal of the revolution was private happiness, it could have ended with a constitutional monarchy devoted to protecting civil liberties and promoting social welfare. If the goal of the revolution was public happiness, it could only have ended with the foundation of a republic. "For the American Revolution, it was a question of whether the new government was to constitute a realm of its own for the 'public happiness' of its citizens, or whether it had been devised solely to serve and ensure their pursuit of private happiness more effectively than had the old regime."[139]

In the Declaration, Jefferson simply ignored these distinctions: "His famous 'felicity of pen' blurred the distinction between 'private rights and public happiness'."[140] The text does not specify what kind of happiness – public or private – all men have the right to pursue.

So "the pursuit of happiness" has at least two senses. It means the right to pursue personal fulfillment in private life without government interference, but it also means the right to the public happiness of political freedom.

> The Declaration of Independence, though it blurs the distinction between private and public happiness, at least still intends us to hear the term "pursuit of happiness" in its twofold meaning: private welfare as well as the right to public happiness, the pursuit of well-being as well as being a "participator in public affairs".[141]

Both of these meanings were originally intended by Jefferson, according to Arendt, but shortly after the Revolution the latter sense of the phrase was almost forgotten. As the revolutionary spirit died out, Americans came to understand the pursuit of happiness primarily in the sense of private happiness:

> For the emphasis shifted almost at once ... from public freedom to civil liberty, or from a share in public affairs for the sake of public happiness to a guarantee that the pursuit of private happiness would be protected and furthered by public power. Jefferson's new formula ... was almost immediately deprived of its double sense and understood as the right of citizens to pursue their personal interests and thus to act according to the rules of private self-interest.[142]

---

[139] OR, 133.   [140] OR, 127–128.   [141] OR, 132.   [142] OR, 135.

244   On Politics and Revolution

The original double meaning of Jefferson's words was eclipsed, and this eclipse showed how quickly Americans forgot the spirit of the Revolution: "The rapidity with which the second meaning was forgotten and the term used and understood without its original qualifying adjective may well be the standard by which to measure ... the oblivion of the spirit that had been manifest in the Revolution."[143]

But the deeper senses of the Declaration have not been wholly forgotten: "the revolutionary notions of public happiness and political freedom have never altogether vanished from the American scene."[144] Most Americans retain the sense that the right to liberty guarantees something more than limited government alone, that freedom means not only the right to be left alone but also the right to participate in politics, and that the Declaration guarantees not just the right to pursue happiness in private life but also the right to enter public life and to work for the well-being of the republic.

"The Consent of the Governed"

Arendt also saw a gap between explicit theory and implicit insight in Jefferson's claim that power is legitimate only when it has the consent of the governed.

The "consent of the governed" is an idea inherited from liberal political theory, which implies that government is based on a contract between a people and a sovereign ruler: the people pledge to obey the sovereign in exchange for his or her protection; and the sovereign pledges to protect the rights of the people in exchange for the right to rule. The contract is consensual. The sovereign has the right to govern only as long as he or she has the consent of the governed. The "consent of the governed" was part of a theory that conceived political power as power-over-others, and that conceived government as a vertical contract between ruler and subjects.

Arendt argued that Americans had learned to organize themselves through an essentially different kind of contract. The earliest colonists had constituted themselves as political bodies through horizontal contracts based on mutual promises among equals. Such constitutions generated political power – power that could be invested in elected leaders but that was essentially nonhierarchical (power-to-do rather than power-over-others). Such power derived its legitimacy not from the "consent of the

---

[143] OR, 132.   [144] OR, 138.

The Declaration of Independence

governed" but from the support of the group for its constitution. The revolutionaries inherited this practical understanding of political power:

> The men of the American Revolution understood ... [that] power came into being when and where people would get together and bind themselves through promises, covenants, and mutual pledges; only such power, which rested on reciprocity and mutuality, was real power and legitimate, whereas the so-called power of kings or princes or aristocrats, because it did not spring from mutuality but, at best, rested only on consent, was spurious and usurped.[145]

Arendt noted this practical understanding of power is implicit in the mutual pledge that closes the Declaration of Independence: "the colonists ... knew of the enormous power potential that arises when men 'mutually pledge to each other [their] lives, [their] Fortune and their sacred Honour.'"[146]

There is a tension in the Declaration between two different notions of power and legitimacy: the traditional theory that political power is generated through a vertical contract between ruler and ruled, and that such power is legitimated by the consent of the governed; and the nontheoretical insight that political power can be generated through horizontal contracts among equals, and that such power is legitimate as long as that contract has the support of the group.

> [The revolutionaries] argued in the same terms as their French or English colleagues, and even their disagreements were by and large still discussed within the framework of commonly shared references and concepts. Thus, Jefferson could speak of the "consent" by the people from which governments "derive their just powers" in the same Declaration which he closes on the principle of mutual pledges, and neither he nor anybody else became aware of the simple and elementary difference between "consent" and mutual promises, or between the two types of social-contract theory.[147]

The nature of consent in a political community is essentially different from consent in a community divided into rulers and ruled. In the latter case, the governed consent to a constitution that gives the ruler the right to make decisions and to command their obedience; support of the constitution entails obedience to the will of the ruler.[148] Arendt noted that the revolutionaries still thought about power and legitimacy in terms of rulership – command and obedience – without seeing that these terms failed to grasp the nature of law in a republic: "The men of the

---

[145] OR, 181.   [146] OR, 176.   [147] OR, 176–177.   [148] RJ, 47.

eighteenth-century revolutions ..., unhappily, still talked about obedience – obedience to laws instead of men; but what they actually meant was support of the [constitutional] laws to which the citizenry had given its consent."[149] In the case of political communities, on the other hand, consent means support for a constitution that gives citizens an equal right to participate in the process of common deliberation and decisions; to consent to such a constitution implies an obligation to respect the laws produced through the political process. But this respect for the law in a polity of equals is something essentially different from the obedience to a ruler and consent to be ruled.

"An Absolute Tyranny over These States"

The revolutionaries accused the king of trying to establish an absolute tyranny. How did they understand tyranny? What did it mean to say the king was a tyrant?

In one sense, tyranny is lawless monarchy, and a tyrant is a ruler who uses public power for his own private ends. Arendt noted that this concept of tyranny goes back at least to Aristotle. "Since the end of antiquity, it had been common in political theory to distinguish between government according to law and tyranny, whereby tyranny was understood to be the form of government in which the ruler ruled out of his own will and in pursuit of his own interests, thus offending the private welfare and the lawful, civil rights of the governed."[150] To accuse the king of tyranny in this sense was to accuse him of violating the rule of law and trampling the civil rights and civil liberties of his subjects for his own benefit. This accusation is certainly there in the Declaration.

But in its original senses, the word "tyrant" (τύραννος) had other connotations. A tyrant was simply a ruler who had not inherited power but come to power through his own efforts. The prime example of a tyrant in ancient Athens was Peisistratos, who ruled Athens for most of the period between 561 and 527 BC, and who was called a tyrant not because he used power for his own ends but because he had seized power by force. Peisistratos allowed the Council and the Assembly to continue to meet, but he retained for himself the ultimate power to decide and to act. So the word "tyrant" had the connotation of a ruler who gutted institutions of self-government and concentrated the power of government in his own hands.

---

[149] OV, 40–41.   [150] OR, 130.

The Declaration of Independence

After George III dissolved the colonial assemblies and took from the colonists the power to tax themselves, the revolutionaries saw his actions as an attempt to undermine self-government in the colonies and to seize power for himself. When they accused him of tyranny they accused him not merely of violating their civil liberties but also of depriving them of political freedom.

> Tyranny, as the revolutionaries came to understand it, was a form of government in which the ruler, even though he ruled according to the laws of the realm, had monopolized for himself the right of action, banished the citizens from the public realm into the privacy of their households, and demanded of them that they mind their own, private business. Tyranny, in other words, deprived [citizens] of public happiness, though not necessarily of private well-being, while a republic granted to every citizen the right to become "a participator in the government of affairs", the right to be seen in action. The word "republic", to be sure, does not yet occur; it was only after the Revolution that all non-republican governments were felt to be despotisms.[151]

The accusation of tyranny had two senses. In one sense, it accused the king of violating the principles of limited government and rule of law. If that was all there was to the accusation, the remedy for tyranny would not have been revolution but restoration, the replacement of a bad ruler with a better one. In another sense, it accused the king of trying to dissolve institutions of self-government and to monopolize power for himself. It was only in light of this latter sense that the revolutionaries came to think that monarchy as such was inherently tyrannical, and that the remedy for tyranny could only be the constitution of a republic.

"To Alter or to Abolish It, and to Institute New Government"

From the principles set down in the Declaration's Bill of Rights, Jefferson deduced a right to revolution: "That whenever any form of government becomes destructive of these ends, it is the right of the people to alter or to abolish it, and to institute new government, laying its foundations on such principles and organizing its powers in such form, as to them shall seem most likely to effect their safety and happiness." Much could be said about this final principle. Let us focus on just a few key points.

The right to revolution is a principle of principles. It is a principle that describes the conditions under which a people may lay down new

[151] OR, 130.

principles as the foundation of a new form of government. At the same time, it lays down the right to revolution as one of the founding principles of the new American government. The principle of revolution describes the act of foundation that the Declaration performs. And it *performs* the revolutionary act it *describes*. The principle of revolution is the self-reflexive moment in the Declaration – the moment it turns on itself and tries to account in theory for what it is doing in practice.

This self-reflexive moment generates a paradoxically self-grounding structure. The act of foundation was justified by the right to revolution; but the right to revolution was officially laid down by the act of foundation. The act of laying down the right to revolution as a principle of a new government could only be justified by the right to revolution itself. The revolutionaries justified the act of establishing new principles of government on the basis of the very principles they meant to establish. They had to posit – as a fundamental principle of government – the right of the people to posit fundamental principles of government.

This self-reflexive self-grounding structure can be read in two ways.

If we assume the principles of the Declaration are self-evidently true, then the right to revolution as a principle of American government rests on a natural right to revolution. This natural right to revolution would be the logical consequence of the more basic principles of the Declaration. It is only because all men are endowed with inalienable rights, and because governments are instituted to secure them, that people have the right to alter or abolish any form of government that becomes destructive of these ends. The act of positing the right to revolution as a principle of government would be justified by a natural right to revolution. Positive right would rest on natural right.

But if the principles of the Declaration are neither self-evident nor grounded in natural rights, as Arendt argued, this self-grounding structure appears viciously circular. The act of positing new principles of government would be justified only by the posited principles themselves. Positive right would appear to rest only on itself. The self-grounding structure of the Declaration would be a response to the vicious circle in which all radical beginnings are caught. Precisely because the revolutionaries sought to establish new principles of government, they could not justify their actions on the basis of established principles; they could only justify the institution of new principles of government on the basis of the very principles they instituted.

The appeal to self-evident truths is an attempt to escape from this vicious circle. In order for the revolutionaries to justify the act of

The Declaration of Independence 249

revolution, they had to take for granted that they already possessed the rights they meant to claim. Hence the ambiguity of the Declaration's language – the revolutionaries had to assume that a natural right to revolution already existed, and that the Declaration merely described (constatively) a right that in fact it (performatively) instituted as a new principle of government. This conflation of performative and constative language is essential to the act of laying foundations. Every attempt to establish new rights must claim merely to recognize as given the very rights it aims to establish.[152]

It seems as though the act of laying down basic principles can only be legitimated on the basis of the principles thus laid down. The act of laying foundations would itself be groundless. In a sense this is true, but only to the extent that we understand "principles" as propositions. Arendt argued that the legitimacy of the Declaration derived from principles in a deeper sense of the word – not the theoretical propositions explicitly enumerated by Jefferson, but the practical principles that implicitly governed the act of declaring independence. These practical principles are legible in the text read not as a theoretical statement but as an act of revolution.

"Absolved from All Allegiance to the British Crown"

The act of laying down new principles of government, in the Declaration, was linked to the act of organizing the powers of government into new forms: "whenever any form of government becomes destructive of these ends, it is the right of the people to alter and abolish it, and to institute new government, laying its foundations on such principles, and organizing its powers in such form, as to them shall seem most likely to effect their safety and happiness." How was power understood in the Declaration? How was power to be organized in the new form of government? How did this new organization of power differ from that of the British monarchy?

The monarchy had the form of a "vertical" contract between ruler and ruled. Power was generated by mutual promises between the monarch and his or her subjects: the subjects swore to obey the monarch, and the monarch was bound in turn to protect the subjects' rights and liberties.

---

[152] My argument here is indebted to Jacques Derrida's reading of the Declaration of Independence. Derrida emphasized that this conflation of performative and constative language is essential to any attempt to establish new rights: "This obscurity, this undecidability between, let's say, a performative structure and a constative structure, is required in order to produce the sought-after effect. It is *essential* to the very positing or position of a right as such." Jacques Derrida, "Declarations of Independence," *New Political Science* 15 (1986), 7–15 (italics added).

On Politics and Revolution

This vertical contract between ruler and ruled was sustained by oaths of allegiance. Each colonist in America had to be willing to swear an oath of allegiance to King George III. One such oath read:

> I, _____, do sincerely promise and swear that I will bear true allegiance to His Majesty King George the Third.–So help me God.[153]

Another read:

> I, _____, do sincerely and faithfully promise and swear that I will with Heart & Hands, Life and Goods, maintain and defend His Majesty's Government and the Laws and Constitution of the Province of North Carolina, against all persons whatsoever who shall attempt to alter, obstruct or prevent the due administration of the Laws & the Public Peace and Tranquillity of said Province. So help me God.[154]

These oaths exemplified the kind of political contract described by Locke, which Arendt described as "an agreement in which an individual person resigns his power to some higher authority and consents to be ruled in exchange for a reasonable protection of his life and property."[155] It was this kind of allegiance that the revolutionaries renounced when they declared that the people of the colonies were "absolved from all allegiance to the British Crown."

The Declaration exemplified a different form of power. It ends with a pledge of mutual commitment among the revolutionaries and the people they represented: "And for the support of this Declaration, with a firm reliance on the protection of Divine Providence, we mutually pledge to each other our lives, our fortunes, and our sacred honor." This pledge was not a contract by which people gave up their power to a government in exchange for its protection; it was a contract by which the revolutionaries formed a new union of states, and generated their power to act in concert. The Declaration exemplified what Arendt called a "horizontal" contract among equals.

> The mutual contract by which people bind themselves together in order to form a community is based on reciprocity and presupposes equality; its actual content is a promise, and its result is indeed a "society" or "cosociation" in the old Roman sense of *societas*, which means alliance. Such an alliance gathers together the isolated strength of the allied partners and binds them into a new power structure by virtue of "free and sincere promises."[156]

---

[153] *The Colonial Records of North Carolina, Volume 7 – 1765 to 1768*, ed. William Laurence Saunders (Raleigh, NC: Josephus Daniels, 1890), 804.
[154] *The Colonial Records of North Carolina, Volume 7 – 1765 to 1768*, 804.   [155] OR, 169.
[156] OR, 170.

The Declaration of Independence 251

These two oaths – the vow of allegiance to King George III and the mutual pledge of support between the revolutionaries – imply two different ways of understanding power. The American understanding was not explicitly articulated in theoretical terms, but it is implicit in the text of the Declaration as an act of revolution. Arendt argued that the revolutionaries knew, not in theory but in light of practical experience, "the enormous power potential that arises when men 'mutually pledge to each other [their] lives, [their] Fortunes and their sacred Honour'."[157]

"We Mutually Pledge to Each Other"

The questions remain: What gave the revolutionaries the political authority to declare independence? What was the ultimate ground of their political authority?

Like every revolutionary act, the Declaration was caught in a vicious circle: precisely because it laid down new principles of government, it could only legitimate itself on the basis of the principles it laid down. The only way out of this circle seemed to be an appeal to self-evident truths about absolute standards of right.

Arendt argued the appeal to self-evident truth was the solution to a false problem. In her view, it is an error to try to ground political authority on claims to absolute truth.

> One is tempted to conclude that it was the authority which the act of foundation carried within itself, rather than the belief in an immortal Legislator, or the promises of reward and the threats of punishment in a "future state", or even the doubtful self-evidence of the truths enumerated in the preamble to the Declaration of Independence, that assured stability for the new republic. This authority, to be sure, is entirely different from the absolute which the men of the revolutions so desperately sought to introduce as the source of validity for their laws and the fountain of legitimacy for the new government.[158]

The authority of the Founders was not based on the *theoretical* principles laid out in the Declaration; it was ultimately based on the *practical* principles that inspired and governed the act of foundation itself. These practical principles are not listed in the Declaration's Bill of Rights but are implicit at the end of the Declaration in the pledge of mutual support: "The principle out of which the republic was eventually founded was

---

[157] OR, 176.   [158] OR, 199.

present enough in the 'mutual pledge' of life, fortune, and sacred honor."[159] How did she understand these "practical" principles?

Arendt's understanding of principle was linked to her concept of free action. Free action is *groundless* in the sense that it is not wholly determined by what preceded it; action is free insofar as it is not entirely governed by goals, motives, conditions, or force of circumstances. But action is not really free if it is completely groundless and arbitrary. Free action is *grounded* in the sense that it is inspired and guided by principles that govern how the action is performed and that set the standards by which action is evaluated. In this sense, honor was the principle of action in the aristocratic ethos of Homer, just as equality by law and public spirit were principles of action the democratic ethos of classical Athens. Practical principles in this sense, Arendt argued, are different from either motives or goals: "Principles do not operate from within the self as motives do . . . but inspire, as it were, from without; and they are much too general to prescribe particular goals, although every particular aim can be judged in the light of its principle once the act has been started."[160] The principle of an action only becomes manifest in the performance of the action, and yet principles transcend any particular action: "In distinction from its goal, the principle of an action can be repeated time and again, it is inexhaustible, and in distinction from its motive, the validity of a principle is universal, it is not bound to any particular person or to any particular group."[161] Principles can inspire and guide the concerted actions of groups made of individuals with very different motives and goals. The key point, for Arendt, is that principles confer a kind of authority on actions, insofar as principled action is bound to inspire the respect of those who share the same principles.

In her view, this notion of principle was essential to political authority in Rome. For the Romans, political authority was based on fidelity to the traditions that tied the Romans back to the founders. The greatness of the founders was manifest in the principles that inspired and governed the act of foundation, and these principles constituted the proper spirit of Roman politics. "The genius of Roman politics – not only according to Virgil but, generally, according to Roman self-interpretation – lay in the very principles which attend the legendary foundation of the city."[162] The act of foundation set the basic principles of Roman politics; hence the acts of the founders became examples and precedents that were handed down by tradition. To follow tradition was to be faithful to the founding principles

---

[159] OR, 130.   [160] BPF, 152.   [161] BPF, 152.   [162] OR, 210 (italics added).

The Declaration of Independence

of the city and to the spirit of the founding fathers. Political authority in Rome was not based on claims to absolute truth; it was based on fidelity to the principles that inspired and governed the act of foundation.

Arendt noted that when the American revolutionaries turned to history for examples that could illuminate their situation, they primarily looked to Rome: "It was ultimately the great Roman model that asserted itself almost automatically and almost blindly in the minds of those who, in all deliberate consciousness, had turned to Roman history and Roman political institutions in order to prepare themselves for their own task."[163] If in their theories the Americans remained uncritically indebted to Christian concepts of law, in their actions they deliberately followed the example of the Romans: "they thought of themselves as founders because they had consciously set out to imitate the Roman example and to emulate the Roman spirit."[164]

Arendt suggested that on a nontheoretical level the revolutionaries saw political authority in light of the colonial experience of founding new polities, and, like the Romans, they understood that the authority of America's founding documents would not come from claims to self-evident truth or appeals to a divine lawmaker, but from the principles that inspired and guided the act of foundation itself.

> The very fact that the men of the American Revolution thought of themselves as "founders" indicates the extent to which they must have known that it would be the act of foundation itself, rather than an Immortal Legislator or self-evident truth or any other transcendent, transmundane source, which eventually would become the fountain of authority in the new body politic. From this it follows that it is futile to search for an absolute in which all beginning is inevitably caught, because this "absolute" lies in the very act of beginning itself. In a way, this has always been known, though it was never fully articulated in conceptual thought...[165]

The "absolute" that lies in the very act of beginning is the principle that inspires and governs the action.

> There exists a solution for the perplexities of beginning which needs no absolute to break the vicious circle in which all first things seem to be caught. What saves the act of beginning from its own arbitrariness is that it carries its own principle within itself, or, to be more precise, that beginning and principle, principium and principle, are not only related to each other, but are coeval. The absolute from which the beginning is to derive its own validity and which must save it, as it were, from its inherent

[163] OR, 199.　　[164] OR, 203.　　[165] OR, 204.

254   On Politics and Revolution

arbitrariness is the principle which, together with it, makes its appearance in the world. The way the beginner starts whatever he intends to do lays down the law of action for those who have joined him in order to partake in the enterprise and to bring about its accomplishment. As such, the principle inspires the deeds that are to follow and remains apparent as long as the action lasts.[166]

The deepest principles of the Declaration are not the theoretical propositions listed in the Bill of Rights but the practical principles that governed the act of foundation.

What were these principles?

In early 1776 the Continental Congress did not have the authority to declare independence from Britain. The congressional delegates had specific instructions from the colonial assemblies to seek reconciliation with Britain rather than independence, and the colonial assemblies themselves derived their authority from the support of the people who had elected them. As Pauline Maier noted in *American Scripture*, the delegates knew that the people "were our power, & without them our declarations could not be carried into effect."[167] The delegates who favored independence asked the colonial assemblies to call for town or county meetings to deliberate on the question of independence. The stakes of the debate were clear – a declaration of independence would be an act of treason. The punishment for treason under British law was loss of life and property. So the towns were being asked not only for a decision, but for a commitment of support. The Assembly of Massachusetts, for example, asked each town to debate this question: if the Continental Congress should pass a measure declaring the colonies independent of Britain, would the men of each town "solemnly engage with their Lives and Fortunes to Support the Congress in the Measure"?[168]

Between April and July of 1776, more than ninety towns, counties, and colonial assemblies wrote "declarations" that renounced allegiance to Britain and promised to support the cause of independence. Many of the local or colonial declarations ended with pledges of mutual commitment. The New Hampshire assembly told its delegates in the Continental Congress "to join with the other Colonies in Declaring the thirteen United Colonies, a free & independent State," and pledged to support that declaration "with our lives and fortunes."[169]

---

[166] OR, 212–213.   [167] Quoted by Pauline Maier, *American Scripture*, 58.
[168] Quoted by Pauline Maier, *American Scripture*, 59.
[169] Quoted by Pauline Maier, *American Scripture*, 64.

The Declaration of Independence

By June 28 every colony (except New York) had authorized its delegates to vote for independence. On July 1 the Continental Congress held a plenary session on a motion to declare independence. At first the representatives of only nine colonies supported the motion, but after two days of deliberation the delegates reached a consensus: twelve colonies voted in favor of independence and one abstained. On July 4 the Congress agreed on the final draft of a declaration of independence, and sometime afterwards they signed their names beneath its pledge of mutual support: "And for the support of this declaration, with a firm reliance on the protection of Divine Providence, we mutually pledge to each other our lives, our fortunes, and our sacred honor."

Arendt argued the act of declaring independence was guided by the same principles that governed the town meetings and colonial assemblies – the practical principles of *consent, equality, nonviolence, common deliberation*, and *mutual promises*.

> The American Revolution tells an unforgettable story and is apt to teach a unique lesson; for this revolution did not break out but was made by men in common deliberation and on the strength of mutual pledges. The *principle* which came to light during those fateful years when the foundations were laid – not by the strength of one architect but by the combined power of the many – was the interconnected *principle* of mutual promise and common deliberation; and the event itself decided indeed, as Hamilton had insisted, that men "are really capable ... of establishing good government from reflection and choice," that they are not "forever destined to depend for their political constitutions on accident and force."[170]

The greatness of the Declaration of Independence, in her view, lies in its achievement not as a work of theory but as an act of revolution – as an example, a precedent, an action that brought to light and made manifest *the practical principles* of American politics: "No doubt there is a grandeur in the Declaration of Independence, but it consists not in its philosophy and not even so much in its being 'an argument in support of an action' as in its being the perfect way for an action to appear in words."[171] The authority of the Declaration does not rest primarily on the appeal to self-evident truths and to the laws of nature and of nature's God; it rests on the practical principles that inspired and guided the act of declaring independence.

---

[170] OR, 214 (italics added).   [171] OR, 130.

The Lost Heritage of the Revolution

What then was the heritage of the Revolutionaries? How has it been forgotten?

In her answer to these questions, Arendt focused on phrases used by the revolutionaries: "the spirit of the revolution," "the revolutionary spirit," "the spirit of 1776." In her view, these words point to something essential to revolution – something no longer clearly understood.

Arendt thought "the spirit of 1776" was born of a new experience of politics. The crisis with Britain pushed the colonists to take action, and the demands of action forced them to participate in politics with unprecedented commitment and intensity. From 1765 to 1775 they learned to organize meetings, demonstrations, boycotts, civic associations, committees of correspondence, committees of public safety, militias, illegal assemblies, and finally Continental Congresses. Once support for the British authorities collapsed, the revolutionaries were forced to improvise institutions with which they could govern themselves. It was this experience of action – "the speech-making and decision-taking, the oratory and the business, the thinking and the persuading, and the actual doing" – that revealed to them their capacity for public freedom and self-government. The struggle for liberation led the revolutionaries to rediscover among themselves a way of being together in which they could decide what to do and how to live together through mutual persuasion and common deliberation.

People who have experienced the nonviolent revolutions since 1989 have a sense of this spirit. They saw how events unfolded: the deepening crises in public authority; the first protests; the unforeseen days when mass demonstrations took on a momentum of their own; the opening of the public realm; the emergence of popular movements crystallized around a demand for freedom; the suspension of business as usual; the sudden collapse of support for established regimes; and the peaceful and anarchic transitions to new forms of government. But they also saw how these events altered public life: how public events overshadowed private life; how people who were normally apolitical became engaged in politics; how the public realm was no longer ruled by fear; how those who moved to the center of the crisis in order to join with others and to act in concert found themselves bound by an impersonal solidarity; how revolutionary action was largely inspired by patriotism and love of freedom; how in order to succeed the revolutionaries had to act in a spirit of mutual commitment to one another and to the polity as a whole; and how revolutionary situations

The Lost Heritage of the Revolution

alter not just the atmosphere of public life, but also the very principles that inspire and guide political action.

The principles that inspired and guided the revolutionaries in 1776 had to be other than the principles that ruled private life: not self-interest but public spirit; not individual liberty but public freedom; not personal fulfillment but public happiness. Arendt suggested that it was these principles of action that the revolutionaries meant by "the spirit of 1776."

> If we leave aside personal motives and practical goals and identify this spirit with the principles which, on both sides of the Atlantic, originally inspired the men of the revolutions, we must admit that the tradition of the French revolution – and that is the only revolutionary tradition of any consequence – has not preserved them any better than the liberal, democratic and, in the main, outspokenly anti-revolutionary trends of modern political thought in America. We have mentioned these principles before and, following eighteenth-century political language, we have called them public freedom, public happiness, public spirit.[172]

When the revolutionaries spoke of "the spirit of 1776" they were speaking obliquely of the principles that inspired and guided action in the revolutionary situation.

But this spirit weakened after the revolution, according to Arendt. In this respect the experience of the American revolutionaries was not unique. Modern history has been punctuated by the abrupt appearance and sudden loss of the spirit of revolution.

> The history of revolutions – from the summer of 1776 in Philadelphia and the summer of 1789 in Paris to the autumn of 1956 in Budapest – which politically spells out the innermost story of the modern age, could be told in parable form as the tale of an age-old treasure which, under the most varied circumstances, appears abruptly, unexpectedly, and disappears again, under different mysterious conditions, as though it were a fata morgana. There exist, indeed, many good reasons to believe that the treasure was never a reality but a mirage, that we deal here not with anything substantial but with an apparition, and the best of these reasons is that the treasure has thus far remained nameless ... And yet, if we turn our eyes to the beginnings of this era, and especially to the decades preceding it, we may discover to our surprise that the eighteenth century on both sides of the Atlantic possessed a name for this treasure, a name long since forgotten and lost – one is tempted to say – even before the treasure itself disappeared. The name in America was "public happiness," which, with its overtones of "virtue" and "glory," we understand hardly better than its French counterpart, "public freedom". . .[173]

---

[172] OR, 221.   [173] BPF, 5.

258   On Politics and Revolution

The spirit of 1776 is part of the lost heritage of the Revolution. Why was it lost?

Arendt gave two reasons.

First, the revolutionaries failed to establish institutions where most citizens could engage in political action governed by the principles of consent, equality, nonviolence, common deliberation, and mutual promises. The revolutionary spirit was born when the crisis in public authority drew ordinary citizens into political action—into meetings, demonstrations, boycotts, civic associations, committees, assemblies, and conventions. These actions had to be governed by the principles of public spirit, public freedom, and public happiness. And yet when the revolution ended, the founding fathers failed to establish institutions where ordinary citizens could continue to participate meaningfully in public life. Since the founders were concerned with government at the state and federal level, they focused on questions of representation rather than local participation, and they founded a republic in which representatives engage in politics but where citizens have little access to the political realm:

> The Revolution, while it had given freedom to the people, had failed to provide a space where this freedom could be exercised. Only the representatives of the people, not the people themselves, had an opportunity to engage in those activities of "expressing, discussing, and deciding" which in a positive sense are the activities of freedom.[174]

The Constitution made citizens out of Americans without establishing local spaces where as citizens they could meet, deliberate, and act on matters of common concern – where they had to confront different points of view and were expected to submit their opinions to the test of free and open criticism, where they had to work through their differences through mutual persuasion, where they were expected to speak and act for the common good, where they could initiate and organize projects, and where they could decide what to do and how to live together.

Arendt in particular lamented the failure of the founding fathers to incorporate the town meetings into the state and federal constitutions. She agreed with Emerson that the townships were "the unit of the Republic" and the town meetings "the school of the people" in political matters.[175] In this respect the town meetings in America were similar to the 139 *deme* assemblies established by Cleisthenes in classical Athens: they opened a

---

[174] OR, 235.   [175] OR, 235.

The Lost Heritage of the Revolution

space where citizens could learn the ethos of democratic politics through the practice of local self-government. The experience of self-government on a local level taught them the realities of political life and instilled in them the practical principles of American politics. But the founders failed to incorporate town meetings into the structure of the republic.

> The failure to incorporate the townships and the town-hall meetings, the original springs of all political activity in the country, amounted to a death sentence for them. Paradoxical as it may sound, it was in fact under the impact of the Revolution that the revolutionary spirit in America began to wither away, and it was the Constitution itself, this greatest achievement of the American people, which eventually cheated them of their proudest possession.[176]

This failure contributed to the demise of the town meeting as an institution and to the loss of spaces where ordinary citizens could actively engage in politics.

In addition, the institutions the Founders did establish were bound to distort American views of politics. The *poleis* of classical Greece lacked two institutions that now tend to seem essential to political life: political representation and elections. Especially in classical Athens, decisions were made not by elected representatives but by the citizens themselves, not just in the citywide assembly but also in the 139 local *deme* or neighborhood assemblies. There were positions of authority in Athens, but citizens were chosen for those positions not by election but by lot. The Founders of the United States, perhaps by necessity, instituted a representative government in which leaders are chosen through elections, and these institutions have understandably skewed our view of politics, foregrounding the struggle among politicians for the power of elective office, and relegating to the background the actions of citizens deliberating over and working for the common good. Representative government altered but left intact the division of the polity into those who rule and those who are ruled. It made the rulers accountable to the ruled, but it did not establish political arenas where citizens could meet as equals and govern their own affairs. The government of the United States is not a democracy in the original sense of the word, Arendt thought, but has become an elected oligarchy.

> That representative government has in fact become oligarchic government is true enough, though not in the classical sense of rule by the few in

---

[176] OR, 239.

On Politics and Revolution

the interests of the few; what we today call democracy is a form of government where the few rule, at least supposedly, in the interest of the many. This government is democratic in that popular welfare and private happiness are its chief goals; but it can be called oligarchic in the sense that public happiness and public freedom have again become the privilege of the few.[177]

The revolutionary spirit disappeared in part because the founders failed to found institutions where, in Jefferson's words, ordinary citizens could become "participators in the government of affairs."

But the heritage of the Revolution was lost for a second reason. Arendt argued that the revolutionaries failed to translate their nontheoretical understanding of politics into a set of concepts that could articulate the meaning of their experience and preserve it for future generations: "The American failure to remember can be traced back to this fateful failure of post-revolutionary thought. For if it is true that all thought begins with remembrance, it is also true that no remembrance remains secure unless it is condensed and distilled into a framework of conceptual notions within which it can further exercise itself."[178]

> The loss, at any rate, perhaps inevitable in terms of political reality, was consummated by oblivion, by a failure of memory, which befell not only the heirs but, as it were, the actors, the witnesses, those who for a fleeting moment had held the treasure in the palms of their hands, in short, the living themselves. For remembrance, which is only one, though one of the most important, modes of thought, is helpless outside a pre-established framework of reference, and the human mind is only on the rarest occasions capable of retaining something which is altogether unconnected. Thus the first who failed to remember what the treasure was like were precisely those who had possessed it and had found it so strange that they did not even know how to name it ... The tragedy began ... when it turned out that there was no mind to inherit and to question, to think about and to remember. The point of the matter is that the "completion," which indeed every enacted event must have in the minds of those who then are to tell the story and to convey its meaning, eluded them; and without this thinking completion after the act, without the articulation accomplished by remembrance, there simply was no story left that could be told.[179]

The failure of post-revolutionary thought was not a failure to think about the revolution but a failure to refine the terms in which it was understood.

---

[177] OR, 269.   [178] OR, 220.   [179] BPF, 6.

The Lost Heritage of the Revolution

It was not that the revolutionaries failed to understand the revolution but that they failed to work out concepts that could adequately grasp and make explicit the nontheoretical understanding they derived from their experiences. So the deepest insights of the revolutionaries were veiled beneath the false clarity of inherited concepts.

This failure of post-revolutionary thought led to a failure of memory – not a failure to record the facts of the revolution but a failure to grasp and preserve its meaning. The revolutionaries told the story of the Revolution, but they interpreted their story in terms of traditional concepts rather than rethinking traditional concepts in light of their experience. The failure was not that events were forgotten but that the meaning of the revolution was concealed beneath superficial interpretations. In Arendt's view, this concealment still prevails. Today Americans proudly conserve the failures of post-revolutionary thought and memory.

These failures are evident today in the most common interpretations of the Revolution, according to Arendt. The Revolution is remembered as a triumph of classic liberalism – as a rebellion against a lawless and over-reaching tyranny, and as the establishment of a limited government based on civil rights and the rule of law. It is remembered as the founding of a Christian nation – a nation whose laws are founded on the laws of nature and of nature's God. And it is remembered as a pseudo-revolution – as a change of government that left existing social structures intact. Arendt thought these interpretations distort and conceal the meaning of events: the American Revolution was not just a fight for civil liberties, limited government, and rule of law; it was also a struggle for political freedom. It did not end with the birth of a Christian nation; it ended with the birth of a secular political realm. It was not a moment of social upheaval, but of political innovation. The Revolution was a moment in the modern age when the political clearly reappeared as a way of life and as a distinct sphere of human existence.

These failures are also evident in common readings of the Declaration of Independence. The Declaration is commonly understood in terms of the political theories from which the revolutionaries inherited their concepts, rather than in light of the actual practice of self-government. Readings of the Declaration have missed the tensions between explicit theory and implicit insight. They have failed to fully grasp the nontheoretical understanding of power and authority implicit in the text. And they have identified the principles of the Declaration with its theoretical propositions rather than the practical principles that actually governed the act of declaring independence.

On Politics and Revolution

This failure is also evident in our thoughtless use of traditional concepts. We will not fully understand the meaning of American history until we critically dismantle the inherited terms in which we think: action, power, authority, law, principle, contract, government, citizenship, rights, equality, opinion, judgment, persuasion, rhetoric, consent, dissent, and freedom. Above all, we have to rethink inherited concepts of the political.

Conclusion: The Political Today

Politics in America is now commonly seen in light of anti-political prejudices: Power is essentially a matter of rule. The most basic political question is "Who rules Whom?" Political life consists not in the self-government of citizens but in a war for power over citizens. Politics is ultimately the struggle to seize government offices and to advance a partisan agenda by any means whatsoever – advertising, lobbying, propaganda, disinformation, smear campaigns, dirty tricks, scapegoating, fear-mongering, misdirection, deception, and outright lies. In the words of Arendt, it is commonly assumed that "domestic policy is a fabric of lies and deception woven by shady interests and even shadier ideologies, while foreign policy vacillates between vapid propaganda and the exercise of raw power."[1] The problem with these prejudices is not that they are false, since they largely reflect the pathetic reality of American politics today. The problem is that they obscure any other possible understanding of politics, and so make our current praxis seem natural and inevitable.

But the problem is not just prejudices. These prejudices are reinforced by the basic theoretical terms in which we think about politics, terms inherited from a philosophical tradition that from the start has been to a large extent anti-political. "Our tradition of political thought . . . far from comprehending and conceptualizing all the political experiences of Western mankind, grew out of a specific historical constellation . . . the conflict between the philosopher and the *polis*."[2] One of Arendt's great achievements was to show that these basic terms were not derived from experiences proper to the political realm, but were abstracted from other spheres of life, and that they do not allow us to grasp the nature of politics but rather distort or efface the specificity of the political realm. In her view, the Western tradition of philosophy "has never has a pure concept of the political." Instead of conceiving political phenomena in light of the

---

[1] PP, 98.   [2] HC, 12.

263

264 Conclusion: The Political Today

experience of political action, it "eliminated many experiences of an earlier past that were irrelevant to its immediate political purposes and proceeded until its end ... in a highly selective manner."[3] We are indebted to this tradition not just for the specific theories of political philosophers, but for the theoretical language in which we think about politics. Her primary concern was not simply to critique traditional political philosophies, but to critically dismantle the inherited concepts in which politics is commonly understood.

These concepts are so familiar they seem self-evident. *Power* is conceived as rule over others, rather than as the capacity of groups to act in concert. *Authority* is conceived as a matter of controlling others through demands for obedience, rather than influencing others through the ability to inspire respect. *Violence* is conceived as the most flagrant manifestation of power – a basic tool of rulership used by the strong, rather than as a substitute for authority used by the incompetent and the weak. *Government* is conceived as an institution to which individuals give up their power for the sake of security and prosperity, rather than the institutions through which the power of citizens to act together is organized and directed. *Consent* is conceived as acquiescence to government rule, rather than as the active support through which the power of political institutions is sustained. *Laws* are conceived as commands that limit freedom, instead of rules that create a space of freedom within a polity. *Freedom* itself is conceived as a matter of sovereign will and choice, rather than as the space of what it is actually possible for us to do.

Arendt argued this framework of concepts is built into the language of American political thought, whose terms were set in the founding documents written by the American revolutionaries. Historians have shown how the revolutionaries were indebted to the philosophical tradition, and Arendt argued that the revolutionaries, instead of rethinking traditional concepts in light of their practical insights, distorted their practical insights by forcing them into this framework of traditional concepts.

But Arendt also argued that the core texts of American political thought contain authentic insights into the basic realities of political life, insights born of the actual experience of self-government and revolutionary action. These insights were not laid out explicitly in the texts' theoretical claims; they were left implicit in the texts' practical language. The most profound truths of the Declaration of Independence are located not in the "self-evident" "truths" of its bill of rights, but in the nontheoretical insights

---

[3] HC, 12.

Conclusion: The Political Today 265

into power, authority, and freedom implicit in the text as an act of revolution. This reserve of authentic understanding is the hidden legacy of the Revolution.

This legacy can help us rethink the meaning of politics. But this rethinking requires an approach to political theory different from traditional forms of political philosophy. The task of political theory is not to withdraw from the realm of opinion, to use reason to discover absolute standards of right that transcend politics, and to use those ideal standards to measure the relative justice or injustice of actual polities. The work of thinking is more complex. Arendt's approach to political theory involved six tasks: to lay out the terms in which political phenomena are traditionally conceived; to trace the genealogy of these terms back to their native sphere in order to explicate their original meanings and delimit the areas within which they make sense; to bring these terms to bear on concrete examples of political phenomena; to ask what these phenomena are in essence; to sense the limitations of traditional concepts, and to point out in the phenomena what these concepts distort or conceal; and to revise and refine the terms in which we think in order to grasp and bring to light what has been obscure or invisible to thought. The aim of thought is not to measure the actual against the ideal, but to illuminate what so far has been hidden or obscure: "not to rule or otherwise determine the chaos of human affairs, but in 'shining brightness' to illuminate their darkness."[4]

This way of thought is no substitute for action. When the chips are down, and our political situation calls for action, pure theory is at best ineffective and at worst an abdication of the responsibility to act. There is more than a grain of truth in the perspective of the women and men in the political arena, for whom devoting oneself to pure thought means devoting oneself to doing nothing.

But this way of thought does have a political significance. While it is not a substitute for action, it illuminates and makes meaningful the sphere in which effective action is possible: "the activity of understanding is necessary; while it can never directly inspire the fight or provide otherwise missing objectives, it alone can make it meaningful and prepare a new resourcefulness of the human mind and heart, which perhaps will come into free play only after the battle is won."[5]

---

[4] BPF, 113.   [5] EU, 310.

Works Cited

All citations are from the following works. Most of this book was written before *Was Ist Politik?* was translated into English, so some of the translations are my own.

Ackerman, Bruce. *We the People: Foundations*. Cambridge, MA: Harvard University Press, 1991.

Aeschylus. *Oresteia*. Edited and translated by Alan H. Sommerstein. Cambridge, MA: Harvard University Press, 2008.

Agamben, Giorgio. *Homo Sacer: Sovereign Power and Bare Life*. Stanford: Stanford University Press, 1998.

    Means without Ends: Notes on Politics. Minneapolis: University of Minnesota Press, 2000.

Arendt, Hannah. "Action and the 'Pursuit of Happiness.'" In *Politische Ordnung und Menschliche Existenz*, pp. 1–16. Munich: Verlag C. H. Beck, 1962.

    Between Past and Future. New York: Penguin, 1968.

    Crises of the Republic. New York: Harcourt Brace, 1972.

    Eichmann in Jerusalem. New York: Penguin, 1963.

    Essays in Understanding. New York: Harcourt Brace, 1994.

    The Human Condition. Chicago: University of Chicago Press, 1958.

    The Jewish Writings. New York: Schocken Books, 2007. Edited by Jerome Kohn and Ron H. Feldman.

    Lectures on Kant's Political Philosophy. Edited by Ronald Beiner. Chicago: University of Chicago Press, 1982.

    Letters: Hannah Arendt and Martin Heidegger. Edited by Ursula Ludz. Translated by Andrew Shields. New York: Harcourt Brace, 2004.

    The Life of the Mind. New York: Harcourt Brace, 1978.

    "For Martin Heidegger's Eightieth Birthday," in *Martin Heidegger and National Socialism,* ed. Gunther Neske and Emil Kettering. (New York: Paragon House, 1990), 207–209.

    Men in Dark Times. New York: Harcourt Brace, 1968.

    On Revolution. New York: Penguin, 1962.

    The Origins of Totalitarianism. New York: Harcourt Brace, 1951.

    On Violence. New York: Harcourt Brace, 1969.

    "Philosophy and Politics." *Social Research* 57, 1 (1990): 73–103.

    The Promise of Politics. Edited by Jerome Kohn. New York: Schocken, 2005.

Works Cited

Responsibility and Judgment. Edited by Jerome Kohn. New York: Schocken, 2003.

Thinking without a Banister. Edited by Jerome Kohn. New York: Schocken, 2018

Was Ist Politik? Edited by Ursula Ludz. Munich: Piper Verlag, 1993.

Arendt, Hannah, and Karl Jaspers. *Hannah Arendt/Karl Jaspers: Briefwechsel 1926–1969.* Edited by Lotte Köhler and Hans Saner. Munich: Piper Verlag, 1985.

Hannah Arendt/Karl Jaspers: Correspondence 1926–1969. Edited by Lotte Köhler and Hans Saner. Translated by Robert and Rita Kimber. New York: Harcourt Brace, 1992.

Aristotle. *Eudemian Ethics.* Translated by H. Rackham. Cambridge, MA: Harvard University Press, 1971.

Metaphysics. Translated by Hugh Tredennick. Cambridge, MA: Harvard University Press, 1989.

Nicomachean Ethics. Translated by H. Rackham. Cambridge, MA: Harvard University Press, 1994.

Politics. Translated by H. Rackham. Cambridge, MA: Harvard University Press, 1998.

Poetics. Translated by Stephen Halliwell. Cambridge, MA: Harvard University Press, 1995.

The Politics and The Constitution of Athens. Edited and translated by Steven Everson. Cambridge: Cambridge University Press, 1996.

Beard, Charles. *An Economic Interpretation of the Constitution.* New York: Macmillan, 1936.

Becker, Carl. *The Declaration of Independence: A Study in the History of Political Ideas.* New York: Random House, 1922.

Benhabib, Seyla. *The Reluctant Modernism of Hannah Arendt.* New York: Alta Mira, 2000.

Berkowitz, Roger. "Misreading 'Eichmann in Jerusalem'." *The New York Times.* July 7, 2013.

Berlin, Isaiah. *Four Essays on Liberty.* Oxford: Oxford University Press, 1969.

Bernstein, Richard J. "'The Banality of Evil' Reconsidered." In *Hannah Arendt and the Meaning of Politics*, pp. 297–322. Edited by Craig Calhoun and John McGowan. Minneapolis: University of Minnesota Press, 1997.

Birmingham, Peg. *Hannah Arendt and Human Rights: The Predicament of Common Responsibility.* Indianapolis: Indiana University Press, 2006.

Campbell, Douglas. *The Puritan in Holland, England, and America*, vol. 2. New York: Harper and Brothers, 1892.

Cartledge, Paul. *Democracy: A Life.* New York: Oxford University Press, 2016.

Covenant of the First Church in Boston. www.firstchurchbostonhistory.org/covenant.html.

Derrida, Jacques. "Declarations of Independence." *New Political Science* 15 (1986): 7–15.

Works Cited

Cosmopolitanism and Forgiveness. Translated by Mark Dooley and Michael Hughes. New York: Routledge, 2001.

Descartes, René. *Selected Philosophical Writings.* Translated by John Cottingham, Robert Stoothoff, and Dugald Murdoch. Cambridge: Cambridge University Press, 1990.

Detienne, Marcel. *The Masters of Truth in Archaic Greece.* Translated by Janet Lloyd. New York: Zone Books, 1996.

Deutscher, Max. *Judgment after Arendt.* New York: Routledge, 2016.

Diogenes Laertes. *Lives of Eminent Philosophers*, vol. 1. Translated by J. D. Hicks. Cambridge, MA: Harvard University Press, 2006.

Disch, Lisa Jane. *Hannah Arendt and the Limits of Philosophy.* Ithaca: Cornell University Press, 1994.

Dolan, Frederick M. *Allegories of America: Narratives, Metaphysics, Politics.* Ithaca: Cornell University Press, 1994.

Dreyfus, Hubert, and Paul Rabinow. *Michel Foucault: Beyond Structuralism and Hermeneutics.* Chicago: University of Chicago Press, 1983.

Epicurus. *The Essential Epicurus.* Translated by Eugene O'Connor. Buffalo, NY: Prometheus Books, 1993, 83.

Euripides. *Complete Greek Tragedies.* Edited and translated by David Grene and Richmond Lattimore. Chicago: University of Chicago Press, 1958.

Helen; Phoenician Women; Orestes. Edited and translated by David Kovacs. Cambridge, MA: Harvard University Press, 2002.

Suppliant Women; Electra; Heracles. Edited and translated by David Kovacs. Cambridge, MA: Harvard University Press, 1998.

Trojan Women; Iphigenia among the Taurians; Ion. Edited and translated by David Kovacs. Cambridge, MA: Harvard University Press, 1999.

Farrar, Cynthia. *The Origins of Democratic Thinking: The Invention of Politics in Classical Athens.* New York: Cambridge University Press, 1988.

Finkelman, Paul, ed. *Dred Scott v. Sandford.* Boston: Bedford Books, 1997.

Finley, M. I. *Democracy: Ancient and Modern.* New Brunswick, NJ: Rutgers University Press, 1973.

Politics in the Ancient World. Cambridge: Cambridge University Press, 1983.

Foner, Eric. *The Story of American Freedom.* New York: W. W. Norton, 1998.

Foucault, Michel. *Power/Knowledge.* Edited by Colin Gordon. New York: Pantheon, 1980.

Fearless Speech. Edited by Joseph Pearson. Los Angeles: Semiotext(e), 2001.

"The Subject and Power," in the Afterword of Hubert Dreyfus and Paul Rabinow, *Michel Foucault: Beyond Structuralism and Hermeneutics.* Chicago: University of Chicago Press, 1983, 221.

Gasché, Rodolphe. "Abbau, Destruktion, Deconstruction." In *The Tain of the Mirror*, pp. 109–120. Cambridge, MA: Harvard University Press, 1986.

Goody, Jack. *The Theft of History.* New York: Cambridge University Press, 2012.

Gottsegen, Michael. *The Political Thought of Hannah Arendt.* Albany: SUNY Press, 1994.

Works Cited 269

Habermas, Jürgen. *Philosophical-Political Profiles*. Translated by Frederick G. Lawrence. Cambridge, MA: MIT Press, 1983.

Heidegger, Martin. *Basic Problems of Phenomenology*. Translated by Albert Hofstadter. Indianapolis: Indiana University Press, 1988.

Being and Time. Translated by Joan Stambaugh. Albany: SUNY Press, 1996.

Hölderlin's Hymn "The Ister." Translated by William McNeill and Julia Davis. Bloomington: Indiana University Press, 1996.

Introduction to Metaphysics. Translated by Gregory Fried and Richard Polt. New Haven: Yale University Press, 2000.

Off the Beaten Track. Edited and translated by Julian Young and Kenneth Haynes. New York: Cambridge University Press, 2002.

Sein und Zeit. Tübingen: Max Niemeyer Verlag, 1986.

Herodotus. *The History*. Translated by David Grene. Chicago: University of Chicago Press, 1987.

The Persian Wars, Volume II. Translated by A. D. Godfrey. Cambridge, MA: Harvard University Press, 1921.

Hill, Melvyn A. *Hannah Arendt: The Recovery of the Public World*. New York: St. Martin's Press, 1979.

Hobbes, Thomas. *Leviathan*. Edited by Richard Tuck. Cambridge: Cambridge University Press, 1991.

A Dialogue between a Philosopher and a Student of the Common Laws of England. Edited by Joseph Cropsey. Chicago: University of Chicago Press, 1997.

Homer. *The Iliad*. Translated by Richmond Lattimore. Chicago: University of Chicago Press, 1961.

Homeri Opera: Iliadis I–XII. Edited by David B. Monro and Thomas W. Allen. Oxford: Oxford University Press, 1989.

Honig, Bonnie. "Toward an Agonistic Feminism: Hannah Arendt and the Politics of Identity." In *Feminists Theorize the Political*, pp. 215–238. Edited by Judith Butler and Joan W. Scott. New York: Routledge, 1992.

"Declarations of Independence: Arendt and Derrida on the Problem of Founding a Republic." *American Political Science Review* 85, 1991: 97–113.

Hull, Margaret Betz. *The Hidden Philosophy of Hannah Arendt*. New York: RoutledgeCurzon, 2002.

Isakhan, Benjamin, and Stephen Stockwell. *The Secret History of Democracy*. New York: Palgrave Macmillan, 2011.

Kant, Immanuel. *Critique of Judgment*. Translated by J. H. Bernard. New York: Hafner, 1951.

Kateb, George. *Hannah Arendt: Politics, Conscience, Evil*. Totowa, NJ: Rowman & Allanheld, 1984.

Kirk, Russell. *The Conservative Mind*. Washington, DC: Regnery Publishing, 1985.

Kramnick, Isaac, and R. Laurence Moore. *The Godless Constitution*. New York: Norton, 1997.

Lacoue-Labarthe, Philippe, and Jean-Luc Nancy. *Retreating the Political*. Edited by Simon Sparks. New York: Routledge, 1997.

Works Cited

Lévinas, Emmanuel. *Totality and Infinity*. Translated by Alphonso Lingis. Pittsburgh: Duquesne University Press, 1969.

Locke, John. *An Essay Concerning Human Understanding*. London: Oxford University Press, 1904.

 The Second Treatise of Government. Edited by Thomas Pearson. Indianapolis: Bobbs-Merrill Publishing, 1980.

Loraux, Nicole. *The Invention of Athens*. Translated by Alan Sheridan. Cambridge, MA: Harvard University Press, 1986.

Maier, Pauline. *American Scripture: Making the Declaration of Independence*. New York: Knopf, 1997.

McGowan, John. *Hannah Arendt: An Introduction*. Minneapolis: Minnesota University Press, 1998.

McGowan, John, and Craig Calhoun, eds. *Hannah Arendt and the Meaning of Politics*. Minneapolis: University of Minnesota Press, 1997.

Mill, John Stuart. *On Liberty*. New York: Penguin, 1984.

Moe, Barbara A, ed. *The Charter of the Massachusetts Bay Colony: A Primary Source Investigation*. New York: Rosen Publishing Group, 2002.

Mouffe, Chantal. *On the Political*. New York: Routledge, 2005.

Nancy, Jean-Luc. "Is Everything Political?" *The New Centennial Review* 2, 3, Fall 2002: 15–22.

Neske, Günther, and Emil Kettering. *Martin Heidegger and National Socialism: Questions and Answers*. Translated by Lisa Harries. New York: Paragon House, 1990.

New Greek–English Interlinear New Testament, The New Revised Standard Version. Edited by J. D. Douglas and translated by Robert K. Brown and Philip W. Comfort. Wheaton, IL: Tyndale House Publisher, 1990.

Nietzsche, Friedrich. *On the Genealogy of Morality*. Edited by Keith Ansell-Pearson and translated by Carol Diethe. New York: Cambridge University Press, 1997.

 Twilight of the Idols/The Anti-Christ. Translated by R. J. Hollingdale. New York: Penguin, 1990.

Oakeshott, Michael. *Philosophy, Politics, and Society*. Edited by P. Laslett. Oxford: Oxford University Press, 1956.

Ober, Josiah. *Mass and Elite in Democratic Athens*. Princeton: Princeton University Press, 1989.

 The Rise and Fall of Classical Greece. Princeton: Princeton University Press, 2015.

Paine, Thomas. *Common Sense*. New York: Penguin, 1986.

 The Rights of Man. New York: Penguin, 1985.

Parekh, Bhikhu. *Hannah Arendt and the Search for a New Political Philosophy*. Atlantic Highlands, NJ: Humanities Press, 1981.

Passerin d'Entrèves, Maurizio. *The Political Philosophy of Hannah Arendt*. New York: Routledge, 1994.

Pitkin, Hanna. *Hanna Fenichel Pitkin: Politics, Justice, Action*. Edited by Dean Mathiowetz. New York: Routledge, 2016.

Works Cited

Plato. *The Gorgias*. Translated by Walter Hamilton and Chris Emlyn-Jones. New York: Penguin, 1960.

Theaetetus/Sophist. Translated by Harold North Fowler. Cambridge MA: Harvard University Press, 1987, 121 [173e].

Phaedrus and Letters VII and VIII. Translated by Walter Hamilton. New York: Penguin, 1985.

The Republic. Translated by Paul Shorey. Cambridge, MA: Harvard University Press, 2000.

Ryan, Alan. *On Politics*. New York: W. W. Norton, 2012.

Saunders, William Laurence, ed. *The Colonial Records of North Carolina, Volume 7–1765 to 1768*. Raleigh, NC: Josephus Daniels, 1890, 804.

Schmitt, Carl. *The Concept of the Political*. Translated by George Schwab. Chicago: University of Chicago Press, 1996.

Schürmann, Reiner. *Heidegger on Being and Acting: From Principles to Anarchy*. Bloomington: Indiana University Press, 1990.

Sen, Amartya. "Democracy as a Universal Value." *Journal of Democracy* 10, 3, 1999: 3–17.

Strauss, Leo. *Natural Right and History*. Chicago: University of Chicago Press, 1965.

The Rebirth of Classical Political Rationalism. Chicago: University of Chicago Press, 1989.

What Is Political Philosophy? Chicago: University of Chicago Press, 1988.

Strong, Tracy B. *Politics without Vision: Thinking without a Banister in the Twentieth Century*. Chicago: University of Chicago Press, 2012.

Thucydides. *The Landmark Thucydides*. Edited by Robert B. Strassler. Translated by Richard Crawley. New York: Free Press, 1996.

Treaties and Other International Acts of the United States of America, vol. 2. Edited by Hunter Miller. Washington: United States Government Printing Office, 1931.

Vernant, Jean-Pierre. *The Origins of Greek Thought*. Anonymous translation. Ithaca: Cornell University Press, 1982.

Villa, Dana. *Arendt and Heidegger: The Fate of the Political*. Princeton: Princeton University Press, 1996.

(ed.). *The Cambridge Companion to Hannah Arendt*. New York: Cambridge University Press, 2002.

Politics, Philosophy, and Terror. Princeton: Princeton University Press, 1999.

Socratic Citizenship. Princeton: Princeton University Press, 2001.

Virgil. *The Aeneid*. Translated by Robert Fitzgerald. New York: Random House, 1981.

Vlassopoulos, Kostas. *Unthinking the Greek Polis*. New York: Cambridge University Press, 2007.

Vollrath, Ernst. "Hannah Arendt: A German-American Jewess Views the United States – and Looks Back to Germany." In *Hannah Arendt and Leo Strauss: German Émigrés and American Political Thought after World War II*, pp. 45–58. Edited by Peter Graf Kielmansegg, Horst Mewes, and Elisabeth Glaser-Schmidt. Cambridge: University of Cambridge Press, 1997.

Works Cited

Weir, David A. *Early New England: A Covenanted Society.* Grand Rapids, MI: Eerdmans Publishing Company, 2005.

Wills, Garry. *Inventing America: Jefferson's Declaration of Independence.* New York: Random House, 1978.

Young-Bruehl, Elisabeth. *Hannah Arendt: For Love of the World.* New Haven: Yale University Press, 1982.

Why Arendt Matters. New Haven: Yale Press, 2006.

Zuckerman, Michael. "The Social Context of Democracy in Massachusetts." *The William and Mary Quarterly* 25, 4, October 1968: 523–544.

Index

the absolute, problem of, 182, 225–227,
 231–232
action(s), 1–3, 26–27, 29–31, 40–41, 137, 211,
 214
 American colonists' understanding of,
 201–202
 deliberation as a form of, 69–70
 freedom and, 62–63, 140–141, 184, 186, 252
 instrumental concept of, 22–24, 127–128,
 135–136
 vs. labor, 26–27
 vs. making, 22–24, 124–129, 135–136
 natality and, 186–187
 plurality and, 203
 principle(s) and, 161–162, 187–188, 253–254
 revelatory power of, 64–65, 93–94
 thought and, 15–16, 25–26, 31, 40–41, 84,
 128–129, 265
Adams, John, 157–158, 191–192, 204–205,
 210, 242
Agamben, Giorgio, 135n77, 137n89
agonism, politics as, 6, 63–64
American colonists. *See also* American
 revolutionaries
 as anti-democratic, 198–199
 experiences of, 198–211
 inherited concepts and, 191–192, 211
 nontheoretical understanding of political
 matters, 198–199
 self-government and, 191, 198–211, 215–217,
 222, 239–240
 understanding of freedom, 208–210
American Revolution, 27, 164, 188–189, 196,
 211–221
 Arendt's interpretation of, 7, 192–198
 Christian interpretations of, 194–196, 261
 classic liberal interpretations of, 193–194, 196,
 261
 forgotten legacy of, 1, 190–192, 198,
 256–262, 264–265
 revolutionaries' views of, 197, 218–219

 social interpretations of, 195–197, 261
 spirit of, 256–258
American revolutionaries, 157–158, 197–198,
 253–254. *See also* American colonists
 choice of republic over monarchy, 193–194,
 213–214, 216–217
 failure to articulate practical understanding in
 theoretical terms, 192, 196–197
 failure to articulate the meaning of the
 Revolution, 191–192
 failure to establish institutions for political
 engagement, 258–260
 gap between political theories and
 nontheoretical understanding of politics,
 197–198, 218–221, 225, 227, 230–232,
 261–262, 264–265
 insights preserved in nontheoretical writings
 and practical political documents, 196–197
 self-government and, 218–220, 225, 256–260
 understanding of law, 227
 understanding of political authority, 225,
 253–254
 understanding of power, 219–220, 244–245
 understanding of principle(s), 157–158, 164
antagonism, politics as, 6
anti-essentialism, 111n9
appearing, 84, 86–87, 117, 123–124
appearance(s), vs. being, 86n4
 as mere semblance or illusion, 123–124
 opinion and, 64–65, 87–88, 117, 123–124
 the polis as space of, 64–65
 as self-showing of beings themselves, 123–124
arche and *archein*, 130–132, 161–162
Arendt, Hannah, readers of,
 Benhabib, Seyla, 75–76
 Birmingham, Peg, 75–76
 Gottsegen, Michael, 78
 Hull, Margaret Betz, 74–75
 Kateb, George, 75–76, 78
 McGowan, John, 75–77
 Parekh, Bhikhu, 75–76

273

Index

Arendt, Hannah, readers of (cont.)
  Passerin d'Entrèves, Maurizio, 77, 168–169
  Pitkin, Hanna, 78
  Villa, Dana, 6–7, 78, 102
  Young-Bruehl, Elisabeth, 7, 75–76
Arendt, Hannah, works of, 20–31
  biography of Rahel Varnhagen, 11
  Crises of the Republic, 27
  Eichmann in Jerusalem, 27–29, 91–92
  The Human Condition, 26–27, 40–41, 132–133
  Introduction into Politics (*Einführung in die Politik*), 6–7, 24, 26
  "Karl Marx and the Great Tradition" (lecture series), 23–24
  The Life of the Mind: Thinking, 30–31, 132
  The Life of the Mind: Willing, 30–31
  Love in Saint Augustine, 11
  Men in Dark Times, 91–92
  Origins of Totalitarianism, 20–22, 234–235
  Between Past and Future, 27, 36–37
  On Revolution, 27, 41, 157–158
  "Thinking and Moral Considerations," 29–30
  "The Totalitarian Elements in Marxism," 22–23
  On Violence, 17n27, 82–83, 167, 190
Aristotle, 7, 23–25, 42–46, 55, 87–89, 111–113, 127, 130–139
  concept of essence, 134–135
  distortion of Greek understanding of politics, 108–109, 131n63, 136–139
  on human nature, 134–135, 138–139
  metaphysical understanding of politics, 134–139
  metaphysical terms derived from the sphere of making, 131–134
  Metaphysics, 130–139, 135n77, 161–162, 186
  Nicomachean Ethics, 133–136, 161–162, 162n175
  Politics, 23–24, 51–52, 106n62, 134–136, 142–143
  on principle(s), 161–163, 187–188
assemblies
  Athenian, 54–59, 81–82, 246–247, 258–260
  colonial, 188, 208–211, 219, 240–241, 254–255, 258–260
Athenian politics, 53–66, 72, 81–82, 142, 233–234, 246–247, 252, 258–260
  Cleisthenes, 54–55, 173–174, 258–260
  demes, 54–55, 258–259
  Isagoras, 54–55
  Peisistratos, 54–55, 173–174, 246–247
  Solon, 54–55, 91
authority, 27, 44–45, 82–83, 139, 148–157, 202, 211. *See also auctoritas*
  American revolutionaries' practical understanding of, 225, 253–254
  Arendt's definition of, 175–176

Aristotle and, 151–152
  in Declaration of Independence, 251–255
  doctrine of ideas and, 150–151, 156
  as foreign to Greek politics, 149–150
  foundation and, 152–153, 155–156, 251–254
  genealogy of, 155–157, 222–223
  law(s) and, 157–160
  moral, 175–176
  natural law and, 151–152, 156
  Plato and, 150–152, 154–156
  power and, 154–157, 168, 175–176
  principle(s) and, 161, 252–253
  problem of, 221–224
  religion and, 152–155, 194, 205–206, 222–227
  Roman understanding of, 152–155, 161
  secular politics and, 221–222
  tradition and, 152–155

Beard, Charles, 195–196
Becker, Carl, 238
being
  vs. appearance, 84, 86
  as appearing, 86n4, 86
Berlin, Isaiah, 140
Bolshevism, 20–23

Cartledge, Paul, 53n20
charters, 198–203
Charter of the Massachusetts Bay Company, 199–200, 204–205
Cicero, 154–155
citizenship, 59, 204–205
  Black and Native Americans deprived of, 236–237
  in the polis, 55–56
  as "the right to have rights," 236–238
  valued over rulership, 143
civil disobedience, 17, 27
civil liberties, 208–209, 213–217, 219, 240–241
civil rights, 194, 208–209, 213–214
coercion, 69, 170–171, 175–176
command, 21–22, 44–46, 68–70, 124–126, 167–168, 245–246
  authority and, 175–176
  law(s) and, 168–169, 181–182
  power and, 170–173
commonality and plurality, 67, 74–75
common good, 67–68, 74–75, 77, 100–101, 203, 210–211
common interest, action and, 203
communities, 100–101, 181–182, 204–205
  political vs. nonpolitical forms of, 82–83
  political vs. ruled by one man, 72, 81–82, 245–246

Index

275

compacts, 198, 201–202, 204–208, 211, 219–220, 222, 229
  Mayflower Compact, 200–201
concepts, pure, 170n15
consensus, 202, 208, 236–237
consent, 208, 211, 255, 258–260, 262, 264
  as fictitious, 207
  of the governed, 193–194, 244–247
  law and, 206–208
  responsibility and, 207–208
  tacit, 207–208
constitutional monarchies, 213–214
constitution-making, 219–222
Continental Congress, 213, 254–255
contracts, 178–180, 184–186, 201–203
  American colonists and, 199–203
  horizontal, 178–180, 202–208, 219–220, 244–245, 250–251
  as means by which power is generated and sustained, 178–180
  vertical, 178–180, 202–204, 206–208, 219–220, 244, 249–250
covenant of first church of Boston, 200
covenants, 198–203, 211, 219–220
critical dismantling, 34–38, 119–121
  Destruktion, 34–36, 42–46
  Konstruktion, 34, 37–38, 42–46
  Reduktion, 34, 36–37, 42–46

Declaration of Independence, 7, 188, 194, 196–197, 209–210, 219–255
  as act of foundation, 247–252, 255
  as act of revolution, 228, 255, 264–265
  Bill of Rights in, 213, 227–255
  as horizontal contract, 250–251
  legitimacy based on practical principles implicitly governing act of Declaring Independence, 245–246, 248–249, 251–255, 261–262, 264–265
  modeled on colonial compacts, 229
  modeled on mathematics, 229–232
  as performative, 247–249, 255
  political authority in, 251–255
  principle(s) in, 164
  rooted in practical experiences of colonists, 198
  self-evident truths in, 231–233, 248–249, 251–252
  self-reflexive self-grounding structure of, 248–249, 251–252
  as statement of political theory, 228
  two different forms of discourse in, 229–232
  two notions of power and legitimacy in, 245–246, 249–251

deliberation, 22–23, 56–58, 69–72, 84–85, 106, 115–116, 124–129, 138, 202–203, 210–211, 237–238, 245–246, 255, 258–260
  common, 56, 99–100, 105–107, 124–126, 202–203, 237–238, 245–246, 255, 258–260
  reduction of deliberation to instrumental thinking, 136–137
  Socratic thought and, 113–115
democratic politics, 31–33, 82–83, 108–109, 168, 198–199
Derrida, Jacques, 48n4, 249n152
Descartes, René
  on principle(s), 162–163
despotism, 61, 70
dialogue, 84–85, 108–111, 115–116
Dio Cassius, 149
Diogenes Laertes, 109n4
dissent
  principle(s) of, 208
  right to, 188, 206–208
domination, 21–22, 50, 81–83, 142, 183, 204–205
doxa, 87, 105–106, 110. *See also* opinion
Dred Scott v. *Sandford*, 236–237

Economics and politics, 60–61, 77–78
Eichmann, Adolf, 27–30, 91–92, 98–99, 114–115
Epictetus, 144–147, 182–183
Epicurus, 25
equality, 68–69, 77, 202–205, 255, 258–260, 262
  Declaration of Independence and, 233–234
  freedom and, 233–234
  legal, 54–57, 77, 143–144, 193–194, 233–234, 252
  natural inequality, 233–234
  political, 77, 233–234
  principle of, 68–70
essence, 130–132
  Aristotle's concept of, 134–135
  as idea, 120–124, 126–127
  as measure, 117–120
  Plato's concept of, 119–121
  Socratic thought and, 110–113
essentialism, 111n9
Euripides
  Ion, 59
  The Phoenician Women, 58–59
  The Suppliant Women, 58–59, 81–82, 143–144
events, 20, 92, 94, 96–98
  historical meaning of, 94

Index

events (cont.)
  limited perspective on, 190–191
  novelty of, 94–98, 103–104, 137
  singularity of, 94–98, 103–104
evil, 27–28, 114–115
examples, thinking in, 91–92
  prime examples in phenomenology,
    79–80
experience as basis of thought, 7–8, 31, 36–37,
    47, 225

family, vs. the polity, 81
fascism, 4, 79–80
Finley, M. I., 3–4, 52n19, 53n20, 55–56, 78–81,
    158–159
force, 44–45, 82–83, 174–175
Foucault, Michel, 3–5, 78–80, 167–168
foundation(s)
  authority and, 152–153, 155–156, 221–222,
    251–254
  Connecticut, founding of, 201–202, 204–205
  Declaration of Independence as act of,
    247–249
  principle(s) and, 187–188
freedom, 13, 27, 60, 137, 139–140, 186–187,
    211, 252
  action and, 62–63, 184, 186, 188
  American colonists' understanding of,
    208–210
  vs. arbitrariness, 187
  autonomy and, 182–183
  causality and, 186
  Christian concepts of, 145–147, 182–183
  contracts and, 184–186
  elevated over life, 143
  and enfranchisement, 215
  equality and, 233–234
  exemplar shifts from citizen to the sovereign,
    145
  experienced in action, 140–141
  as freedom of choice, 79–80, 145, 239–240
  Greek understanding of, 58–59, 141–145
  as horizon of possibilities, 188, 214, 239–240
  inner freedom as derivative, 184
  law and, 159, 169
  liberation and, 143, 146–148, 182–183,
    208–209, 214–215
  natality and, 186–187
  negative, 140, 147–148, 182–186, 214,
    239–241
  nonsovereign, 183–186
  nontheoretical understanding of, 140
  not understandable by returning to ancient
    political philosophy, 140
  plurality and, 183–186

politics and, 62–63, 70, 81, 143–144, 186
  and the power to act, 184–186, 214, 239–240
  principled action and, 187–188
  self-government and, 208–210, 214–215,
    239–240
  sovereignty and, 142–143, 145, 147–148,
    169, 182–186
  Stoic philosophy and, 147
  from subjection to arbitrary will of others,
    208–209
  from subjection to necessities of life, 142
  transposition of worldly to spiritual, 144–147
  will and, 147–148, 182–183
freedom of assembly, 188, 215, 237–238
freedom of choice, 184–186
freedom of movement, 214
freedom of speech, 56–59, 103–105, 143–144,
    188, 214–215, 237–238
freedom of thought, 105
free obedience, 124–126
French Revolution, 27, 195, 215, 217–218

Glorious Revolution of 1688, 213
government, 27
  based on contract, 244–245
  as distinct from politics, 73
  power as essence of, 177
  republican, 193–194, 213–214, 216–217,
    219–220
  supposed ends of, 166–167
  understood as forms of rule, 42–46, 49,
    123–126, 168
Greek political thought, 17, 66, 108–109,
    149–150, 156–157
  authority as foreign concept in, 149–150
  distorted by the Western philosophical
    traditions, 108–109
  exemplarity of, 66
  nontheoretical discourse of, 52–53
  understanding of freedom in, 58–60, 141–145
  understanding of politics, 50–66 (see also the
    polis)

Habermas, Jürgen, 172n21
happiness, 241–242
  American revolutionaries and, 242–244
  in Declaration of Independence, 241–244
  political life and, 135–137, 241–242
  private vs. public, 242–244, 257–260
Hegel, G. W. F., 34, 95
Heidegger, Martin, 10–11, 13, 26–27, 41,
    50–51, 80
  Being and Time, 10–11, 38–40
  Introduction to Metaphysics, 86n4
  on being and appearance, 86n4

Index

on *Destruktion*, 34–35, 119–121
on *Konstruktion*, 37
on Plato's view of truth, 122–123
on the political, 50–52, 79
on *Reduktion*, 36
on theory, 38–39
on three tasks of critical dismantling, 34–37
Herodotus, 43–44, 70, 142–143, 161
  The History, 68
hierarchy, 129, 151–152
  authority and, 175–176
  law(s) and, 181–182
  as only one possible power structure, 171
historiography, Greek and Roman, 96–98
history, 27, 84, 96–98, 137–138
  Arendt's approach to, 43–44, 98–99
  complexity of historical truth, 98
  distorted by concepts of causality, 94–95
  distorted by concepts of laws of, 22–23
  distorted by concepts of process, 94, 96
  distorted by concepts of progress, 94–95
  distorted by concepts of *telos* of, 95
  distorted by delusion of human control
    over, 95
  modern philosophies of, 94–96
  totalitarian views of, 21–22
Hobbes, Thomas, 4–5, 168–169, 178–180
Homer, 161, 252
  Achilles in, 63–64, 91, 161
  Athena in, 57–58
  Hector in, 63–64
  Odysseus in, 161
  as exemplar of impartiality, 100–101
  The Iliad, 63–64, 100–101
Honig, Bonnie, 72n87
the household (*oikos*) vs. the polity, 60–63, 81,
    124–126
Hugh of St. Victor, 24–25
human nature
  Arendt on, 234
  Aristotle on, 134–135, 138–139
  natural rights and, 166–167, 234
  political rights and, 234
human rights, 193–194, 235–238
Hutcheson, Francis, 238–239

the ideal, 127
  essence and, 120–123, 127
  as measure of the actual, 120–122
idea(s), 119–124, 130–132, 166–167
  essence as, 120–124, 126–127
  Plato on, 95–96, 150–151, 156
  as transcending politics, 166–167
imagination, 84–86, 90–91, 99, 102–104
impartiality, 100–101, 123–124, 210–211

the individual
  powerlessness of, 174
  sovereignty of, 182–183
  strength and, 174
instrumental thinking, 22–24, 127–128,
    176–177
interpretation, tasks of, 197–198
isegoria, 56–59, 143–144
isonomy, 43–44, 54–59, 68, 81–82, 143–144,
    233–234. *See also* equality

Jaspers, Karl, 10–13, 23–24
Jefferson, Thomas, 164, 188, 191–194,
    209–210, 238–239, 244–251, 258–260. *See
    also* Declaration of Independence
  happiness and, 241–244
  self-evident truths and, 228–234
Jouvenel, Bertrand de, 167–168
judgment, 29–31, 84–86, 89, 99, 102, 115–116,
    123–124, 138, 210–211
  determinant, 89–90
  reflective, 89–90, 103–104
  as seeing things in their singularity, 89–90

Kant, Immanuel, 10, 25–26, 182–183
  "enlarged way of thinking," 99, 104–105
  on history, 94–95
  on representative thought, 99, 105
  on two kinds of judgment, 89
Kirk, Russell, 4–5

law(s), 27, 139, 211, 222–223
  as artificial, 158–160, 206–208
  authority and, 157–160, 227
  commandments and, 159–160, 168–169,
    181–182, 225–227
  concepts of, 167, 181–182, 225–227, 262, 264
  as directives, 181–182, 206–208, 227
  divine, 157–160, 194, 217–218, 222–223,
    225–227
  freedom and, 159, 169
  genealogy of, 225–227
  Greek understanding of *nomos*, 158
  as imperatives, 159–160, 181–182, 206–208,
    227
  legitimacy of, 206–208
  natural, 151–152, 156, 158–160, 222–224, 234
  new understanding of in American politics,
    206–208, 227
  Roman understanding of *lex*, 158, 225–227
  secular, 159, 225–227
  set above men, 166–167
  sovereignty and, 159, 181–182
  Ten Commandments as model of, 159,
    225–227

Index

leadership, vs. rulership, 124–126
legitimacy
  in Declaration of Independence, 245–246
  problem of, 158–160, 166–167, 182, 221
Lévinas, Emmanuel, 3–4, 78–80, 167
liberalism, 193–194, 208–209, 214
liberation, 147, 215–216, 218
  as emancipation from subjection, 208–209,
    214
  freedom and, 146–147, 182–183, 214–215
  sovereignty and, 145
liberty, 238–244
  as end of politics, 49
  vs. freedom, 143, 182–183
  negative, 184–186, 239–241
  positive, 182–183
  as right to limited government, 215, 240–241
  as right to self-government, 240–241
life, as the end of politics, 49, 238–244
life of the mind, vs. life of action, 15–16
Locke, John, 238
  appeal to "God in Heaven," 224
  on political contracts, 249–250
  on principle(s), 163–164
  self-evident truths in, 228–229

Madison, James, 222
Maier, Pauline, 216n63, 254
making, 119–121, 126–127, 132–134
  vs. acting, 95–96, 124–129, 135–136
Mao Zedong, 168
Marx, Karl, 21–24, 95–96
  debt to the Western philosophical traditions, 23
  totalitarianism and the philosophy of, 21–23
measure, 88, 101, 120–124
  essence and, 117–120
  Plato and, 117–120
memory. *See also* remembrance
  failures of, 192, 260–262
  the polis as space of, 65–66
metaphysics
  Aristotle and, 130–139, 161–162, 186
  critical dismantling of, 119–121
  political philosophy and, 130–131
Mill, John Stuart, 147–148, 182–183
Mills, C. Wright, 167–168
monarchies, 72, 168, 181–182, 213–214,
  249–251
  rejected by American revolutionaries, 193–194
  vertical contracts and, 249–250
Montesquieu (Charles-Louis de Secondat, Baron
  de La Brède et de Montesquieu)
  on principle(s), 187–188
  The Spirit of the Laws, 163–164
Mouffe, Chantal, 3–4, 6, 167

Nancy, Jean-Luc, 4
narrative thought, 92–99
  anecdotes, 98
  life stories, 93–94
natality, free action and, 186–187
National Socialism (Nazism), 4, 9, 20–22,
  27–31, 77. *See also* Nazis
natural law(s), 151–152, 156, 158–160,
  222–224, 234
natural right, 193–194, 224, 234, 248–249
Nazis, 9, 11–12, 31–33, 98
Nietzsche, Friedrich, 25, 102
nontheoretical discourse, 40–42, 47, 52–53, 85,
  197–198
nontheoretical thought, 38–42, 84–86, 197–198,
  218–221, 225, 230–231
nonviolence, 69–70, 170–171, 255, 258–260
nonviolent revolutions, 256–257

Oakeshott, Michael, 3–4, 78–80
obedience, 21–22, 29–30, 44–46, 49, 68, 72,
  124–126, 167–168, 170–171, 175–176,
  245–246
  authority and, 168,
  power and, 170–173
objectivity, 102
  impartiality and, 101, 123–124
  plurality of perspectives and, 104–106
  in political thought, 101–102, 104–106
  scientific, 101–102
oligarchies, 72, 168, 178–180, 258–260
opinion, 84–88, 99–106, 110, 117–119,
  123–126, 208
  measure and, 118–119
  perspective and, 88, 99–101, 123–124
  Platonic demotion of, 123–124
  political thought and, 86–89
  reconceived by Arendt in light of her
    phenomenological concept of appearing,
    87–88

Paine, Thomas, 213n53
partisanship, 100–101, 263–265
Paul, St., 145–147, 159, 182–183
perspective(s), 16, 64–65, 90–91, 102n55, 102,
  105, 117–119, 190–191
  opinion and, 88, 99–101, 123–124
  plurality of, 88, 101–106, 102n55
  political thought and, 101–102
  representative thought and, 99–101
persuasion, 57–58, 69, 71–72, 85,
  103, 117, 124–126, 150, 175–176. *See also*
  rhetoric
phenomenology, 7, 26, 34, 39–41, 43–44,
  86–88, 120, 148

Index
279

philosophers
philosopher-kings, 126–127, 150, 154–155, 228–229
political role of, 115–116, 121–122
philosophy, 40–41, 85
political (*see* political philosophy)
political theory and, 20
politics and, 18–19, 24–27, 84–85, 91, 102, 108–109, 116–117, 129, 138–141, 263–264
phronesis, 89
Plato, 7, 23–25, 42–46, 84, 111–113, 116–129, 140, 191–192
allegory of the cave, 121–124
anti-political philosophy, 123–126, 129
authority and, 150–152, 154–156
concept of measure in, 117–120
concept of rule in, 124–126
departure from Socrates, 116–117
distortion of Greek understanding of politics, 108–109, 123–126, 129
doctrine of ideas, 95–96, 150–151, 156
Gorgias, 24
on opinion, 123–124
philosopher-kings and, 124–126
politics and, 23–24, 108–109, 120, 123–129, 136, 150–151
on politics as matter of rule, 123–127, 129, 150–151
The Republic, 129
self-evident truths and, 163, 228–229
Seventh Letter, 117
on task of political philosopher, 121–124
truth and, 122–124, 163, 228–229
Platonic thought, vs. Socratic thought, 109
plurality, 67, 74–75, 88
action and, 203
as a condition of politics, 47, 67, 74–75
freedom and, 183–186
objectivity and, 102n55, 104–106
of perspectives, 101–106, 102n55, 123–124
power and, 184–186
rights and, 237–238
truth and, 102n55, 104–106
the polis, 24, 50–66, 108, 140
Aristotle on, 134
distinctive character of, 66, 79–80
the family vs., 81
Greek understanding of, 50–52
the *oikos* and, 60–61, 81, 124–126, 143
as the prime example of political community, 43–44, 79–80
as space of appearances, 64–65
as space of freedom, 62–63
as space of memory, 65–66

as space of struggle, 63–64
vs. three other kinds of communities, 60–61
two institutions defining, 55–56
the political
Arendt's concept of, 26, 41–42, 47–48, 74–83
definitions of, 31–33, 76, 78
four distinctions implied by, 71–74
Greeks' understanding of, 50–66 (*see also* the polis)
Heidegger on, 50–52, 79
other concepts of, 78–83
pure concept of, 24, 34, 47–84
seven traits defining, 68–71
political discourse, 71–72, 85, 102–107
vs. philosophical discourse, 84–85, 102
political life, 41, 211, 263–265
Aristotle's debasement of, 138–139
dignity of, 6, 62, 210–211, 217–218, 237–238
happiness and, 135–136, 198–211, 215–216, 241–242
vs. philosophical life, 108, 140–141
Plato's debasement of, 123–124
Socrates' stance toward, 115–116
political philosophy, 18–19, 26, 139
classical, 122–124, 139–165 (*see also* Aristotle; Plato; Socrates)
metaphysics and, 130–131
phenomenology and, 40–41
political questions, vs. technical questions, 73–74
political rights, 237–238
derived from nature of politics, 237–238
human nature and, 234
political sphere, 26–27
definition of, 76
as distinct from other spheres of human existence, 79–82
seven traits defining, 68–71
political theory. *See also* political philosophy
Arendt's approach to, 7, 42–46, 265
vs. nontheoretical understanding of politics, 218–221, 225, 230–232
vs. political philosophy, 20
political thought, 85. *See also* political philosophy; political theory
Arendt's view of, 85
Aristotle's view of, 138
faculties of, 84–91, 102–104
forms of, 91–102
as largely nontheoretical, 7, 84, 88–89, 102, 122–123
objectivity of, 102, 104–106
vs. philosophical thought, 84–85, 91, 102, 123–124, 129
Plato's view of, 122–124

280   *Index*

politicization, 71–72, 77
politics, 47, 62, 134
  conditions of, 74–75
  essence of, 23–24, 71–72
  as matter of rule, 49, 123–127, 129, 166–167
  meaning of, 3–7, 23–24, 26–27, 43–44, 48–50, 167, 265
  as means to an end, 49, 82–83, 136, 166–167
  not a universal and necessary part of human life, 48–49, 74–75, 82–83, 166–167
  philosophy and, 18–19, 24–27, 108–109, 116–117, 129, 138–141, 263–264
  prejudices against, 1–3, 48–50, 74–75, 80, 82–83
  as struggle for power to rule, 21–22, 50, 82–83, 167
  as technical expertise and management, 124–126, 129, 136
  totalitarianism as death of, 21–22
power, 1–2, 27, 44–45, 81–83, 167–169, 204–205, 211, 214
  American colonists' understanding of, 201–202, 219–220, 244–245
  Arendt's definition of, 172–173
  authority and, 154–157, 168, 175–176, 222–223
  command and, 170–173
  contracts as means to generate, 178–180
  in Declaration of Independence, 245–246, 249–251
  de jure vs. de facto, 73
  domination and, 82–83
  as essence of government, 177
  horizontal contracts and, 245–246
  inherited concepts of, 44–46, 170–174, 262, 264
  nonhierarchical forms of, 171
  plurality and, 184–186
  as power-over-others, 167–168, 173–174, 219–220, 244–245
  as power-to-do, 173–174, 178–180, 184–186, 214, 219–220, 239–240
  precedes distinction between means and ends, 176–177
  revolutions and, 44–45, 170–171
  sovereignty and, 82–83
  strength and, 174
  two levels of, 173–174
  tyranny and, 173–174
  vertical contracts and, 245–246
  violence and, 168, 170–172, 176–177
prejudices against politics, 1–3, 48–50, 74–75, 80, 82–83, 263–264
  end of politics as liberty, 49
  end of politics as life, 49

politics as means to an end, 49
politics as struggle for power to rule, 49–50
politics as universal and necessary part of human life, 48–49
principle(s), 130–132
  actions and, 161–162, 187–188, 252–254
  American revolutionaries and, 157–158, 164
  Aristotle on, 161–163, 187–188
  authority and, 161, 252–253
  in Declaration of Independence, 164
  Descartes on, 162–163
  freedom and, 187–188
  genealogy of concept of, 161
  Locke on, 163–164
  Montesquieu on, 163–164, 187–188
  practical, 251–255
  as self-evident truths, 162–163
  as "spirit of the laws," 163–164
private happiness, 242–244
private sphere, 193–194, 208–209
  vs. public sphere, 21–22, 70–72, 104–106, 106n62, 124–126
promises, mutual, 184–186, 202–204, 210–211, 222, 244–245, 250–255, 258–260
public happiness, 209–211, 215–216, 241–244, 257–260
public sphere, 67, 70, 74–75
  vs. private sphere, 70–72, 104–106, 106n62, 124–126
public spirit, 210–211, 257–260
pure concepts, definition of, 170n15

questions
  political vs. social, 77–78, 195
  political vs. technical, 73–74

representative government, 193–194, 258–260
representative thought, 99–102, 104–105
  Kant on, 99, 105
  Socratic thought and, 113–114
responsibility, 114–115, 207–208
revolution(s), 27, 77, 94, 98–99, 164, 211–213
  as change of rules, 181–182
  Cuban revolution, 27
  definition of, 27, 211–213
  distinguished from similar phenomena, 211–213, 217
  as fight for political freedom, 216–217
  as founding of new form of government, 211–213, 217
  genealogy of concepts of, 27
  history of, 170–171
  Hungarian Revolution, 27, 170–171
  nonviolent, 170–172, 256–257
  pathos of novelty in, 137, 217

Index

281

power and, 44–45, 170–171
problem of authority and, 221–222
secularization and, 217–218
vicious circle of legitimation in, 221
violent, 170–171
rhetoric, 57–58, 84–85, 123–124, 262
rights, 235–236
belonging to human beings in the plural,
235–238
citizenship as the right to have, 236–238
human nature and, 166–167, 234–235
natural, 193–194, 223–224, 234, 248–249
right to revolution, 247–251
Robespierre, Maximilien, 195, 224
Rome, Ancient
authority in, 149, 152–156, 161, 222–223,
252–253
founding of, 152–154, 156, 187–188
as model for American revolutionaries, 253
religion in, 152–155
tradition in, 17
Rousseau, Jean-Jacques, 147–148, 178–180,
182–183
rule, 42–46, 49, 81, 126–127, 129, 263–265
concept taken from household, 124–126
excluded from political life, 68, 70, 72–73,
82–83, 124–126, 142–143, 204–205,
209–210, 217
as "fundamental problem of political
philosophy," 169–170
politics as matter of, 49, 150–151
rulership, 72, 81–82, 124–126, 129, 245–246
vs. citizenship, 68, 70
vs. leadership, 124–126
Ryan, Alan, 124n39

Schmitt, Carl, 3–4, 51, 78–80, 167
secular politics, 149, 217–218, 221–222
self-evident truths, 228–233
Arendt's view of, 231–232
Jefferson and, 228–234, 248–249, 251–252
Locke and, 228–229
Plato and, 163, 228–229
self-government, 198–203, 211, 263–265
American colonists' experience of, 198–211,
215–220, 222, 239–240, 256–260
arising out of practical considerations,
198–199, 202–203
freedom and, 208–210, 240–241
self-sufficiency, ideal of, 184–186
Seneca, 143
singularities/singularity, 92–98, 103–104
of events, 96
judging, 89–92
of persons, 103–104

slavery, 69, 142, 145, 147
in ancient Greece, 53–55
in the United States, 236–237
social and political equality, 77
social histories of the American Revolution, 195–196
Socrates, vii, 87, 91–92, 108–116, 129
as model of politically engaged thinker, 108–109
trial and death of, 116–117, 142n103, 150,
228–229
Socratic thought, 109–116
cognition and, 113–115
deliberation and, 113–115
dialogue, 87, 108–109, 115–116
essences and, 110–113
judgment and, 113–115
vs. Platonic thought, 109n4, 109
relevance to political life, 115–116
representative thinking and, 113–114
sovereignty, 81–82, 140, 147–148, 219–220
citizenship and, 142
freedom and, 142–143, 147–148, 169,
182–186
illusion of, 183–184
law and, 159, 181–182
political power and, 82–83, 169
of the will, 182–183
"spirit of 1776," 256–258
"spirit of the laws," 163–164
Strauss, Leo, 123n38, 128n50, 129, 136n84
strength, 44–45, 82–83
power vs., 174

Taney, Roger, 236–237
technical questions, vs. political questions, 73–74
telos, 94–95, 130–136, 161–163, 166–167,
187–188
theory, 38, 88–89, 138, 197, 229–230
Arendt's concept of, 38, 41
history and, 43–44
limits of, 197–198
nontheoretical discourse and, 40–42
nontheoretical thought and, 29–30, 38–42,
84, 197–198
phenomenology and, 39–41
scientistic conceptions of, 22–23
thinking, 7–8, 30–31
action and, 15–16, 25–26, 84, 128–129, 265
essences and, 110–111
everyday speech and, 41
in examples, 91–92
experience of, 14–15
in narrative, 92–99 (*see also* narratives)
remembrance and, 198, 260–262
representative (*see* representative thought)
tasks of, 14–16, 265

Index

thoughtlessness, 114–116
Thucydides, 102
Tocqueville, Alexis de, 196
totalitarianism, 98–99
  as anti-political, 21–22, 24, 31–33, 176–177
  as eluding terms of traditional political theory, 17–18
  essence of, 20–22
  Marxism and, 21–23
  "politicization" of everything within, 4
  unprecedented nature of, 20
town meetings, 202, 208–211, 240–241, 255, 258–260
tradition(s), 7–8, 17–20
  authority and, 152–155
  Destruktion and, 34–36
tradition(s), internal differences in17n27
truth(s), 27, 84, 87–88, 93–94, 98, 123–124. *See also* self-evident truths
  as correspondence, 122–124
  as illumination or *aletheia*, 98, 122–123
  plurality of perspectives and, 104–106
tyranny, 59, 61, 81–82, 246–247
  Oedipus and, 61
  Peisistratos, 54–55, 173–174, 246–247
  powerlessness generated by, 173–174
  Thirty Tyrants and, 115

the universal, 130–132, 137–138
U.S. Constitution, 194–196, 258–260
  exclusion of Black and Native Americans from, 236–237
  Founders' failure to incorporate town meetings in, 258–260
  God not mentioned in, 224–225, 227
  understanding of authority implicit in, 261, 264–265

violence, 44–45, 78, 82–83, 124–126, 175–176, 204–205
  excluded from political life, 69–72, 76–77, 176–177
  as extra-political condition of politics, 176
  power and, 168, 170–172, 176–177
Virgil, 161, 187–188, 252–253
  the *Aeneid*, 153–154
vita activa, 24–27, 40–41, 84, 108, 138–140, 210, 242
vita contemplativa, 24–27, 40–41, 84, 108, 135–136, 138–141, 210, 242
Voltaire (François-Marie Arouet), 167–168

will, 30–31, 140, 147–148, 169
  freedom and, 147–148, 182–183
Wills, Garry, 238–239

Printed in the United States
by Baker & Taylor Publisher Services